God on High

God on High

Religion, Cannabis, and the Quest for Legitimacy

Laurie Cozad

LEXINGTON BOOKS
Lanham • Boulder • New York • London

Published by Lexington Books
An imprint of The Rowman & Littlefield Publishing Group, Inc.
4501 Forbes Boulevard, Suite 200, Lanham, Maryland 20706
www.rowman.com

Unit A, Whitacre Mews, 26-34 Stannary Street, London SE11 4AB

British Library Cataloguing in Publication Information Available

Library of Congress Cataloging-in-Publication Data Available

ISBN 978-1-4985-0404-1 (cloth : alk. paper)
ISBN 978-1-4985-0405-8 (electronic)

∞™ The paper used in this publication meets the minimum requirements of American National Standard for Information Sciences Permanence of Paper for Printed Library Materials, ANSI/NISO Z39.48-1992.

Printed in the United States of America

THIS BOOK IS DEDICATED TO

My family, Joel, Winston, and Jesse and to my friends Kim Fleming, Kirsten Dellinger, and Robbie Etheridge. I deeply appreciate your creative ideas, love, and support, all of which went into the pages of this book. I also want to thank those founders and members of cannabis-based religions: Roger Christie, Share Christie, Danuel Quaintance, Mary Quaintance, Daniel Jeffrey, and Craig Rubin who stand at the breach between religious freedom and the law.

Contents

Preface

As a historian of religions I have come across myriad religious traditions. Some that worshipped a single omnipotent deity, some that worshipped a variety of deities, and some that worshipped objects, animals, the natural environment, and/or mortal men and women. And in the 20-plus years that I have studied, taught, and published about religion, I have come to understand that if a set of beliefs and practices is to be correctly identified as "religious," it must incorporate one essential element: it must foreground some sense of the transcendent. Defining "transcendence" is a tricky business all on its own, but if we reduce it to its foundation rather than enumerate its effects one can define transcendence as follows: the presence of that which lies beyond mundane reality.

As we look around at religious traditions throughout the world, one can see that there are almost as many ways to gain access to the sacred as there are religions. And many of these traditions require substances to be used ritualistically to allow for communion between a human being and the transcendent. I would call these substances "powerful substances." Cannabis has a long and distinguished history as a powerful substance; one that has been used both to effect medicinal healing and to develop a sense of sacred communion.

As one who has experienced the spiritual power of cannabis, I understand the raison d'être of those religious groups who would use cannabis as a sacramental substance. Thus, when I found out that two academics had been instrumental in denying the Church of the Universe—a cannabis religion—the status of a "legitimate" religion, I was moved to examine this court case more closely. As it turned out, the two academics acting for the prosecution of this church relied upon an orthodox definition of religion that did not fit the framework of the Church of the Universe. That is why it is crucial for academics to be critically aware of how they are defining religion, for how one defines religion determines how the judiciary defines religious freedom. Moreover, the consequences of using a method reliant upon a laudry list of orthodox elements had a severe impact on the Church of the Universe, as two of its founding members were imprisoned. Thus, the stakes are very high for those who would use cannabis as a sacramental substance, and one would hope that an academic choosing to appear in a courtroom would be able to rise to the occasion.

Having watched the course of this trial and its outcome, I was moved to take action. This action took the form of looking into cases wherein a religious group was being tried by the judiciary for their belief in and use of cannabis as a sacrament. It did not take long to find such a group as a quick search of the internet revealed that a Hilo, Hawai'i, minister, Reverend Roger Christie, his wife Share Christie, and 12 other members of the Hawai'i Cannabis (THC) Ministry had recently been arrested by federal agents for using cannabis as a sacrament.

After communicating with Roger Christie from his jail cell and interviewing several members of the ministry for over a year, I was persuaded that the THC Ministry was a legitimate church and deserved the protection afforded churches under the First Amendment of the Constitution. The ways and means by which one might come to such a conclusion lies at the core of this book. For now, suffice it to say that I agreed to act as an expert witness for the defense of the THC Ministry, thus moving from a scholar of religion to an advocate of a religious group that I believed was being wrongfully prosecuted by the federal government. Moreover, having reviewed the Government's Memorandum against Christie, I concluded, under penalty of perjury, that "the THC Ministry's beliefs and practices mandated that the Ministry cultivate cannabis sacrament plants and distribute [them] to its members."[1]

The debate over the legalization of cannabis is extremely divisive at the moment, and not surprisingly, this divisiveness shows up in the state and federal judicial systems. In this context, courts are often split as to whether or not cannabis religions should even be recognized as religions. Given the shifting target represented by the judicial system at present, I would hope that scholars of religion will be more rather than less active in helping courts understand unfamiliar religions. However, scholars are no different than other people when it comes to forming an opinion around controversial subjects. For this reason, the scholar of unorthodox religions must always be conscious of the fact that we "too, have brought different sets of agendas into play."[2]

Thus, having armed oneself with knowledge of one's own subjectivity, religious studies scholars provide a necessary service in setting up a template through which the judiciary can make sense of an unfamiliar religion. And, as academicians, we do this work not merely to render ourselves as tolerant and respectable members of academia; we do this work to allow those practitioners of unfamiliar religions a chance to keep alive those practices which they hold most sacred.

NOTES

1. *United States v. Roger Cusick Christie*, Sherryanne L. Christie, In the U.S. District Court for the District of Hawaii, CR. NO. 10-00384 LEK, Supplemental Declaration of Laurie Cozad, Ph.D., 22.

2. Elisabeth Arweck, *Researching New Religious Movements: Responses and Redefinitions* (London: Routledge, 2006), 7.

Introduction

Why Would You Want to Get High in Church?: An Introduction to Pot, Politics, and the Law

In the spring of 2011, I was teaching a course on religion and politics in which students were asked to bring in articles that would broaden our perspective on the intersections between these two fields of study. One of the students brought in a series of articles about the Church of the Universe, a self-proclaimed cannabis ministry located in Ontario, Canada. Their founder, Walter Tucker, described his beliefs stating that "My religion is about worshipping God, and my communication thereto, and the use of the cannabis marijuana plant, the tree of life, for my health and for my spiritual well-being."[1] I found this ritual use of cannabis fascinating, but what struck me at the time was the intolerance demonstrated by my students—a class full of 20-year-old collegians. Without hesitation, each and every one of these students deemed the Church of the Universe a sham and discounted their use of cannabis in this setting as opportunistic at best and sacrilegious at worst.

As I looked further into the Church of the Universe, I found that they had been battling the Canadian government for more than a decade to have their cannabis ministry recognized as a legitimate religion. In 2011, two of their members were put on trial for drug trafficking but attempted to overturn the charges by using a Religious Freedom defense. It was then that I realized my students were not the only ones to discount this group. During these proceedings, the Crown invited three professors of religion to act as expert witnesses to help the justices decide whether or not the Church of the Universe could be categorized as a legitimate religion. While one of the professors held a neutral stance, the other two saw the Church of the Universe in a very negative light. One of the latter replied that "she could not see anything in the Church of the Universe that resembled ritual, sacred spaces or symbols, or helped its members deal with life's paradoxes. The only 'scripture' or other literature she could find was from *Cannabis Culture* magazine, a secular journal, and some information on a website."[2] Further, the prosecuting attorney, Nicholas Devlin, called their use of a Religious Freedom defense an "inside joke among people who like to smoke marijuana."[3] I was not surprised to find that a public prosecutor would deem a Religious Freedom defense "an inside joke," but I was surprised to find that two of my colleagues had passed judgment on this group using a definition of religion that seemed reductionist, biased, and reliant on a skewed methodology.

THE PURPOSE OF THIS BOOK

Thus began my research into the triangular relationships between cannabis, religion, and the law, and the ways in which the shifting discourse of medical science impacts this trio. I quickly found that, in addition to the Church of the Universe in Canada, there were several cannabis religious groups that had been recently active in the United States. The largest of these included the Church of Cognizance, the Hawai'i Cannabis Ministry, and Temple 420. The Church of Cognizance was founded by Dan and Mary Quaintance in 1991. the Hawai'i Cannabis Ministry was founded in 2000 by Roger Christie. And Temple 420 was founded in 2006 by Craig Rubin. Among other things, all of these groups understood cannabis to be a sacramental substance that opened the mind to sacred experience. Another element common to these groups is that every single one of these church founders had been charged with possession of a controlled substance and/or drug trafficking and all had been prosecuted for one or more of these felonies. In other words, their claims of being legitimate churches protected by the First Amendment, or in the case of the Church of the Universe, protected by the Canadian Charter of Rights and Freedoms, had been rejected.

What is at stake here can be summed up with the following questions: What constitutes a religion? And following closely upon that question: How has the judiciary in both Canada and the United States used its power to define the category of religion and thus religious freedom? While the latter question will be the focus of chapter 5, it is important to examine the former question for those who are new to the study of religion.

As one looks for a definition of religion, one soon realizes that there is no single definition that is accepted by scholars and religious practitioners alike. There are, however, several definitions that have guided the study of religion over the past century. One of the earliest definitions is that of Edward B. Tylor, a nineteenth-century scholar who states: "[Religion is] the belief in Spiritual Beings."[4] Emile Durkheim, a sociologist whose book *The Elementary Forms of the Religious Life* was published in 1912, states: "Religion is a unified system of beliefs and practices relative to sacred things, that is to say, things set apart and forbidden—beliefs and practices which unite into one single moral community called a church, all those who adhere to them."[5] In this definition Durkheim sets up a binary system in which the sacred is set off from all else and limits religion to those who practice exclusively in a group "called a church."

Moving to the mid-twentieth century, Paul Tillich, a philosopher and theologian who played a role in the U.S. Supreme Court's definition of religion, broadens Tylor's focus: "[Religion is] the state of being grasped by an ultimate concern, a concern which qualifies all other concerns as preliminary, and a concern that in itself provides the answer to the question of the meaning of our life."[6] Tillich, moves away from theism (that which imbues deities with absolute power and authority) to substitute "ultimate concern," a methodological move that expands the definition of religion by expanding that which constitutes the transcendent. I am using the term transcendent here and throughout this book to express that which rises above subjective reality to allow us a glimpse of ultimate reality. Charles Long, a twentieth-century historian of religions not only provides a space for the transcendent but also brings up race as he believes that too many scholars focus their research on the religious practices of those at the top of the social ladder, namely, Caucasians. Moreover, he guides scholars away from church settings as a vast number of people do not limit their religious practices to a church.

> Given the situation of Americans of African descent . . . the church was not the only context for the meaning of religion. For my purposes, religion will mean orientation—orientation in the ultimate sense, that is, how one comes to terms with the ultimate significance of one's place in the world.[7]

While both Tillich and Long open up space for a broad understanding of the transcendent, Clifford Geertz, a twentieth-century cultural anthropologist, closes down that space.

> A religion is: (1) a system of symbols which acts to (2) establish powerful, pervasive, and long-lasting moods and motivation in men by (3) formulating conceptions of a general order of existence and (4) clothing these conceptions with such an aura of factuality that (5) the moods and motivations seem uniquely realistic.[8]

In clothing his definition of religion in "man"-made actions, Geertz positions himself as a social constructionist, one who believes that men are responsible for the creation of religion.

While all of the scholars listed above refer to the phenomenon of religion in gender exclusive language, Mary Daly, a twentieth-century feminist theologian, pushes gender politics to center stage in her statement that "patriarchy is the prevailing religion of the entire planet. . . ."[9] And for Daly, this means that patriarchy has been elevated to an exalted ideology in which men are to be seen as having ultimate power and authority. Catherine Albanese, a twentieth-century historian of religions also uses gender-inclusive language as she brings us back to Durkheim in highlighting "community": "[Religion is] a system of symbols (creed, code, cultus) by means of which people (a community) orient themselves in the world with reference to both ordinary and extraordinary powers, meanings and values."[10] Albanese breaks her likeness to Durkheim, however, in refusing to separate the "ordinary" and "extraordinary." In so doing, she locates the transcendent not merely in the realm of religious activities but also in ordinary moments.

Frederick Streng, a twentieth-century philosopher of Asian religions provides a definition that focuses on the experiential effects of religion: "Religion is a means to ultimate transformation."[11] I, too, have spent my career in the realm of Asian religions and have found that, in both East and South Asia, one discovers not only an emphasis on transcendent experience as noted by Streng but also an emphasis on orthopraxy, as ritual practices are expected to bring forth transformative experiences.

The above discussion points out that those academics based in different academic disciplines will use different methods in their scholarly pursuits; for instance, sociologists will focus on the practices of social groups while theologians will focus on knowing and explicating God. While theology once held pride of place in academia, at present, theology and the academic study of religion exist side by side, each using different methodological tools. The academic study of religion asks students and scholars of religion to look across time and cultures to examine the diverse ways that a plurality of human beings, including men, women, indigenous peoples and those disenfranchised by their respective societies, have experienced the sacred and codified that experience. According to Rita Gross,

> The single greatest change that enabled religious studies to emerge as an academic discipline was the recognition that one could understand a religious position without adhering to it. I believe that this recognition was made possible by the study of non-Western religions; more removed from sectarian battles within culturally familiar religious settings, scholars realized that they could understand and appreciate, with great empathy, a point of view that they did not share. Therefore, such understanding could also be taught to others.[12]

While this list is hardly exhaustive, it includes those definitions that focus on both race and gender, and, at the same time, provides an understanding of the differences between theists, social constructions, and those who, like Tillich, Long, Albanese, and Streng, leave room in their definitions for what Rudolf Otto called the *mysterium tremendum.*[13] My methodological approach as a twenty-first-century historian of religions includes the following: analyzing discourse to deconstruct the ways in which those in power control knowledge; and leaving space open for the numinous.

Discourse is comprised of myriad modalities through which knowledge is conveyed. This knowledge is, among other things, designed to control social behavior and shape public opinion, but can be so pervasive and persuasive that it can pose as self-evident information rather than socially constructed ideology. The modalities through which knowledge is conveyed include, but are not limited to, legal statutes, governmental dictates, textbooks, social media sources, films, television commercials, song lyrics and, perhaps most importantly, the voices of those closest to one.

This list could stretch on to incorporate any and all forms of communication that serve to shape the way one thinks about any given subject. However, two important caveats must be raised at this point. First, even discourse controlled by those in power is never univocal and contains those voices that would challenge the knowledge produced. For example, the issue of cannabis legalization prominently demonstrates a discursive divide between the federal government and, at present, 29 state governments. Second, within any society there are counter-discourses raised by those disenfranchised by those in power. This book contains many of these counter-discourses as I present the knowledge produced by those belonging to the cannabis-based religions under review. I must stress again, however, that even counter-discourses aimed at changing the rules that govern society or altering public opinion around a particular topic are not univocal and may disintegrate over ideological differences.

When it comes to the other element of my methodological approach, it can be summed up with the following: I leave space in my methodology for the numinous rather than reifying the social construction of religion. So, in leaving space for the numinous, one does not force a grid over what, where, and how the transcendent enters into one's life; the irruption of *kairos* into *chronos*.

As we turn back to the specific type of religiosity central to this book—namely, cannabis-based religions—one must acknowledge that many people, scholars, and the general public alike, would not perceive these groups to be religious. Rather, as was highlighted at the trial of the Church of the Universe, a cannabis-based religion was characterized as a joke. In order to avoid such pejorative casting of unfamiliar religions, the term "new religious movement" or (NRM) is often applied to such religions. This is because the term NRM will shield unfamiliar religions from being characterized pejoratively as its members stray from orthodox practices and doctrines.

Of course the term "orthodox" literally means "ortho" (right) and "dox" (teaching) and refers to the "right teachings" that are drawn from canonical texts; examples of which include the Old and New Testaments of the *Bible*, the *Qu'ran*, and the *Avesta*. However, like all other binary systems, what is right versus what is wrong varies according to its own time and place. In other words, these binary taxonomies are framed within and dependent upon the cultural context in which they exist, and what is considered "right" in one context may be considered very "wrong" when applied to another time and/or place. For example, human sacrifice was considered essential to the Aztecs as a practice that anchored their belief system—needless to say a practice that would be frowned upon today. However, one might argue that the death penalty mirrors the practice of human sacrifice in significant ways. I would argue that both practices have been understood in their time and culture to allow the body politic to be strengthened—in the former, by the energy of the sacrificed and in the latter by the removal of the deviant, each enclosed within their respective discourses but achieving the same objective.[14]

Given that ideas around what constitutes "right teaching" are culturally and historically sensitive, we can see this title of "new religious movement" as an attempt to protect those ideas that might be seen as irrelevant or even dangerous to established religions and thus threaten orthodox ideas and establishments. However, it is a problematic term, for as it emphasizes the label "new" it removes our gaze from the fact that contemporary religions have roots that extend from ancient times and places. Thus, as the members of contemporary cannabis religions come to construct their particular manner of being religious, they are building a religious framework from the bricks and mortar of religious practices that were used in other cultures and historical times. That is why Levi-Strauss used the word *bricoleur*, or bricklayer, when he discussed the ways in which religions come into being.

> The "bricoleur" is adept at performing a large number of diverse tasks. . . . His universe of instruments is closed and the rules of his game are always to make do with "whatever is at hand," that is to say with the set of tools and materials which is always finite and is also heterogeneous because what it contains bears no relation to the current project, or indeed to any particular project, but is the contingent result of all the occasions there have been to renew or enrich the stock or to maintain it with the remains of previous constructions or deconstructions.[15]

Viewed this way, it is clear that none of these religions are "new." Rather, those who have experienced the power and glory brought on by a religious experience will enhance this experience with bits and pieces of rituals, myths, and symbols that are relevant to their religious reality making this generation of builders, contemporary *bricoleurs*. I will be using the term cannabis-based religions rather than "new religious movements" throughout this book to describe the Church of the Universe, the Hawai'i Cannabis Ministry, the Church of Cognizance, and Temple 420.

As the term "ritual" is central to the subject matter presented in this book, it, too, needs to be defined. Defining the term "ritual" is a tricky proposition, for there are so many scholarly interpretations of ritual actions that Ritual Studies has become a subset within the academic study of religion. Rather than list a coterie of scholars who define ritual in their own way, I will list several ways in which scholars theorize about what motivates those who would engage in ritual activity. Rituals recreate the original order of creation and thus are believed to sustain order in society. Rituals solidify the ties within social groups. Rituals are not only performed by people, but also perform people, as they are used to endow members of society with new social roles. Rituals are enacted to purify that which has been made impure through profane actions, sickness, group disharmony, etc. Rituals are enacted both to propitiate and/or celebrate deities. Rituals provide the space to form a connection between humans and the divine. Rituals will sometimes use powerful substances both to initiate the connection between humans and the divine and to further enhance that connection.

In the cases listed above, rituals tend to be both formulaic and formalistic in order to achieve their objective. As noted by Catherine Bell, however, "[t]oday there is a growing social legitimacy for many types of ritual improvisation as well as the unprecedented visibility of the very dynamics of ritual invention."[16] Moreover, there is a whole school of thought that tears down the wall between ritual activity enacted at the sacred level and ritual activity enacted at the mundane level. As stated by Seligman, Weller, Puett, and Simon, "[r]itual, we will claim, provides an orientation to action and hence a framing of action that is relevant in understanding human activities beyond what may be done in temples, churches, mosques—or the houses of Parliament for that matter."[17]

I am very much in agreement with this attitude toward ritual, for I have found in studying these cannabis religions that both founders and practitioners find transcendence through ritual in, out, and beyond sacred times and locations. Moreover, from my study of cannabis religions, I have found that practitioners tend to engage in four of the ritual explications noted above: first, they engage in "ritual improvisation" to make relevant their goal of sacred communion; second, they are motivated to partake in these rituals to form a connection between members of their group as well as, third, to forge a connection to the divine;[18] and fourth, they use powerful substances to forge that connection to the divine.

Returning to the concept of the *bricoleur*, another historian of religions, Jonathan Z. Smith, builds on this concept as he turns to the past to make unorthodox religions "intelligible."[19] In his analysis of Peoples Temple in Jonestown, Guyana, Smith states that if a group claims to be religious, we have a "professional obligation" to interpret them within that framework, regardless of the fact that they may be a "scandal in the original sense of the word."[20] One achieves this knowledge by looking to history and/or other cultures to find a template that allows us to frame an unorthodox religion within its own sphere of signification.

> As students of religion, we have become stubbornly committed to making the attempt (even if we fail) at achieving intelligibility. We must accept the burden of the long, hard road of understanding. To do less is to forfeit our license to practice in the academy, to leave the study of religion open to the charge of incivility and intolerance.[21]

Thus, when J. Z. Smith looked for a religious pattern that allowed him to render Peoples Temple meaningful, he had Levi-Strauss's work to guide him back across time and across cultures to find patterns that rendered unfamiliar religions intelligible. Looking all the way back to the second century BCE, Smith found a description of a "Dionysic cult" practiced by the Bacchics in Rome that reflected certain significant components of Peoples Temple. More importantly, this method provided Smith with a means for framing Peoples Temple not within a contemporary religious structure but through "the Dionysiac *pattern*, as classically established by Euripides,"[22] a method that allowed him not only to analyze this group's actions within a religious context but also to compare cross-culturally and cross-temporally the very structures that give religion meaning.

This is a wonderful use of both the comparative method and discursive analysis, as any project that attempts to render a religious group "intelligible" must first convey a categorical definition of religion that can include that group within its parameters; for it is at the structural level, the contextual level, that a religious system or any system is rendered meaningful.[23] As Smith analyzed this second-century BCE group, he did so in order to provide a template for a certain type of religiosity:

> The utility of this model reminds us that the prime purpose of academic inquiry, most especially in the humanities, is to provide *exempli gratia,* an arsenal of classic instances which are held to be exemplary, to provide paradigmatic events and expressions as resources from which to reason, from which to extend the possibility of intelligibility to that which first appears novel.[24]

In regarding this second-century BCE group as an exemplary model he stated, "I suggest no simple parallels. There are profound differences between Dionysiac cults and Peoples Temple Christian Church."[25] This, of course, reflects Levi-Strauss's understanding that because religions are created using the *bricolage* at hand—these bits and pieces will be put together in novel ways and, as such, will not provide a mirror of their predecessors but rather a mosaic. As stated by Smith, when we supply "some instances of familiarity [from one to the other, we do so] to seek to understand the other."[26] This is an exceptionally important point when it comes to the study of cannabis-based religions, for it is only as we find historical or cross-cultural precedents that we are able to make "the attempt (even if we fail) at achieving intelligibility."[27]

With California's passage in 1996 of Proposition 215, which legalized the use of cannabis for medical purposes, the public's image of cannabis shifted dramatically.[28] When once this drug was primarily associated with the counterculture of the 1960s, now cannabis is seen by many as a healing agent for such medical conditions as glaucoma, Alzheimer's, diabetes, nervous system disorders, gangrene, multiple sclerosis, AIDS, and cancer. Moreover, as of this writing, 28 more states as well as the District of Columbia have joined California in legalizing medical marijuana, and 8 states as well as the District of Columbia have legalized marijuana for both medicinal and recreational purposes.[29]

While cannabis use is expanding into every sector of society, with 6,000 Americans trying it for the first time each day, marijuana remains a Schedule 1 controlled substance in the eyes of the federal government and every 37 seconds a cannabis user is arrested.[30] Given that a number of medical studies now depict marijuana as improving aspects of physical well-being, it is not surprising that religious groups promoting cannabis as improving mental and spiritual well-being have become more visible during this period. However, the federal judicial systems in the United States and in Canada do not accept these claims. One can thus see a discursive clash happening between two powerful discursive streams, namely, that of medical science and that of the law. Moreover, as noted earlier, neither of these streams is univocal and within judicial discourse, there is a huge clash occurring between state and federal law.[31] There is also a subtle clash within various levels of the judiciary, as certain judges remain open to the idea that cannabis-based religions are not only legitimate religions but also should be allowed to operate if certain precautions are instilled into their practices. This is an important point and one that I will return to in chapter 5.

Bruce Lincoln is especially helpful in analyzing these types of discursive shifts. Lincoln believes that it is timing, the presentation of a persuasive message, and the ability to garner a receptive social group that allows "discourse the capacity to shape and reshape society itself."[32] I would argue that the discursive shift responsible for legalizing medical cannabis on the state level has both made cannabis religions more visible and provided an opening for more cannabis-based religious groups to appear. However, as federal law enforcement has turned its attention to these cannabis-based religions, a battle has emerged over the question of what constitutes a religion, a question that has serious legal ramifications if one's religious practices are judged illegitimate.

Therefore, the purpose of this book is fourfold: First, to demonstrate that these cannabis-based religions have not arisen *ex nihilo* but rather are a *bricolage* of beliefs and practices from other times and other places. Second, to use J. Z. Smith's methodology to contextualize these cannabis religions by looking at the patterns presented by earlier renditions, such as the Rastafari religion, the Ethiopian Zion Coptic Church (EZCC), and The Farm. Third, to provide case studies of these cannabis religions in order to understand better both their routine use of cannabis and the ways in which these routine practices reveal a deeper religious significance. Fourth, to examine the medical and legal discourses around cannabis to determine whether or not cannabis-based religions challenge their imposed discursive boundaries to the extent that they promote a more inclusive definition of religion.

It was J. Z. Smith's focus on "the *skandalon* of Jonestown" and his insistence that such a phenomenon "requires . . . the effort of understanding" that defined for him the reason to study unorthodox religions. However, to my mind, there is a much more compelling reason for understanding unorthodox religions that outweighs leaving "the study of religion open to the charge of incivility and intolerance,"[33] and that involves the necessity of bringing religious studies scholars into the realm of the judiciary. I would argue that it is imperative for scholars to monitor the scope of congressional and judicial authority in defining what counts as a religion and thus what counts as religious freedom. If one's religion is judged as illegitimate, the federal and state judiciaries have the power to place one in prison in an attempt to force one to conform to socially acceptable practices. This statement seems almost surreal in what we imagine to be our pluralistic, democratic society; however, both the United States' and Canada's judiciaries have prosecuted every founder of the cannabis-based religions discussed in this book. And it is not simply because these religions use cannabis in their sacramental rituals. However, since the ratification of the First Amendment designed to protect religious pluralism, our judicial system has slowly but surely moved to a position in which religious freedom is seen as an exemption from the law rather than a legal right. Moreover, this exemption is granted only if the adherents of an unorthodox religion are judged to be sincere in their beliefs.

This leads to the following question: How can a judge discern whether or not a defendant is sincere in his or her beliefs? The answer is simple: she cannot. That is why when we look at the judicial history of religious freedom from 1778 to 2016 we see a strangely divisive discourse in which unfamiliar religions, whether or not they involve illegal substances, are labeled as nonreligious. This precedential judicial treatment of unfamiliar religions basically nullifies the First Amendment Clauses involving religious freedom.[34] So, the search for a more inclusive application of legal standards is a goal that may require the scholar of religion to become an advocate for religious practitioners—a role that members of the academy rarely support nor often shoulder.

Perhaps we, as academicians living in a postmodern world, are unwilling to undertake the role of advocate because we will then be subject to displaying our own subjectivity. The scholar of unorthodox religions is particularly vulnerable to becoming a mouthpiece for her subjects, as there is little evidence available with which to frame one's subject apart from the following: the evidence produced by that subject and the historical and cross-cultural frameworks belonging to earlier religious renditions that can be used to contextualize these religions. One's challenges grow when these unorthodox religions are no longer in operation, so that one's links to information is limited to voices, documents and memories from the past. Elisabeth Arweck makes a good point when she notes that academics are no different than other interested parties when it comes to their participation within the "shifting alliances and hostilities" that work to construct a pattern around the always controversial subjects of unorthodox religions. For this reason, the scholar of unorthodox religions must always be conscious of "the processes by which knowledge is acquired."[35]

Given this set of challenges, I have attempted to gird myself with a hermeneutic of suspicion as it forces me to examine carefully the evidence gathered. In so doing, I have checked the facts and tried to find corroborating evidence for claims made and sources cited. If no corroborating evidence can be found to support a claim or source, I have either left it out or attributed it directly to the speaker. I have also tried to make my own agenda as transparent as possible—stating at the outset of this study that I believe an injustice was done to the Church of the Universe, and other cannabis-based religions, when a scholar of religion categorized this group as nonreligious. So, this study will rely on the method developed by J. Z. Smith of seeking *exempli gratia* in order to critically contextualize these religions within an intelligible framework. The groups I will review have all experienced cannabis to be a "powerful sacramental substance." Thus, in choosing historical examples that provide the best pattern for understanding cannabis religions, the mechanism or "trigger point" for their inclusion is the fact that they all position cannabis as a powerful substance, one that has been used historically and cross-culturally as a substance capable of effecting a change from the mundane to the sacred.

When exploring the category of powerful substances, India provides us with a wealth of examples where such substances are used ritualistically to provide a portal to sacred space: the various substances produced by cows such as dung, milk, and ghee (clarified butter), Ganges water, and, in the category of substances that alter consciousness, soma (most probably mushrooms or some other type of natural hallucinogenic) as well as cannabis. As we see in this list, a powerful substance can be almost anything that is identified as creating a transcendent disposition in the user as it is perceived as providing access to the divine.

It is, however, the arena of institutionalized power—namely, the government—that in the West provides the ultimate litmus test of a powerful substance. This occurs when the government identifies those substances that by definition must be "controlled" as they are considered too powerful to be "uncontrolled." In 1970, during the Nixon administration, Congress established the Controlled Substances Act (CSA), which set up a Schedule of Controlled Substances. This Schedule is topped by those substances deemed so powerful that they cannot be handled even within the medical arena, much less the general populace. These Schedule 1 substances are described by the U.S. Drug Enforcement Agency (DEA) as follows.

> Substances in this schedule have a high potential for abuse, have no currently accepted medical use in treatment in the United States, and there is a lack of accepted safety for use of the drug or other substance under medical supervision. Some examples of substances listed in schedule 1 are: heroin, lysergic acid diethylamide (LSD), marijuana (cannabis) peyote, methaqualone, and 3, 4-methylenedioxymethamphetamine ("ecstasy").[36]

As cannabis is deemed by the U.S. government to be a highly dangerous substance, only those presiding within institutionalized structures of power are eligible to control its usage. According to Durkheim, that degree of control is the *sine qua non* of both the sacred and the taboo: that which is so powerful it is kept away from any but the most powerful in society. In fact, from Durkheim's perspective, it is only as something is socially controlled that it is rendered powerful.[37] But Durkheim was a sociologist and a social constructionist and therefore was especially intrigued by those things that were rendered powerful only as society categorized them as such. Levi-Strauss, an anthropologist, furthers this line of reasoning in his understanding that categorizing a substance as powerful and keeping it in its established place is the only means for maintaining social order:

> A native thinker makes the penetrating comment that "all sacred things must have their place."[38] It could even be said that being in their place is what makes them sacred for if they were taken out of their place, even in thought, the entire order of the universe would be destroyed. Sacred objects therefore contribute to the maintenance of order in the universe by occupying the places allocated to them.[39]

Looking through Levi-Strauss's lens, cannabis can be a very antinomian substance as it disrupts the position to which it has been allocated by the federal government, especially as it produces an effect on anyone who can get their hands on it.

These cannabis-based religions, however, seek to change the position to which cannabis has been allocated and recontextualize cannabis as something that contributes to both physical and spiritual well-being. Thus, as exhorted by J. Z. Smith, framing cannabis as a powerful substance propels our passage down "the long, hard road of understanding" that allows us to contextualize these contemporary cannabis religions within a religious framework.[40]

Finally, while I have explained my methodology, what really interests me about this project, and really any project I undertake as a historian of religions, is the interplay between religion and politics, an interplay in which religion can function as a force for social liberation—for example, the role that the African American churches played in the 1960s civil rights movement—or as a force for social oppression—for example, the practice of profiling Muslims as potential terrorists and working to keep Muslims from entering this country. Lastly, religion is a force in and of itself. I think Wilfred Cantwell Smith said it best when he wrote, "God, as we have said, does not reveal a religion, He reveals Himself; what the observer calls a religion is man's continuing response."[41] I very much like the word "response." It denotes that one is responding to some kind of experiential calling—something outside of oneself, outside of one's culture, and beyond one's frame of reference: the ineffable experience of the sacred.

CHAPTER OUTLINE

Chapter 1, The Forerunners of Cannabis-Based Religions, brings contextual depth to our analysis of the Hawai'i Cannabis Ministry, the Church of the Universe, the Church of Cognizance, and Temple 420. Borrowing from Levi-Strauss and J. Z. Smith, I argue that every religion is a *bricolage,* as they are built, in some fashion, on the practices and beliefs of those movements that preceded them. To bring this analysis to life we will begin with the earliest historical instances of sacramental cannabis use around the globe and then move on to the Rastafari religion, the EZCC, and The Farm. In exploring these fore-runners of these cannabis-based religions, we unearth what Smith called *exempli gratia,* "an arsenal of classic instances which are held to be exemplary, to provide paradigmatic events and expressions as resources from which to reason, from which to extend the possibility of intelligibility to that which first appears novel."[42]

Chapters 2 and 3 examine the cannabis-based religions that collectively inspired the writing of this book: the Hawai'i Cannabis Ministry, the Church of Cognizance, Temple 420, and the Church of the Universe. Having demonstrated the exemplary structure grounding cannabis-based religions in chapter 1, we are poised to examine the ways in which these groups practice their sacramental rituals, establish their communal relations, engage in the political arena, and forge their connection to the divine. Chapter 2 begins with an exploration of the Church of the Universe, the religious group responsible for catalyzing this project, and continues with the exploration of the Church of Cognizance, and Temple 420. Included in this chapter are interviews with Danuel Quaintance of the Church of Cognizance and Craig Rubin of Temple 420. In chapter 3, I focus on both Roger Christie and the Hawai'i Cannabis Ministry as this group is the most recently active of the four cannabis religions under review, thus allowing me the best access to members of the ministry. I have been corresponding with Reverend Roger Christie for four years, and our dialogue has been extremely helpful in detailing the ways in which this particular group uses cannabis and answering an intrinsic question: Why would one want to get high in church?

Chapter 4, The Discourse Shifts: Public Reactions to the Science and Medical Effects of Cannabis, documents the discursive shifts that have recontextualized the meaning and accepted uses around cannabis in the last two decades and includes an interview with Dr. Mahmoud ElSolhly. ElSohly speaks to the science of cannabis and the active ingredients responsible for both affecting medical conditions and effecting a psychic "high." It is important to understand both the scientific basis and the medical usage of cannabis for two reasons: First, I make the argument that it is the shift in medical discourse that has both changed public perception around the religious use of cannabis and challenged the judiciary to examine their legal parameters around the sacramental use of cannabis. Second, without an understanding of how cannabis works in the body, we will be unable to understand why cannabis is seen as a unique sacramental substance by these cannabis-based religions. There is only one federally approved cannabis field in the country and that is controlled by ElSohly. We are able to visualize this field and its facilities in chapter 4, as ElSohly takes me on a tour of the University of Mississippi's cannabis field.

Having developed an understanding of these cannabis-based religions by seeing the ways in which cannabis is used and the deeper significance underlying this use, chapter 5 allows us to explore the labyrinthine relationships between religious freedom, cannabis, and the law. This chapter delves into the seminal law and court cases leading us to our present predicament in which the federal government and state governments are facing off in a duel not seen since the Civil War. In this chapter, we look at the legal precedents that pertain to religious freedom and the ways in which our cannabis-based religions have attempted both to conform to and to subvert these laws.

These cannabis-based religions provide us with a marvelous case study as they stand in that interstitial place between orthodox religions and what passes as the moral lens of the law. Walter LaFleur puts it best when he states: "There are, in fact, a lot of adjustments between the strict ethical axioms that are laid down at the base of a tradition and the moral reality of everyday life in the present. There have to be. And these adjustments that take place 'in between' are, in fact, the tradition."[43] According to LaFleur's analysis, that is why the founders and members of these churches, temples, and ministries claim pieces of orthodox religions while rejecting others and undertake great risks to introduce new practices into their religious lives—they do so to make their religious lives relevant.

As noted, two representatives of the academy denied the Church of the Universe's legitimacy during their trial on charges of drug trafficking. However, as this study concludes with, The Evolution of Religious Freedom, I will do two things: First, describe the ways and means through which the judiciary and these cannabis-based religious groups have worked together, in certain instances, to allow for the continued existence of the latter. And second, to recall the reader to the deep religious significance of the practices demonstrated by these cannabis-based religions.

NOTES

1. "Church of the Universe Argues That Marijuana Is a Sacrament Protected by Freedom of Religion," Centre for Constitutional Studies, July 9, 2010, http://ualawccsprod.srv.ualberta.ca/ccs/index.php/constitutional-issues/25-other/78-Church-of-the-universe-argues-that-marijuana-is-a-sacrament-protected-by-freedom-of-religion.
2. Charles Lewis, "Updated: 'Pot Church' Member Sentenced to Three Months in Jail," *National Post*, May 30, 2011, http://news.nationalpost.com/holy-post/pot-Church-members-to-be-sentenced.
3. Ibid.
4. Edward B. Tylor, *Primitive Culture* (London: John Murphy, 1903), 424.
5. Emile Durkheim, *The Elementary Forms of the Religious Life* (New York: Free Press, 1912), 47.
6. Paul Tillich, *Christianity and the Encounter of the World Religions* (New York: Columbia University Press, 1963), 4.
7. Charles Long, *Significations: Signs, Symbols, and Images in the Interpretation of Religion* (Aurora, CO: The Davies Group, 1999), 7.
8. Clifford Geertz, *The Interpretations of Cultures: Selected Essays* (New York: Basic Books, 1973), 90.
9. Mary Daly, *Beyond God the Father: Toward a Philosophy of Women's Liberation* (Boston: Beacon Press, 1973), 32.
10. Catherine L. Albanese, *America: Religions and Religion* (Belmont, CA: Wadsworth, 1992), 11.
11. Frederick Streng, *Understanding Religious Life* (Belmont, CA: Wadsworth Publishing Company, 1985), 2.
12. Rita Gross, *Feminism and Religion: An Introduction* (Boston: Beacon Press, 1996), 7.
13. Rudolf Otto, John W. Harvey trans. (New York: Oxford University Press, 1948), 12.
14. Kay Almere Read, *Time and Sacrifice in the Aztec Cosmos* (Indiana: Indiana University Press, 1998).
15. Claude Levi-Strauss, *The Savage Mind* (Chicago: University of Chicago Press, 1966), 17.
16. Catherine Bell, *Ritual: Perspectives and Dimensions* (New York: Oxford University Press, 1997), 224.
17. Adam B. Seligman, Robert P. Weller, Michael J. Puett, and Bennett Simon, *Ritual and Its Consequences: An Essay on the Limits of Sincerity* (New York: Oxford University Press, 2008), 5.
18. The definition of "ritual" and the importance of studying ritual practices has become *de rigueur* in the field of religious studies; so much so that it has become a subfield within the History of Religions. The major debate among scholars when working with this term is along the lines of whether ritual is to be consistently linked with religion or if ritual fits more clearly into the realm of everyday practices.
19. J. Z. Smith, *Imagining Religion from Babylon to Jonestown* (Chicago: University of Chicago Press, 1982), 113.

20. Ibid., 104.
21. Ibid.
22. Ibid., 112.
23. Michel Foucault, *The Archaeology of Knowledge*, translated by A.M. Sheridan Smith. (London: Routledge, 2002).
24. Smith, 113. "*Empli gratia*" from the Latin, literally means for the sake of an example.
25. Ibid., 115
26. Ibid.
27. Ibid., 104.
28. Lydia Saad, "Majority Continues to Support Pot Legalization in U.S.," Gallup, November 6, 2014, http://www.gallup.com/poll/179195/majority-continues-support-pot-legalization.aspx?utm_source=genericbutton&utm_medium=organic&utm_campaign=sharing.
29. These states include Alaska, Arizona, Arkansas, Colorado, Connecticut, Delaware, Florida, Hawaii, Illinois, Maine, Maryland, Massachusetts, Michigan, Minnesota, Montana, Nevada, New Hampshire, New Jersey, New Mexico, New York, North Dakota, Ohio, Oregon, Pennsylvania, Rhode Island, Vermont, Washington, West Virginia, and the District of Columbia. The states that have legalized cannabis for recreational purposes include Alaska, California, Colorado, Maine, Massachusetts, Nevada, Oregon, Washington, and Washington, D.C.
30. K. K. Repp and A. L. Raich, "Marijuana and Health: A Comprehensive Review of 20 Years of Research," Washington County, Oregon, Department of Health and Human Services, October 20, 2014, available at http://www.co.washington.or.us/HHS/News/upload/Marijuana-review.pdf.
31. While not a state, I am counting the District of Columbia in this statement.
32. Bruce Lincoln, *Discourses and the Construction of Society: Comparative Studies of Myth, Ritual, and Classification*, 2nd ed. (Oxford: Oxford University Press, 2014), 7.
33. Smith, 104.
34. "Congress shall make no law respecting an establishment of religion, or prohibiting the free exercise thereof. Two Clauses of the First Amendment concern the relationship of government to religion: the Establishment Clause and the Free Exercise Clause." Introduction to the Establishment Clause of the First Amendment, University of Missouri-Kansas City, accessed July 23, 2016, http://law2.umkc.edu/faculty/projects/ftrials/conlaw/estabinto.htm.
35. Elisabeth Arweck, *Researching New Religious Movements: Responses and Redefinitions* (London: Routledge, 2006), 7.
36. U.S. Department of Justice, "Controlled Substance Schedules," accessed November 9, 2012, http://www.deadiversion.usdoj.gov/schedules/index.html.
37. Emile Durkheim, *The Elementary Forms of the Religious Life* (Mineola, NY: Dover Publications, Inc., 2008).
38. Z. C. Fletcher, "The Hako: A Pawnee Ceremony," *22nd Annual Report, Bureau of American Ethnology* (1900–1901) (Washington, DC: Government Printing Office, 1904), 34.
39. Levi-Strauss, 4.
40. Smith, 104.
41. Wilfred Cantwell Smith, *The Meaning and End of Religion* (Philadelphia: Fortress Press, 1962), 129.
42. Smith, 113.
43. William LaFleur, *Liquid Life: Abortion and Buddhism in Japan* (Princeton: Princeton University Press, 1992), 12.

ONE

The Forerunners of Cannabis-Based Religions

Exempli Gratia: *For the Sake of an Example*

The current discourse around cannabis can be split into three categories: medical usage, recreational usage, and the law. In other words, the current discussion of cannabis does not contextualize cannabis as a ritual substance and we do not find a category within dominant discourse that pairs cannabis and religion. This was not always the case. In fact, this chapter will begin with a look not only at the earliest uses of cannabis but also at its role as a "sacrament," a word which in Greek translates to *musterion* or mystery. We will then examine the Rastafari religion, the Ethiopian Zion Coptic Church (EZCC), and The Farm in order to see if they provide us with a template by which to judge the legitimacy of the more contemporary cannabis-based religions.

CANNABIS USE ACROSS TIME AND SPACE

When one is looking back in history for the origins of a practice, the evidentiary trail gets murky. And while there is a plethora of speculation and hypotheses around the question of when and where cannabis was first used, the only reliable evidence comes from archaeological artifacts, stone inscriptions, or texts—and even then the information gleaned from these can be ambiguous. Earnest Abel suggests that the Chinese were the earliest users of hemp, drawing his evidence from archeological artifacts and the *Book of Rites*. In verse 23 of the *Book of Rites*, dated somewhere in the vicinity of the fifth century BCE to the third century BCE, it is stated that "During the three years of the mourning rites (for parents), the king . . . when he went to transact any business, the ropes (for his chariot) were made of hemp (and not silk)."[1] In terms of the archaeological evidence, Abel states that a Chinese artifact, dating back to the Stone Age, was found at a site containing pottery fragments: "Dispersed among the pottery fragments were some elongated rod shaped tools, very similar in appearance to those later used to loosen cannabis from their stems."[2] And in "The Origin and Use of Cannabis in Eastern Asia," by Li, we read the following:

> While traces of early Chinese fabrics have all but disappeared, in 1972 an ancient burial site dating back to the Chou dynasty (1122–249 B.C.) was discovered. In it were fragments of cloth, some bronze containers, weapons, and pieces of jade. Inspection of the cloth showed it to be made of hemp, making this the oldest preserved specimen of hemp in existence.[3]

Another country where one finds the early use of cannabis is India. One of the most popular ways that cannabis has been used over the centuries and continues into the present involves mixing it into a drink called bhang, which also contains such ingredients as poppy seed, cloves, cinnamon, and milk—cannabis, however, is the major ingredient. The *Atharva Veda*, dated at approximately 900 BCE and the fourth of the Vedic texts, states that the God Siva is the Lord of Bhang. This is not a surprising role given that Siva is the God of creation and destruction, love and death, and, as stated by Wendy Doniger, erotica and asceticism.[4] As such, he is the perfect God to enjoy bhang, a drink that frees people from their inhibitions. While bhang is used on many occasions, two of the most important of these are Sivaratri, literally "the night of Siva," and the festival of Holi. Holi lasts for one or two days and it comprises a celebration of the wonders of life and love with bonfires, water fights, singing, dancing, throwing paint, and drinking bhang.

The ancient Aryans, those responsible for bringing the Vedas to India somewhere between 1,500 BCE and 1,200 BCE, are thought to have stopped in Persia along the way. For this reason, it is not surprising that we find Bhang in Persia as well as India. According to Mircea Eliade, Zoraster, circa seventh century BCE, "may have been a user of bhanga and may have relied on its intoxication to bridge the metaphysical gap between heaven and earth."[5]

Given that Africa had a major part to play in the Rastafari religion of Jamaica, "Africans have had a long tradition of smoking hemp in gourd pipes . . . [and] that by 1884 the King of the Baluka tribe of the Congo had established a riamba,"—a religious ritual utilizing cannabis.[6] Further, cannabis was used in Africa for medical purposes such as "restoring appetite and relieving the pain of hemorrhoids."[7]

Moving to Greco-Roman history, "[t]he first undisputed mention of the intoxicating properties of cannabis is found in "Researches" (450 BC) by the Greek historian Herodotus, known as the father of history, who describes a Scythian burial ceremony in a small hut with a pit for hot stones. The Scythians threw cannabis on the stones, producing smoke, which they inhaled."[8] This piece of evidence was further confirmed when "Rudenko, a Russian anthropologist, unearthed the remnants of a Scythian burial site and found a bronze cauldron filled with burned Cannabis seeds. . . ."[9] Among the Romans in approximately 70 CE, a Greek physician by the name of Diosorides mentioned cannabis as a healing plant in his *Materia Medica*. In this text he noted that while cannabis "was not very useful for manufacturing strong ropes . . . the juice of its seeds was also very beneficial in treating earaches and in diminishing sexual desires."[10]

Looking at the Western traditions, we find in the Old Testament of the Bible two verses that the Women of Reformed Judaism, as well as others engaged in Biblical hermeneutics, argue is referring to the sacramental use of cannabis. In Genesis 1:29, "See, I have given you every plant yielding seed that is upon the face of all the earth, and every tree with seed in its fruit; you shall have them for food." And in Exodus 30:22 we are told that the Lord said to Moses to make a "sacred anointing oil blended as by the perfumer; it shall be a holy anointing oil."[11] *Kanabos/kaneh bosem* is one of the ingredients in this oil, and as noted in Ben-Yehuda's Hebrew Dictionary, "the modern Hebrew word transliterated as 'kanabos' is translated as 'hemp,' the English word for cannabis."[12]

Do all scholars translate *kanabos* or *kaneh bosem* as cannabis? I asked two Old Testament scholars, and they both agreed that it was nearly impossible to make a scholarly case for *kaneh bosem* being cannabis. They based this opinion on the fact that *kanabos* and *bosem* used in combination, show up in only two places in the Hebrew Bible, both in Exodus 30:23 wherein they are usually translated as "fragrant cinnamon" or "aromatic cane." And while there is a phonetic similarity, that similarity does not signify that *kaneh bosem* is cannabis.[13] So, the idea that these verses are referring to cannabis is a minority opinion.

Moving forward several centuries to Britain, we find a short pharmaceutical reference to hemp in Phillip Miller's 1724 *The Gardener's Dictionary*, in which he notes: "This Plant is propagated in the rich fenny parts of Lincolnshire in great quantities for its bark which is so useful for cordage, cloth, etc., and the seeds afford an oyl which is used in medicine."[14] In 1813, when information was gathered by the British from India, the English dictionaries were able to flesh out the entries dealing with hemp and note that cannabis sativa, bhang (bangue), and ganja (ganjah) were all names for the same plant.

> Ganja (Tamil, Duk and Malay), Kanub (Arab), Hemp Cannabis Sativa, Vijya, Sanjica (Sanskrit). Ganja is the Tamool name of the plant from which Bangie and Majum are prepared. The leaves are frequently add-

> ed to tobacco and smoked to increase its intoxicating power; they are also sometimes, given in case of Diarrhoea and in conjunction with Turmeric, Onions and warm Ginglie oil, are made into an application for painful, swelled and protruded Piles.[15]

Looking to North America, the cultivation of cannabis sativa has been documented in the United States since the early seventeenth century, when settlers brought the plant to Jamestown, Virginia, to produce hemp.[16] The hemp plant's economic importance in America also dates back to this period, when it was used in the production of rope, sails, and clothing.[17] Domestic production for industrial purposes flourished until after the Civil War. In the late nineteenth century, cannabis was introduced into Western medicine and sold openly in pharmacies as a sedative and to reduce inflammation and muscle spasms. Cannabis merited an entry in the 1850 edition of the medical reference book *U.S. Pharmacopeia*, and remained in this medical text for more than 50 years.[18]

MARIJUANA: A NEW LOW

Permissive attitudes toward cannabis would change dramatically in the beginning of the twentieth century, as social reform movements attempted to eradicate the recreational use of cannabis and other substances such as alcohol, morphine, and opium. Local, national, and international jurisdictions codified these prohibitions, passing laws that restricted the nonmedical use of cannabis or banned the substance completely.

> During the period 1909–1995, important and significant changes took place in respect of the drugs involved, as well as the form and extent of their abuse, but it was realized from the very beginning that national efforts aimed at restricting the availability of drugs of abuse to medical and scientific purposes must be supported by international action.[19]

In relation to these international political actions, the United States was one of the primary instigators.

The first international meeting on drug use was held in 1909 Shanghai and dealt primarily with the addictive use of opium. However, at this meeting the subject of cannabis was brought up by the Italian contingent, but was not acted upon until 1925. Two meetings of the International Opium Convention were held in February of 1925. "The second Geneva Convention [of] the International Opium Convention . . . was intended to impose global controls over a wider range of drugs, including, for the first time, cannabis—described as 'Indian hemp' in Article 11 of the Convention."[20] Given the religious significance of cannabis in India, the Indian Delegation objected to the inclusion of cannabis in the treaty:

> The Government of India, however, at the present stage of their examination of the subject point out various serious difficulties of an administrative order in confining the use of hemp drugs to medical and scientific purposes; for example there are social and religious customs which naturally have to be considered, and there is the doubt whether the total prohibition of drugs easily prepared from a wild-growing plant could in practice be made effective.[21]

The convention delegates eventually arrived at a two-part compromise: first, Indian hemp and cannabis could only be exported to countries in which these products were legal; second, the importing country had to provide a license stating that the product was to be used for medical and/or scientific purposes.

Back on the home front during the time of Prohibition and the Great Depression, public and government concern regarding the potential harms of cannabis began to grow, as a series of anecdotal, nonscientific reports linked the use of "marijuana" with violence, insanity, crime, and social deviance. These ideas became instantiated in society largely due to the work of Harry Anslinger, the first commissioner of the Federal Bureau of Narcotics.

> A failed career diplomat, Anslinger used the marijuana issues to revive his fortunes in governmental service. Under his direction, an official picture of marijuana was drawn, in which the drug was held responsible for the poverty and moral apathy of native peoples, such as Mexican farm laborers, and posed a threat to American users. . . . Occurring simultaneously with the rise of xenophobic sentiments against Mexican migrant workers, Anslinger's campaign resulted in severe penalties against the possession, use, and cultivation of marijuana.[22]

William Randolph Hearst, a timber and newspaper baron, was also a staunch supporter of the anti-cannabis campaign as the industrial uses of hemp, particularly its usage as construction material and paper, competed with Hearst's lumber and newspaper empire. As hemp can be made into myriad products as diverse as rope, sails, clothing, food, and oil, it drew fire from other industrial moguls, such as John D. Rockefeller, Jr. Rockefeller had as much to lose as Hearst if hemp were to become a major source of oil as he stood at the head of a petroleum empire. These two industrial magnates along with others such as DuPont, a maker of synthetic clothing, worked in concert with Anslinger to delegitimize the use of cannabis; a campaign that was waged especially through Hearst's newspapers.

By 1931, cannabis was outlawed in 29 states. The film *Reefer Madness* was released in 1936 and showed a cornucopia of madness, murder, and mayhem—all due to the smoking of cannabis. The film brought together sex, criminal gangs, insanity, and murder to inflame the people of America and convince them that "something must be done to wipe out this ghastly menace."[23] Moreover, while the time was ripe for exploiting the negative reaction forming around all uses of cannabis, this film was particularly directed toward parents, both to scare them and to steer them directly into the voting booth. And, in 1937, Congress passed the Marijuana Tax Act, which restricted possession of the drug to individuals who paid an excise tax on certain medical and industrial uses. By 1942, cannabis was removed from the *U.S. Pharmacopoeia*, the nation's official list of medicines.[24]

"The currency of the word [marijuana] increased greatly in the United States in the 1930s in the context of the debate over the use of the drug, the term being preferred as a more exotic alternative to the familiar words hemp and cannabis. . . ."[25] This discursive "exoticism" also enabled U.S. citizens to think of this drug as being in the possession of others, not us; and, in fact, as noted by Mitch Earleywine, marijuana is "a Spanish word purportedly coined in Mexico, [that] originally meant 'cheap tobacco.'"[26] Jack Herer, a pro-cannabis activist, stated the following:

> The actual Spanish word for hemp is "canamo." But using a Mexican Sonoran colloquialism—marijuana—guaranteed that no one would realize the world's chief natural medicine and premier industrial resource had been outflanked, outlawed and pushed out of the language.[27]

Foucault speaks to this linguistic phenomenon: "If [something] is repressed, that is, condemned to prohibition, nonexistence, and silence, then the mere fact that one is speaking about it has the appearance of a deliberate transgression."[28]

In sum, the United States and many other countries had firmly fixed cannabis, now called marijuana, into the context of harmful and illegal substances. However, the use of cannabis as a sacramental substance could not be stopped or controlled, even when it was up against the federal government, international policies, exploitative movies, parental fears, and the looming possibility of criminal incarceration. I would argue that, even in the face of a damning discursive flow, when it comes to religion, there is a higher experiential authority to which one is drawn. When one can replicate a religiously based sensory experience using an illegal substance, it is difficult for a legal system to curtail its use.

I now turn to three groups that have used or continue to use cannabis as a sacrament: The Rastafari religion, the EZCC, and The Farm. As I examine these religious groups, I will apply to each, the following three questions: First, who were the founders and what was the early development of the group? Second, in what ways did each group contextualize and use cannabis as part of their communal practices? And third, what have been the legal consequences for using cannabis as a sacrament? I am keeping these questions broad, as the questions one asks delimit the answers one receives. For this reason, rather than imposing my preconceived notions upon these groups, I will keep my frame of analysis as spacious as possible in order to see what emerges from this examination. After completing my examination of these three groups, I will compare the Rastas, the Coptics, and the members of The Farm to see if these religious groups provide us with a structural template through which we might better understand more recent cannabis-based religions.

FOUNDERS: MARCUS GARVEY, BOB MARLEY, AND THE ORIGINS OF THE RASTAFARI RELIGION

As stated by Lambros Comitas, the trip from India to Jamaica first occurred in the mid-eighteenth century when workers from India were brought to several Caribbean countries as indentured servants.

> The roots of the Jamaican ganja complex can be linked to the Indian subcontinent. During the latter part of the nineteenth century, its prototypical forms were carried to the island by East Indian indentured laborers. . . . Present-day techniques and ganja use, critical parts of the ganja lexicon and much of the justificatory ideology surrounding ganja lend strong support to a claim of a direct India-to-Jamaica diffusion.[29]

Another theory of cannabis dispersion noted by Bilby and Murrell, as well as O'Brian and Carter, claimed that the ideological framework around the Jamaican use of cannabis came from Africa. "West Indian scholars have traced the religious ancestry [of cannabis] through the Revival of the late nineteenth century, back to traditional African belief systems."[30] Most scholars believe that both Africa and India were responsible for the conveyance of cannabis to Jamaica. However, it is the term "Revival," used by Carter and O'Brien, that is particularly striking due to the fact that the word "revival" signals the resurgence of religious *bricolage* from one place or time to another place or time.

One of the primary *bricoleurs* in the transformation of Indian and African cannabis rituals into the Rastafari religion in Jamaica was Marcus Garvey (1887–1940). Over his lifetime, Garvey had a profound effect on religions that centralized black social empowerment, separatism, and self-reliance, and he can be seen as a strong force behind the development of both the Nation of Islam and the Rastafari religion. In relation to Garvey, Roderick states: "Although his contributions to American and global society are only now beginning to be recognized Marcus Garvey was one of the most influential leaders of the African-American community in the early 20th C."[31] In 1914, Garvey founded the Universal Negro Improvement Association. "Garvey's purpose was to demonstrate to all men and women of African descent their essential oneness in the struggle for survival in a hostile White dominated world."[32] And according to I. J. Tafari, Marcus Garvey "established the framework on which Noble Drew Ali,

Prophet W. D. Fard and Elijah Muhammad built the Nation of Islam. . . ."[33]

Part of the ideology stemming from both Africa and India had to do with the ritual use of ganja—the holy herb; but whatever the source of this religious practice, Jamaicans came to make this religious system their own. This process of *bricolage* led to the formation of the Rastafari religion, which currently counts its membership at approximately 1 million members worldwide. Marcus Garvey had proclaimed that a black emperor and living deity would arise from Africa and he used the Bible to confirm his conviction: "Ethiopia shall soon stretch out her hands unto God."[34] In 1930, Ethiopia crowned Ras Tafari Markonnen as Emperor Haile Selassie I, and many Jamaicans and those from other countries such as Trinidad, Tobago, and Guyana believed that Garvey's proclamation had come to pass. Thus, the name of the religion, "Rastafari," came from the term "Ras" which means king or emperor and "Tafari," which was the surname of Haile Selassie I.

THE SACRED HERB AND COMMUNITY PRACTICES

Throughout the 1930s and the following decades, the Rastafari religion developed several distinctive elements. First, the smoking of herb as a sacramental substance—and it is important to note that the Rastas primarily refer to cannabis as herb; second, the acceptance of Haile Selassie I as a living messiah; third, the representation of Ethiopia as Zion—heaven on earth; fourth, the wearing of dreadlocks; and fifth, the maintenance of an "Ital" diet, which eschews foods that are not naturally grown from the earth. As such, most Rastafaris are vegetarians who also do not eat pork or shell-fish, foodstuffs found in Leviticus to be impure.

In addition to Leviticus, the Rastafari religion draws on the Bible as the foundation of many Rasta practices. However, as part of the work of this new generation of *bricoleurs*, the Rastafaris reinterpret orthodox texts and practices to make them relevant to their own religiocultural context. Tahari notes that Numbers 6:5 is taken by Rastafaris as the source for wearing dreadlocks: "All the days of their nazirite vow no razor shall come upon the head; until the time is completed for which they separate themselves to the Lord, they shall be holy; they shall let the locks of the head grow long."[35] The use of herb is similarly perceived to be promoted in Revelation: "Then the angel showed me the river of the water of life, bright as crystal, flowing from the throne of God and of the Lamb through the middle of the street of the city. On either side of the river is the tree of life with its twelve kinds of fruit, producing its fruit each month; and the leaves of the tree are for the healing of the nations."[36] And Genesis 1:29, quoted earlier, which states that "See, I have given you every plant yielding seed that is upon the face of all the earth. . . .[37] The

Bible also enjoins each man to invite his neighbor to dwell under his own fig tree and grape vine, following the Biblical injunction that, "On that day, says the Lord of hosts, you shall invite each other to come under your vine and fig tree."[38] The Rastafari interpret this passage as meaning that they should grow communal gardens whether they live in rural or urban places. Thus, Rastafaris have communal gardens both in villages and in more urban settings, a practice that not only brings people together into a community but also affords self-sufficiency.

In pointing out that white-dominated culture functions to oppress Rastas and all other black people, white culture is denoted as Babylon—described in Jeremiah 51:58: "Thus says the Lord of hosts: The broad wall of Babylon shall be leveled to the ground, and her high gates shall be burned with fire; The peoples exhaust themselves for nothing, and the nations weary themselves only for fire."[39] The Rastafarian connection between white oppressors and Babylon is one of the defining characteristics of the Rastafari religion: "Because of the nature of Rastafarian ideology (rejection of capitalism, rejection of European hegemony, and the upending of white racism) it has been easily incorporated into other nations with similar histories of European and American oppression, such as other Caribbean nations, Ethiopia, Ghana, Senegal, Australia, and New Zealand—particularly among the Maori."[40] Thus, the Rastafaris centralize a political agenda within their religion in an effort to overturn the current social order, so as to destroy white hegemony. As we will see, the importance of a political agenda is shared by all of the cannabis-based religions.

The deification of Haile Selassi I is also believed to derive from Revelation 5:2 wherein the Rastafari believe "the Root of David" refers to Haile Selassi I. "Then one of the elders said to me, 'Do not weep. See, the Lion of the tribe of Judah, the Root of David, has conquered, so that he can open the scroll and its seven seals.'"[41] However, while Haile Selassie I is regarded as the Messiah, one does not need to go through a priest, minister, community leader, or anyone else to forge one's divine connection with him and union with Jah, the name Psalms 68:4 uses for God.[42] Jah encompasses everything and everyone is a part of Jah. The unified nature of all things is a belief held by all three of the cannabis forerunners and most of the contemporary cannabis-based religions.

Like the connection between Babylon and white oppression, the deification of Haile Selassi I is clearly founded on political as well as biblical interpretation. Hamid states that one reason for positioning Haile Selassi I as a divine being had to do with his prowess in maintaining Ethiopia's sovereignty during World War II. "Soon after his ascent to the throne, Ethiopia had been invaded by Mussolini. The Emperor vowed to recapture his land without shedding a drop of Ethiopian blood. . . . [I]n a famous photograph accompanying his many appeals in the major European newspapers, he was shown standing on an unexploded bomb [and] he regained his throne in 1941."[43]

Because the sacramental and biblically mandated use of cannabis is a central practice within the Rastafari religion, it is important to talk about its particular usage among adherents. As noted by Hausman,

> Rastas have created an oral mythology around the use of marijuana. . . . The myths that are associated with the smoking of marijuana come from splinters of Psalms in the Bible and from Ethiopian tales that go back to Solomon's time as king. One of these suggests that ganja plants sprang out of Solomon's grave after he was buried. There are aphorisms that state "to smoke renders one as wise as Solomon" or that "herb is the wine," the blessing of the sacrament, the advocation of the Lord.[44]

In the last few decades, cannabis has been the central component in communal "reasoning sessions," where the herb is passed around to all present to encourage the truth, "since it was through smoking ganja that truth was revealed."[45] Women were initially barred from these sessions, but that is no longer the case. The Rastafari do not find the need for a separate building to house religious activities. Instead, they most often meet in a member's home. "The meetings . . . provide a time for chants, prayers and singing, and for communal issues to be discussed." Cannabis is seen as a God-given gift that elevates "feelings of community and [is used] to produce visions of a religious and calming nature. . . ."[46] Prior to the partaking of the holy herb, those present say a prayer glorifying Jah, the creator of everything. "Glory be to the father and to the maker of creation. As it was in the beginning is now and ever shall be World without end."[47]

This prayer should be familiar to those who have attended a Catholic or Protestant worship service. However, in those services, the words acknowledge the triumvirate of God, Jesus, and the Holy Ghost whereas in Rastafari reasoning sessions, Jesus and the Holy Spirit are replaced by "the maker of creation." To my mind, this reinterpretation of the "Gloria Patri" prayer indicates the unity of all things, including God and the worshipper. One sees the same religious stance in the following: "A Rasta will never [say] 'I am going there' instead it would be 'I and I am going there.' The Rasta does this to show that God is part of him, and that individuals are not separate from any other person."[48]

Those who identify as members of the Rastafari religion do not proselytize. But the Rastafari, while not proselytizing, have a very effective means of disseminating their religion: this is reggae music. "Excuse me while I light my spliff, you know I got to take a leave from reality I just can't drift."[49] And "Live for yourself, you will live in vain. Live for others, you will live again."[50] As noted by O'Brien and Carter, "the movement has been able to communicate its message globally through the medium of reggae music."[51] Some of the greatest reggae musicians were Rastas including Bob Marley, Peter Tosh, and Toots (Frederick Nathaniel Hibbert) from Toots and the Maytals.

Like Mozart, Bob Marley created an amazing amount of music prior to an early death. Marley died at the age of 36 from malignant melanoma and was inducted into the Rock and Roll Hall of Fame posthumously in 1994. Many of his lyrics rejoice in the sacramental power of the holy herb and the need to

> Get up, stand up. Stand up for your rights.
> Get up, stand up. Don't give up the fight.[52]

In terms of the holy herb, "[m]any remember Marley for his public embrace of marijuana and his belief in its healing powers." Marley's website describes the musician: "[i]t's important to note that Marley did not just enjoy weed as a recreational habit. He was instead a staunch supporter of the plant's meditational, spiritual and healing abilities, and a fierce opponent to those ('political forces') who tried using marijuana as a vehicle of oppression, and to keep certain groups of people out of the societal mainstream."[53] Bob Marley's daughter Cedella states: "Creative inspiration was everything for my father—it was like breathing or life to him. . . . Every time he smoked, he was inspired and an open mind was the open door for this creative inspiration. He thought the herb was actually a gift."[54]

In looking at other Rastafari musicians, Peter Tosh elaborates on why the word herb is so important to the Rastafari religion: "Rastas don't smoke marijuana . . . marijuana is a girl from Cuba . . . Ganja is a bird from Australia, I smoke HERB."[55] The importance of using their own linguistic signifiers also comes up in our later cannabis-based religions and is founded on the fact that Babylon, in the case of the Rastafari religion, is said to have torn away the language around cannabis in order to vilify the herb and in so doing vilify those who use the herb.

> Rastas have created a modified vocabulary and dialect known as "Iyaric," to not only take back language but push it forward and reject modern western society, often referred to as "Babylon," which Rastas see as entirely corrupt. So it's for these reasons that Rastas smoke herb "the healing of the nation" and nothing else.[56]

Toots, the lead singer and songwriter of Toots and the Maytals, was not as concerned about using Iyaric as Peter Tosh, but his songs show the same reverence for cannabis. Toots showed his devotion to cannabis by putting out the album Pass the Pipe.[57]

In this song, Toots is extolling not only the virtues of cannabis but also the necessity of praising Jah with song based on Psalms 68:4. "Sing to God, sing praises to his name; lift up a song to him who rides upon the clouds—his name is the Lord—be exultant before him."[58]

THE CONSEQUENCES OF USING THE SACRED HERB

Given that Jamaica has been perceived as the tourist hot spot for cannabis since the mid-1960s, one might be surprised that it was not until 2015 that Jamaica changed its laws to decriminalize cannabis for medical and scientific use. Prior to that time, all three of the musicians discussed above, Bob Marley, Peter Tosh, and Toots had been imprisoned for possession of cannabis; Toots named a song after his prisoner's number, 54–46, and Peter Tosh was beaten up on a street corner in Kingston by several plainclothesmen and then "taken to the local station and badly beaten again. The results were more than several stitches on his head [and] an arm in plaster."[59] And according to the *London Times*, as of 2014, "300 Jamaicans are said to receive criminal records each week."[60]

Bob Marley raised an interesting and relevant question: "How could a plant created by God be made illegal by humans? 'You mean they can tell God that it's not legal?' If growing cannabis is to be a crime then by man's laws God, who made all plants was a criminal too." Bob Marley was not surprised that people who smoke herb were persecuted by "Babylon," the ruling system, as he reminded people: "Them crucify Christ, remember?"[61]

As noted, Jamaica changed their law in 2015 to allow for the decriminalization of cannabis following the pattern of the 23 U.S. states that had already done so. While this change was an extremely popular one in Jamaica, what struck me was a sentence quoted in the *London Times* when the Jamaican Parliament was examining their stance on cannabis: it states that one of the issues that had kept Jamaica from touching laws dealing with cannabis stemmed from "fears that the island could face American sanctions if it legalized the drug."[62] Of course, it is not surprising that the United States has used legal discourse and its punitive effects to create a context for the present-day use of cannabis, but the tremendous reach of American discourse and its hand-in-glove relationship not merely with national law, but international law, is daunting from the standpoint of religious freedom.

I next turn to the EZCC, a "mansion" or offshoot of the Rastafari religion. In so doing, I will pay careful attention to those Rastafari components which the Coptics employ and those from which they abstain as they develop their own practices around cannabis.

THE ETHIOPIAN ZION COPTIC CHURCH: THE FOUNDERS AND EARLY DAYS

The EZCC was operational from 1976–1982 and included at its peak approximately 1,500 members. As noted above, this church developed as a mansion of the Rastafari religion, but, over time, took up strict religious customs that were not practiced by the Rastas. Louva Williams was the founder of the EZCC. "A carpenter's son who began spreading the doctrine in Jamaica in the 1940s. . . . Through Williams, the present Coptic doctrine took form. When he died in 1969, the Church collapsed."[63] In spirit form, Williams passed the torch to George Baker Ivy, who tried to reassemble the Coptics. As noted by Carl Hiaasen of the *Miami Herald,* "Ivy was the first elder to admit whites in the 'camp,' and in fact encouraged disaffected young Americans to come to the island and learn the ways of the ganja Church."[64] The American infusion of the EZCC thus began when a handful of white American men went to Jamaica in the early 1970s to escape from what they found to be a corrupt American society. What they found in Jamaica was a group of Jamaican men in a camp near Kingston calling themselves the Ethiopian Zion Coptic Church and tracing "its origins back 6,000 years."[65] The Coptics also believed that cannabis was a sacrament.

Over the next few years, many more Americans moved to Jamaica and were allowed to be part of this group. If one were to visit the EZCC in those days, one would find black and white people smoking ganja and chanting prayers. During the 1970s, Thomas Francis Reilly, Jr. one of the "disaffected young Americans," also known as Brother Louv, came to be the leader and spokesperson for the EZCC. In 1975, the EZCC was incorporated and the church bought 1,000 acres of farmland in Jamaica and invested more than $3,000,000 in the Jamaican economy—a huge injection of cash that, among other things, proved a help to a very poor, underdeveloped economy. In fact the prime minister of Jamaica at the time, Edward Seaga, stated that "the export of marijuana from Jamaica is a critically important factor in the country's economy."[66] Also in 1975, the Caucasian Coptics bought up land on Star Island in Miami for $270,000 in cash. According to Carl Hiaasen of the *Miami Herald,* "[T]he money was provided by a Jamaican Coptic elder, Keith Gordon," and from this time forward, the EZCC had its headquarters on Star Island.[67]

No one refutes the fact that the enormous amount of money referred to above was acquired by the Caucasian Coptics through the export of sacraments/medicine/drugs (pick your discourse) from Jamaica into the United States. However, raising huge sums of money that is then justified through religious discourse is something that religious institutions have excelled at across time and cultures. The Coptics were, at one time, the major employer of the Jamaican people. While "law enforcement authorities believe the Church is merely a front for a massive pot-smuggling operation, the Florida Supreme Court had recognized the Coptic faith as a true religion whose doctrine stretches back centuries."[68] I now turn to the Coptic's religion and the ways in which the Coptics celebrated their sacrament.

THE SACRAMENT OF CANNABIS AND COMMUNITY PRACTICES

While the EZCC is no longer in operation, one can still gain insight into how the Coptics contextualized cannabis and how it was used sacramentally. The Coptics incorporated both Christian and Rastafari elements into their religion. However, unlike the Rastafaris, they do not believe that Haile Selassie is the messiah. Moreover, unlike Christianity, the Coptics believe that human beings and God are one and that the holy sacrament of ganja highlights and focuses on that connection. As such, the EZCC is a nondualistic religion as God, other humans, and the cannabis sacrament exist in a unified reality; a reality in which the present is all that matters.

The EZCC centered their belief system on the passages of the Bible that felt relevant to their sacramental experiences. As noted, they also believed in the unity of everything, thus God was present in everything and everyone. Members smoked ganja only using a pipe, never a joint, and taking small sips that were to continue all day and into the night. The Coptics were also very strict about eschewing both hard drugs and alcohol and forbidding the use of cannabis outside of church for recreational purposes.

The EZCC drew on Rastafari rituals such as the understanding that cannabis was a sacramental substance given by God for human use. Second, they believed, like the Rastafari, that Marcus Garvey was a prophet. Third, like the Rastas, the Coptics focused on the importance of community; and while the Rastas were brought together through reasoning sessions, the Coptics were brought together through prayer sessions. Prayer sessions happened three times a day, at 3:00 pm, 8:00 pm, and 3:00 am, and would last for approximately two hours. Prior to each session, a designated member would put together a mixture of cannabis and tobacco that would be smoked during these sessions. Biblical scripture was also a central part of these sessions and drew on both the Old and New Testaments of the Bible, such as Psalms 104:14, which particularly praises God for creating plants through which all God's creatures thrive: "You cause the grass to grow for the cattle, and plants for people to use, to bring forth food from the earth."[69] Whether in a group or alone, one was always in the presence of God. The Rastas spoke of one's particular experience of Jah in a very similar fashion: "For Rastafari, communication with God is not mediated through a priest or other Church official: it is a wholly private affair."[70]

As we can see here, the Coptics, like the Rastas, highlighted the individual and experiential connection with God over and above a shared doctrinal tradition. However, while one person alone was "still in the presence of God it is in the collective body of their community that the Coptics 'are God and that humans are to act like God.'[71] God lives in all of us, collectively. We are a part, and God is a whole."[72] The theological position in which one experiences God as "a whole" encompassing all things is a position also held by Rastafaris.[73]

The Coptics intentionally constructed a gender hierarchy: women members of the EZCC were expected to be faithful and subject to their male partners. There is no formal marriage ceremony among the Coptics and[74] in the daily prayer meetings, the women and children sat behind the men. Sexual activity was to be reserved for the purpose of reproduction exclusively. Children raised in the Coptic tradition could ask their parents for cannabis, and while the parents could say no, more often the children of a Coptic couple would be allowed to smoke. Coptics denounced homosexuality, abortion, oral sex, and masturbation as these sexual acts do not lead to procreation. As to these rules, Brother Louv joked, "If it weren't for marijuana . . . we would be the Moral Majority."[75]

Moreover, the Coptics neither aligned themselves with the Rastafari religion in equating Zion with Ethiopia nor did they grant Haile Selassie I divine status. As far as both the Caucasian and the Jamaican Coptics were concerned, Jamaica is Zion—heaven on earth. And while the Coptics considerd themselves to be part of the Rastafari religion as well as founded on Christian elements, they believed that Jesus of Nazareth was a black man born in Jamaica and crucified by non-blacks in a political act of racial hatred. Thus, like the Rastafari, the Coptics combine religion and politics as the Coptics very much sympathized with the oppression of all black people and used a share of their money to bring potential members down to Star Island and away from Babylon—the land of moral corruption, namely, the United States.

While many rules were strictly enforced, Hiassan notes the following: "All oblations [prayer sessions] are voluntary, which becomes a significant consideration at 3 in the morning. . . . If all this is really a fraud, the Coptics are going to epic lengths to preserve the charade."[76] Lastly, neither the Rastafaris nor the Coptics proselytize. However, while the Rastafaris disseminated their message through their music, the EZCC took a more mundane route: they advertised their church in the Miami Yellow pages and printed a free newspaper.

THE CONSEQUENCES OF REVERING CANNABIS

In 1977 and 1978, in a series of raids in Florida, the police confiscated approximately 20 tons of cannabis linked to the Coptics. The IRS revoked the church's tax-exempt status. At the same time all of this was going on, neighbors near Star Island were complaining about the smell of marijuana wafting over their land. In an interesting side note, Dan Rather conducted a televised interview with Brother Louv in 1979, and one of the issues to emerge was the fact that the viewing audience saw children smoking cannabis—and were shocked by seeing what was perceived as a form of child abuse. Moreover, "in November, 1978, news broke of the mass deaths of Peoples Temple in Jonestown, Guyana, and many Miami residents were shocked into wondering if they might not have a potential Jonestown on their doorstep."[77] In the wake of the raids designed to close down the Coptic church, the Florida Supreme Court wrote the following in 1979: "(1) the Ethiopian Zion Coptic Church represents a religion within the First Amendment to the Constitution of the United States," and (2) the "use of cannabis is an essential portion of the religious practice . . ." and "[f]urther, the Ethiopian Zion Coptic Church or religion is not a new church or religion but the record reflects it is centuries old and has regularly used cannabis as its sacrament."[78] Nevertheless, the Florida Supreme Court banned the use of cannabis on the Island, stating that they had "a compelling interest sufficient to override the fundamental interest of any citizen of the United States to practice their religion without governmental interference in it."[79]

The EZCC, by using the "unusable" and uttering the "unsayable," was a danger to the powers that control discourse. As such, the closing down of the Coptic's church and the imprisonment of its members was inevitable. As stated by Foucault: "[B]y locking up, retraining and rendering docile, [prison] merely reproduces, with a little more emphasis, all the mechanisms that are to be found in the social body,"[80] or as a member of the EZCC would probably rephrase it, "the social body of Babylon." When the federal authorities raided Star Island, anyone who lived there full time or who led a prayer service was considered to be an active member of the church and was thus sent off to prison. And after doing their time, there was nothing left of their religious community to which they could return.

As we turn to our last forerunner, The Farm, Farm founder Stephen Gaskin sees the fight for religious freedom pivoting on the fight over the Constitution. Thus, it is clear that the stakes are high for those disenfranchised from their own religious practices.

STEPHEN GASKIN AND THE MONDAY NIGHT CLASS

Stephen Gaskin was born in 1935 in Denver, Colorado, to a working-class family. He joined the Marines at 17 and saw combat in the Korean War. When he returned, he settled in San Francisco in the early 1960s and took classes in English, creative writing, and semantics at San Francisco State College earning a Master's degree in 1964. He then went on to teach at the college, but the *outre* topics he included in his classes, such as Witchcraft, ended that appointment after two years. But something in the amalgam of his upbringing, his time at war, his studies, and the burgeoning free-thinking, free-living, free-loving, drug-loving scene of San Francisco in the early and mid-60s created a man with a vision. He would not only found The Farm, an intentional community called by the *Wall Street Journal*, "[T]he General Motors of American Communes,"[81] but also earn the Swedish Parliament's Right Livelihood Award.[82]

His gift for teaching and reaching out to people experiencing both the horror and fear of the Vietnam War during an unprecedented time for idealistic thinking led him to start Monday Night Class in 1967. These were not formal classes but rather discussions that Gaskin led on subjects across the board, such as religion, politics, Tantric practices, consciousness and being, changing the world, and the sacred nature of cannabis.

Photographs reveal that Stephen Gaskin was an imposing figure: 6′5″, a good-looking man with blond hair and a beard. He once said self-deprecatingly that the key to his success "was an ability to talk intelligently while stoned longer than most people."[83] But you do not galvanize people to action without a lot more on the brain than that: "Twelve people showed up for Gaskin's first class, which was held in a room on the San Francisco State campus. Over the next three years, the class grew, and the venues changed—eventually there were 1,500 people sitting on the floor of a ballroom near the Pacific Ocean."[84] Clearly, Gaskin had a message that people wanted to hear and a wide range of people who wanted to hear it. His audience included hippies, vets, war protesters, "old people and retired people, college dropouts as well as graduates, and a generous sprinkling of ethnic and religious diversity."[85]

In spite of his popularity, Gaskin apparently remained a humble if impassioned man who challenged people to become energetically enlightened: "Enlightenment, he said, is getting off your tail and doing something."[86] In a strange turn of events, members of the usually staid American Academy of Religion started coming to his classes. The American Academy of Religion not only includes academics interested in the history of religions but also those interested exclusively in theology and biblical literature. This latter group is made up of academics as well as religious leaders, and the religious leaders were anxious to find out how to bring young people back to organized religion in these tumultuous times, and hoped that Stephen Gaskin might give them some answers. Gaskin told them that his sessions comprised spiritual events and they were persuaded enough by their own attendance at these meetings to fund a 42-state tour for Gaskin that included stops at many churches and colleges.

His most ardent students and fans wanted to join him, and he said "that any of his students who could manifest a bus and gas money, keep it together, and keep up with him, could join him on this revolutionary caper."[87] They ended up with a caravan of approximately 25 multihued buses, and, after leaving on the evening of October 12, 1970, Gaskin, driving the lead bus, realized he had lost the rest of his caravan before reaching the Golden Gate Bridge.[88] After that, he kept better sight of his group in the rearview mirror and did not encounter any more trouble until he reached his first new state, Oregon, where he was arrested. His fellow travelers paid his bail, mostly with change, and the police turned out to be good transit hosts for the most part, handing him off from one state police group to the next saying "that we were peaceful and were all right and we weren't planning to stop and we weren't taking welfare."[89]

THE SACRALITY OF CANNABIS AND COMMUNITY PRACTICES

Gaskin experienced that "grass," marijuana, was central both to connecting with the divine and with other people. When Gaskin would act as a mediator for members having a conflict of any sort, he would sit down with them and roll a joint. When everyone had smoked a bit, every person was given a chance to talk and share their viewpoint. "One of the things about grass that is neat is that if you get a little meditative, it gives you a sense of perspective on yourself. You see yourself as one person among a whole world population rather than as an absolute personal ego."[90] In talking about the caravan experience, he reiterates the viewpoint that we are all part of a unified reality, something that both the Rastas and the Coptics expressed as central to their belief systems as well.

> I was thinking of inside and outside, and as above so below, that what goes on inside of you is the same as what you make go on outside of you, and that everything that we manifest at the level of us here on the Caravan—what is it, a hundred and fifty of us, two hundred maybe?—is a microcosm of all of mankind. So we're out here working it out for everybody as we're passing through.[91]

This religious viewpoint, in which one exists in an integrated union with God, nature, and the rest of humanity, has a very practical side in that it highlights the necessity for religion to be relevant in daily personal interactions—"as above so below."

> Your religion ought to make a difference to you in your daily life; [i]t ought to help you through the heavy passages of life.[92]

For Gaskin, one of the main ingredients for elevating one's daily life was grass. "Grass is an ally. It naturally engenders spirituality in the people that do it."[93]

The caravan got back to California after traveling for four months and, due to their shared experiences on the road, the caravanners had become a community—a church. Farm historian Michael Traugot describes the early Farm as a "Grass Church."

> Farm folks depended upon marijuana for insight, for ceremonial value and to enhance lovemaking. They shunned, however, commerce in pot. . . . [S]ince pot was a sacrament and an aid to consciousness, one absorbed some of the karma of those who produced and distributed [it].[94]

All of these groups have placed a crucial focus on communal gatherings, sometimes for problem solving, sometimes for prayer, and sometimes as in the case of the Rastas, reasoning sessions. And within the communal gatherings of all three groups, the ritual of smoking cannabis was a central component. Gaskin felt strongly that the communal smoking of cannabis was a powerful spiritual tool.

> With cannabis, you can have one joint and two people, and you can get higher than if one of you smokes it. It just works that way. And if you share it with six people, you still get higher than if just one person smokes it himself. There's a real gentle ritual, in that it gets passed from hand to hand with the gesture of "I'm passing something precious, and we're sharing communion with it." Another reason I use cannabis is because I find open religious experience to be one step closer to God than having a Bible of Latin that only the priesthood understood. You can go to the experience and learn it for yourself. You can use cannabis as a sacrament—not as an end to itself, but as a holy tool to help you to experience reality.[95]

The highlighting of experience over a shared doctrinal tradition is a value held by all of these cannabis religions. And, according to Gaskin, while this sacred experience is logarithmically enhanced when taken communally, it is also experienced in all its sacred particularity by individual members. This is an important point, for while all three of these cannabis-based religions used cannabis communally, the members of all three also performed their ritual use of cannabis when they were alone. The Rastas and the Coptics both sanctified the use of cannabis outside of their respective "reasoning sessions" and "prayer meetings." In fact, what these cannabis-based religions provided for their membership was the creation of a space wherein one might define the context in which one used cannabis as a religious practice.

As noted above, Gaskin experienced that "Grass . . . naturally engenders spirituality in the people that do it." When Gaskin talks about getting high by himself, he notes that one will have the best experience alone if he is "deliberate and ceremonial. . . . Then you can take that deliberate space and time to sit back and let the grass do what it wants to do . . . which is open you up and leave you compassionate. It is also perfectly fine to get stoned and have fun, which is another kind of prayer."[96]

During their travels, Gaskin and his fellow caravanners had come across Summertown, Tennessee, and it looked like a good place to lay down some roots. This is exactly what Gaskin and his followers did in 1971, and, in its heyday, The Farm community numbered approximately 1,600 members. "South of Nashville a thousand acres were purchased in the backwoods of Lewis County, TN, and The Farm was born."[97] The Farm was founded on the principles of collective ownership, and it was not merely an intentional community but an "intentional spiritual community. . . ." The Farm organized itself on a communal basis as in the Book of Acts: "All who believed were together and had all things in common; they would sell their possessions and goods and distribute the proceeds to all, as any had need."[98] The underlying vision for Gaskin was to change the world into a better place; a nonviolent, compassionate place. "We learned that if you really want to change the world, you have to change your soul—you have to change things from the spiritual level."[99]

Al Gore was a cub reporter for *The Tennessean* newspaper when these events were taking place and was sent by his editor to check out the weekly discussions that were going on at The Farm between Gaskin and local ministers. Gore underscored the fact that what might easily have been a shouting match between those of contrasting religious positions was actually a time of listening and informative debate.

> EVERY SUNDAY afternoon and every Monday night for the past four weeks, the minister of Sandy Hook Church of Christ [Reverend Williams] has come with 30 to 40 members of his congregation and several other ministers to share "the word of God" with Gaskin and the estimated 450 members of his commune who live on a farm near here.
>
> EACH SIDE presents its beliefs and then both sides hash out their disagreements. Unlike most communities, the Gaskin group is committed to leading a religious life. His followers look to him for spiritual guidance and he is more than willing to give it to anyone who asks. Gaskin describes his group as a . . . monastery.
>
> TO THE SURPRISE of both sides, they found they share a lot of common ground in the Ten Commandments, the Sermon on the Mount, the Golden Rule, the value of working hard and trying always to tell the truth—and most important, a deep faith in God.
>
> WHILE GASKIN says they no longer grow marijuana, he admits that his followers smoke it. . . . "We strongly disapprove of their use of these things" said Williams, "but we feel it is our duty to teach them New Testament Christianity."
>
> FROM GASKIN'S point of view, it is the Church of Christ that is "making progress" as a result of the meetings. "They're getting so mellow," he explained. "You should have seen them the first week they came."[100]

Like the Rastas and the Coptics, the members of The Farm drew from the Bible and reinterpreted certain passages to be relevant to their own experience. However, unlike the Rastas and the Coptics, they also drew on other religious traditions. The Farm was set up "in the East Indian tradition of 'householder yogis,' where spiritual discovery and family life went hand in hand. Hard work was seen as an act of love and a path to enlightenment."[101] Some of the other essential tenets of The Farm community included the need to be "compassionate, nonviolent, and vegan, to avoid alcohol and hard drugs, to shun consumerism, and to be a good planetary citizen, a 'voluntary peasant.'"[102] Moreover, in terms of gender equality, if two members came together as a sexually active couple, then in the eyes of the community, they were engaged. And if a woman became pregnant, she and her partner were to be married. This is a very different stance from that of the EZCC which made women subservient to men and banned marriage.

Other than gender equality and the modeling of religious traditions outside Christianity, the Coptics and the Rastas embraced most of the teachings listed above. Bob Marley talked a great deal about the evils of capitalism and the Coptics eschewed all types of hard drugs, tobacco, and alcohol, but used cannabis, as do all of our groups, as a sacramental substance. As noted by Stephen Gaskin, "When we want to feel close to the Holy Spirit, we get together before the sunrise and take communion. We sit in meditation for an hour and smoke cannabis if we have it."[103] However, underlying their Grass Church, there was a tension between the importance of community and the importance of their sacramental substance; a tension that played out when local authorities raided their cannabis field.

THE CONSEQUENCES OF BELONGING TO A GRASS CHURCH

In 1974, local authorities found cannabis growing on The Farm's property. Gaskin says that he was against growing cannabis in a place where so many neighbors and others would find problems with the crop. He understood himself as a newcomer to the rural south and wanted to be respectful of local mores. That did not mean that he halted the use of cannabis as a sacramental substance, but he certainly did not want it to be a tourist attraction that could be seen from the local railroad.

> Much to their embarrassment, it turned out that the people tending the pot plants had placed the weed in plain sight, along trails frequented by local hunters. As Gaskin tells the story, Railroad guys were telling people, "As you go through, look to your right. You've got a good chance you're going to see a naked hippie lady playing flute to a pot plant."[104]

When the local authorities stepped in, Stephen Gaskin and three other members of The Farm community were taken into custody. Stephen Gaskin and his three compatriots were eventually made to serve one year in prison. While he and his fellow inmates were doing time, "The Farm members declared a 'grass-fast.'"[105] But it was a blow to Gaskin and his belief in the freedom of religion as stated in the First Amendment of the Constitution.

From 1971 forward, The Farm no longer grew cannabis on its land and, for the most part, this allowed the residents of The Farm to live peacefully with their neighbors and those in law enforcement. However, things took a strange turn in July of 1980.

> On July 11, 1980, a battalion of state police, including two helicopters, some 50 police cars, dogs and over 100 officers raided The Farm in the dark of night. Accompanied by television crews from three Nashville Stations, they converged from all directions on a field of ragweed. As it turned out, an overzealous helicopter pilot on a routine dope-spotting run mistook the overgrown watermelon field, with its neat rows of ragweed that had grown up between the melons, for hemp.[106]

While cannabis was no longer grown on The Farm, Farm residents could still obtain cannabis through donations and barter. However, the ease and freedom which had formerly existed around their sacramental use of cannabis was demolished due to the police surveillance of their community and the earlier incarceration of their founder and three of their members. Due to these events, a tension arose between preserving The Farm community and preserving their sacramental ritual; a tension that resulted in The Farm community losing much of its identity. Without a central ritual to cement their communal ties, The Farm community faltered. They struggled with cash flow problems during the economic downturns of the early 1980s and "[d]uring this period of transition, 700 people left The Farm, and, by the mid-1980s, only the land was held in common."[107] In 1983, Stephen Gaskin stepped down from being a spiritual leader to being just another resident of the community.[108] However, prior to that time in 1980, he called on The Farm's residents to reach out to those in need.

> [They] built 1,200 houses for the victims of a 1976 earthquake in Guatemala, set up volunteer ambulance services in the South Bronx and on an Indian reservation in upstate New York, and started a school lunch program in Belize and an agricultural training program in Liberia. They were among the earliest volunteers to arrive in New Orleans after Hurricane Katrina.[109]

In 1980, Stephen Gaskin founded Plenty International, a charitable organization that is especially active in Central America, the Caribbean, and Africa. He remained on The Farm until his death at age 79, on July 2, 2014. He continued to smoke his sacred sacrament to the end, and leaves us with the following words. "I'm a teacher, not a leader. If you lose your leader, you're leaderless and lost, but if you lose your teacher there's a chance that he taught you something and you can navigate on your own."[110]

Certainly, one of the lessons taught by Gaskin to his followers included the importance of religious freedom, and a determination to not give up his sacred sacrament without a fight. Therefore, prior to the decision to preserve community over cannabis, Gaskin agitated for what he felt to be his God-given right to honor creation through the sacramental use of cannabis.

> Hold fast, friends: we are not finished! Years ago, Pot was not thought to be political. *Rolling Stone, The Nation* and *The Progressive* ignored dope as "not real politics." . . . I believe the "Reefer left" is the most authentic Left in the country. In the Vietnam days everyone knew someone who was drafted or already in "Nam." . . . [E]veryone knows someone who is doing hard "mandatory minimum" time [for smoking cannabis]. These folks have had their lives ruined as surely as if they were wounded or killed in war.[111]

And having stated that mandatory prison sentences for those who smoke marijuana will ruin lives in the same way as those who are "wounded or killed in war," Gaskin spoke eloquently with a plea for change:

> If a lawmaker wants to put the screws to marijuana smokers, he can propose a law that puts marijuana in the same category with heroin. This is scientifically untrue but has been made legally true.[112]

In a quote attributed to Mark Twain, he put this succinctly: "It's not what you don't know that kills you, it's what you know for sure that ain't true."[113] When read as Foucault would have read this statement, it is when we have experienced something as the truth, but are then repeatedly told that our experience is false that we are in real trouble. We are in real trouble because it causes us to be faced with a dilemma: we either fight for what we know to be true or we lay down our arms and submit. At one time or another, all of our cannabis religions have taken on a political commitment to fight for their truth. When Gaskin was arrested for growing cannabis on his land, he took his fight all the way to the Supreme Court. The Supreme Court refused the case and as noted, Gaskin and three other members of The Farm went to jail.

After serving a year in prison, with plenty of time to ruminate, Gaskin made the following assertion.

> I have come to believe that it is not the proscription of a substance but the systematic oppression of a certain kind of people. There have been a whole series of decisions made, on local, state and federal levels, to the effect that hippies . . . are undesirable and are to be banned, interdicted, harassed, discouraged, arrested and pee-tested. It is a blatant use of police power to frighten and intimidate millions of people into giving up a heartfelt spiritual practice and lifestyle.[114]

So, we travel from uncontrollable substances to uncontrollable people and the consequences for both are the same. Both the substances and the people are locked up until they become controllable. For Stephen Gaskin, the authorities believed he was controllable after a year of being contained. For cannabis, we may be waiting a long time until the federal government, with the blessing of the Food and Drug Administration, loosens their hold on cannabis.

EXEMPLI GRATIA

We are now faced with the following question: Have these forerunners provided us with a structural template, a pattern, or, in the words of J. Z. Smith, an *exempli gratia* that will be useful as we strive to understand the Church of the Universe, the Church of Cognizance, Temple 420, and the Hawai'i Cannabis Ministry? I would argue that they have, and would break down this template into the following five structural elements. (1) These forerunners used cannabis as a ritual sacrament both in community and alone. (2) They ingested cannabis to effect a transcendent experience that was profound and irreducible; an irreducible process that obviated the need for what Cantwell Smith defined as "cumulative tradition"—namely, all the fixed features of institutionalized religion. (3) As contemporary *bricoleurs*, they took orthodox texts and practices and reinterpreted them to support and structure their ritual activities. (4) They attracted a community of like-minded people that were non-proselytizing. And (5) they involved themselves in the political process to obtain religious freedom—be it protesting through music, calling for social change, filing endless lawsuits, or keeping track of what politicians were saying about cannabis.

Now, the ways that these groups conducted their sacramental rituals were as varied as their communal formations, their motivations for using orthodox scripture, their particular and individual sacred experiences, and their political aspirations. But the Rastas, the Coptics, and The Farm have provided us with a mirrored mosaic that reflects the contextual significance of the Church of the Universe, the Church of Cognizance, Temple 420, and the Hawai'i Cannabis Ministry. I now turn to chapter 2, where I analyze and compare the Church of the Universe, the Church of Cognizance, and Temple 420.

NOTES

1. *Book of Rites*, chapter 54, verse 23, translated by James Legge (Beijing and Washington, DC: Intercultural Press, 2013), 54.
2. Earnest Abel, *Marijuana: The First Twelve Thousand Years* (New York: Plenum Press, 1980), 4.
3. H. Li, "An Archaeological and Historical Account of Cannabis in China," *Economic Botany* 28 (1924): 437–38.
4. Wendy Doniger, *Siva: The Erotic Ascetic* (New York: Oxford University Press, 1981).
5. Mircea Eliade, *Shamanism: Archaic Techniques of Ecstasy* (Princeton: Princeton University Press, 1964), 399–400.
6. Alfred Dunhill, *The Pipe Book* (London: A & C Black, 1924), 159.

7. "History of Marijuana Use: Medical and Intoxicant," Schaffer Library of Drug History, accessed May 15, 2015, http://www.druglibrary.net.

8. Robert Deitch, *Hemp: American History Revisited* (New York: Algora Publishing, 2003), 10.

9. Ibid.

10. Ibid., 32.

11. *The New Oxford Annotated Bible* (NOAB).

12. Women of Reform Judaism, "Medical Marijuana as Mitzvah: A Study Guide," (New York: Women of Reform Judaism, 2000), http://www.thc-ministry.org/benyehudadictionaryreference.html.

13. Conversation with colleagues March 21, 2013.

14. James H. Mills, *Cannabis Britannica: Empire, Trade and Prohibition 1800–1928* (Oxford: Oxford University Press, 2003), 31–32.

15. Ibid., 33.

16. Cannabis produces both marijuana—a plant that is cultivated to be high in THC and used for human consumption in some form, and hemp—a plant that is cultivated to be low in THC and is used for industrial purposes such as canvas, rope, paper, plastic, and oil. While these two words (hemp and cannabis) are often used interchangeably, the marijuana strain of cannabis is cultivated from the buds just beneath the female flower, hemp plants are usually male and do not flower but are grown to be tall, fibrous stalks. This is a paraphrase from "5 Differences Between Hemp and Marijuana," *Leaf Science*, September 16, 2014, accessed February 27, 2016, http://www.leafscience.com/2014/09/16/5-differences-hemp-marijuana/.

17. Deitch, 16–17.

18. Bruce Meland, *There Was Marijuana in the Garden of Eden!: An Exposé on Marijuana and Hemp* (Bloomington, IN: XLibris Corporation, 2015).

19. I. Bayer and H. Ghodse, "Evolution of International Drug Control, 1945–1995," *UN International Drug Control Programme, Bulletin on Narcotics*, Vol. LI, Nos. 1 and 2 (New York: United Nations, 1999), 1–17.

20. "The History and Development of the Leading International Drug Control Conventions," Canada: Library of Parliament, accessed April 10, 2015, http://www.parl.gc.ca/content/sen/committee/371/ille//library/history-e.htm.

21. Westel Willoughby, *Opium as an International Problem* (Baltimore: Johns Hopkins Press, 1925), 379.

22. Ansley Hamid, *The Ganja Complex: Rastafari and Marijuana* (Lanham: Lexington Books, 2002), xi.

23. *Reefer Madness*, directed by Louis J. Gasnier (1936; United States: Grand National Studios).

24. Rep. Earl Blumenauer and Rep. Jared Polis. "The Path Forward: Rethinking Federal Marijuana Policy," accessed April 11, 2015, http://www.blumenauer.house.gov.

25. "Use of the Word 'Marijuana' Increases in the US," ProCon.org, accessed April 15, 2015, http://www.medicalmarijuana.procon.org.

26. Mitch Earleywine, *Understanding Marijuana: A New Look at the Scientific Evidence* (New York: Oxford University Press, 2002), 126.

27. Jack Herer, *The Emperor Wears No Clothes: Hemp and the Marijuana Conspiracy* (Van Nuys: Hemp Publishing, 1990), 25.

28. Michel Foucault, *The History of Sexuality, Vol. 1: An Introduction* (New York: Random House, 1978), 6.

29. Landrow Comitas, "Occupational Multiplicity in Rural Jamaica," in *West Indian Perspectives: Work and Family Life*, eds. L. Comitas and D. Lowenthal (New York: Double Day, 1973), in A. Hamid, *The Ganja Complex* (Lanham: Lexington Books, 2002), xxxvii.

30. Derek O'Brien and Vaughan Carter, "Chant down Babylon: Freedom of Religion and the Rastafarian Challenge to Majoritarianism," *Journal of Law and Religion*, 18, no. 1 (2002–2003): 220.

31. Bradley Roderick, "A Brief Look at the Roots and Development of the Nation of Islam," *Renaissance: A Monthly Islamic Journal*, accessed March 10, http://www.renaissance.com.pk.
32. Ibid.
33. I. J. Tafari, "The Rastafari Successors of Marcus Garvey," *Caribbean Quarterly*, Vol. 26, No. 4 (1980): 9.
34. Psalms 68:31 (King James Version).
35. NOAB.
36. Revelation 22:1–2 (NOAB).
37. Genesis 1:29 (NOAB).
38. Zechariah 3:10 (NOAB).
39. Jeremiah 51:58 (NOAB).
40. Akeia Benard, "The Material Roots of Rastafarian Marijuana Symbolism," *History and Anthropology* 18, no. 1 (2007): 90.
41. Revelation 5:5 (NOAB).
42. King James Bible.
43. Hamid, 77–78.
44. Benard, 94.
45. Ibid., 97.
46. bbc.co.uk. Worship and customs. The Bible verses that the Rastafaris rely on to position herb as holy substance come from the following verses. Psalm 104:14; Genesis 3:18; Exodus 10:12; Proverbs 15:17.
47. A variation on the Roman Catholic "Gloria Patri" actual quotation is available at https://erowid.org/plants/cannabis/cannabis_spirit1.shtml
48. William Grant, "Rastafarian Culture," accessed on July 7, 2016, https://debate.uvm.edu/dreadlibrary/grant02.htm.
49. Bob Marley, "Easy Skanking," on *Kaya*, Island Studios, 1978.
50. Bob Marley, "Pass It On," on *Burnin'*, Harry J. Studios, 1973.
51. O'Brien and Carter, 221.
52. The Wailers, "Get Up, Stand Up," by Bob Marley and Peter Tosh, recorded April 1973, track 1 on *Burnin'*, Island Records-Tuff Gong, 1973.
53. "Lifestyle: The Lifestyle of a Legend," accessed October 10, 2016, http://www.bobmarley.com/history/.
54. Paige Lavender, "On Bob Marley's Birthday, A Look at What He Had to Say about Government Opposition to Weed," *Huffington Post* online, February 6, 2015, http://www.huffingtonpost.com/2015/02/06/bob-marley-weed-government_n_6631410.html.
55. Joshua Jelly-Schapiro, *Island People: The Carribean and the World* (New York: Knopf, 2016).
56. "Why Rastas Don't Smoke Marijuana," January 6, 2011, accessed July 15, 2015, The Dread Library.
57. Toots and the Maytals, *Pass the Pipe*, Island Records-Tuff Gong, 1979.
58. Psalm 68:4 (NOAB).
59. Barbara Charone, "Peter Tosh in Creem Magazine: 'Peter Tosh: He's the Toughest,'" in *Creem Magazine*, March 1979.
60. Will Pavia, "Home of Reggae and Rastafarians Legalises Its Favorite Herb," *The Times* (London, UK), June 14, 2014, Eire edition, 36.
61. "Kaya: Bob Marley and Marijuana," joewein.de, accessed February 17, 2016, http://www.joewein.de/kaya.htm.
62. Pavia.
63. Carl Hiaasen, "Louv Story: Are Brother Louv and His Zion Coptic Church Facing the Last Judgment?" *The Miami Herald*, August 2, 1981, available at http://www.druglibrary.org/olsen/rastafari/tropic.html.
64. Ibid.

65. Cynthia Mazur, "Marijuana as a 'Holy Sacrament': Is the Use of Peyote Constitutionally Distinguishable from That of Marijuana in Bona Fide Religious Ceremonies?" *Notre Dame Journal of Law, Ethics, & Public Policy* 5 (1991): 700.
66. Edward Seaga in *Square Groupers: The Godfathers of Ganja,* directed by Billy Corben (2011; Magnolia Pictures).
67. Hiaasen.
68. Ibid.
69. Psalm 104:14 (NOAB).
70. O'Brien and Carter, 221.
71. Ibid.
72. Ibid.
73. Michael Cook, *Trinitarian Christology: That Power That Sets Us Free* (Mahwah, NJ: Paulist Press, 2010).
74. Ibid.
75. Hiaasen.
76. Ibid.
77. "Ethiopian Zion Coptic Church," *CBS News—60 Minutes,* Volume xii, Number 7, October 28, 1979.
78. *Town v. Florida,* No. 55987, Supreme Court of FL 377 So. 2d 648 (Fla. 1979), November 1, 1979.
79. Milton Ferrell, Jr., in an interview with Dan Rather, "Ethiopian Zion Coptic Church," *CBS News—60 Minutes,* Volume xii, Number 7, October 28, 1979.
80. Michel Foucault, *Discipline and Punish: The Birth of the Prison* (New York: Vintage Books, 1977), 233.
81. Rupert Fike, ed., *Voices from the Farm: Adventures in Community Living,* 2nd ed. (Summertown, TN: Book Publishing Co., 2012), 10.
82. The Right Livelihood Award has been equated with a Nobel Prize and Stephen Gaskin was presented with his for his humanitarian work through his organization Plenty International.
83. Douglas Martin, "Stephen Gaskin, Hippie Who Founded an Enduring Commune, Dies at 79," *New York Times,* July 2, 2014.
84. Stephen Gaskin, *Monday Night Class* (Summertown, TN: Book Publishing Co., 2005), 9.
85. Stephen Gaskin, *The Caravan,* Rev. ed. (Summertown, TN: Book Publishing Co., 2007), 6.
86. Ibid.
87. William Breathes, "'Holy Hippies' Tells Story of 1971 Pot-Fueled Spiritual Bus Caravan," *Toke of the Town,* July 25, 2011, available at 1http://www.tokeofthetown.com/2011/07/holy_hippies_book_tells_story_of_1971_pot-fueled_b.php/.
88. Gaskin, *The Caravan,* 10.
89. Ibid.
90. Ibid., 74.
91. Ibid., 64.
92. Stephen Gaskin, *Cannabis Spirituality* (New York: High Times Books, 1996), 2.
93. Ibid., 74.
94. Michael Niman, "Out to Save the World: Life on the Farm," *High Times,* February 1, 1995, available at http://thefarmcommunity.com/high-times-1995/.
95. Gaskin, *Cannabis Spirituality,* 40.
96. Gaskin, *Cannabis Spirituality,* 70–71.
97. Fike, 6.
98. Acts 2:44–45 (NOAB).
99. Gaskin, *Cannabis Spirituality,* 29. Paraphrasing Matthew 5:21–22, The New Oxford Annotated Bible
100. Albert Gore, "Church Group Swaps Views with Gaskin's," *The Tennesseean,* March 13, 1972.

101. Fike, 7.
102. Ibid., 8.
103. Gaskin, *Cannabis Spirituality*, 37.
104. Douglas Stevenson, *Out to Change the World: The Evolution of The Farm Community* (Summertown, TN: Book Publishing Co., 2014), 25.
105. Bill Metcalf, "Voices on The Farm: Adventures in Community Living (Book Review)," Rupert Fike, editor, in *Utopia Studies*, Vol. 10, No. 1 (2012), 206.
106. Ibid.
107. Ibid.
108. Jessica Bliss, "Stephen Gaskin, Founder of The Farm, Dies at 79," *The Tennessean*, July 2, 2014.
109. Martin.
110. Bliss.
111. Stephen Gaskin, *Amazing Dope Tales* (Berkeley: Ronin Publishing, Inc., 1999), iv.
112. Gaskin, *Cannabis Spirituality*, 106.
113. Mark Twain, "Quotes," goodreads.com, accessed on March 4, 2016.
114. Gaskin, *Cannabis Spirituality*, 113.

TWO

The Church of the Universe, the Church of Cognizance, and Temple 420

As demonstrated in chapter 1, the forerunners of these cannabis-based religions each have five prominent elements that include (1) the sacramental use of cannabis; (2) the highlighting of transcendent experience over a shared doctrinal tradition; (3) the reinterpretation of orthodox texts to support their ritual activities; (4) access to a community of like-minded people; and (5) the undertaking of political battles to legitimate their religious practices. Beyond this template, chapter 1 revealed that the Rastas, Coptics, and members of The Farm had other elements in common. Within these groups, each member connects with the divine in their own particular way. The groups do not proselytize or demand among their own membership exclusive adherence to their beliefs and practices. And, finally, the groups tend not to have structured, formal services—and, if they do, as is the case with the Coptics, attendance is voluntary.

In looking at three more recently founded groups that centralize cannabis as a sacrament, I will examine whether or not the religious template created by the Rastas, the Coptics, and the members of The Farm holds up. Toward that end, I will explore two churches and one temple in the chronological order of their founding. First, the Canadian Church of the Universe, which was established in 1969; the Church of Cognizance (CoC), which was established in 1991; and Temple 420, which was established in 2006. As there are no scholarly treatments of these groups, I must rely on the media, church literature, and interviews with their respective founders and members to sort out these groups' histories and activities. And, to remain consistent, I will ask the same three questions that I asked of the forerunners in chapter 1. First, who were the founders and what was the early history of the group? Second, in what ways did each group contextualize and use cannabis as part of their religious practice? And, third, what were the legal ramifications of using cannabis as a sacrament?

THE EARLY DEVELOPMENT OF THE CHURCH OF THE UNIVERSE AND CLEARWATER ABBEY

As described earlier, it was the trials and tribulations of the Church of the Universe that provided the catalyst for undertaking this study. And while the Church of the Universe was established significantly earlier than either the CoC, Temple 420, or the Hawai'i Cannabis Ministry, its legal battles have continued into our later time frame, thus making them a useful model for the study of contemporary jurisprudence around cannabis-based religions.

The Church of the Universe was established in Canada in 1969 by Walter Tucker and eight associates at Clearwater Abbey, an abandoned quarry that also included 360 acres of streams and grasslands in Ontario. Tucker leased this land from its owners, Canada Cut and Crushed Stone. In addition to growing cannabis at Clearwater Abbey and surrounding themselves with products made of hemp and cannabis, such as clothes, paper, and food, the Church of the Universe followed a close variation of the golden rule—"Do not hurt yourself. Do not hurt anyone else."[1] They often eschewed clothing at Clearwater Abbey, citing Adam and Eve prior to their fall from grace.

This church is the first of these groups to explicitly name their religion as entheogenic: one that draws sacred inspiration from the ingestion of a plant. Michael Pollan further elaborates the significance of this term in *The Botany of Desire*.

> No one has yet written the natural history of world religion, but we have some idea of the story such a book would tell. Among other things, it would force us to rethink the relation of matter and spirit—specifically, plant matter and human spirituality. For it would tell of how a select group of psychoactive plants . . . were present at the creation of several of the world's religions. . . . What these peoples discovered was that certain plants or fungi (ethnobotanists call them "entheogens," meaning "the god within") opened a door onto another world. The images and words brought back from these journeys—visits of the afterlife, answers to life's questions—were powerful enough to compel belief in a spirit world and, in some cases, to serve as the foundation of whole religions.[2]

Since reading that passage in *The Botany of Desire*, I have discovered a wide assortment of books that explore entheogens, most of which would be described as self-help books. Regardless, there are scholars and writers who have started conversations around religion and plants who are open to shifting a discourse which has historically focused on theistic religions to a discourse that might be truly pluralistic and inclusive of entheogenic practices. Ironically, my computer refuses to acknowledge this term and has demonstrated its discursive control by consistently underlining it in red.

SACRAMENTAL CANNABIS AND COMMUNITY PRACTICES

When it came to cannabis, the Church of the Universe believed that cannabis was the Tree of Life and they reinterpreted portions of the 10 verses found in Genesis, Revelation, and Proverbs that focus on this symbol to provide the central image for their creed.[3] Their creed reads as follows:

> We believe that the Tree of Life is necessary to our understanding and worship of Almighty God.
> We believe that the Tree of Life opens a path to spiritual growth and connection with the Almighty God and us, the Children. We believe that the Tree of Life is for the healing of the nations.
> We believe that everyone has the right to worship God, to explore and create their own understanding of spirituality and growth in connection with God.
> First God, then Humanity, then Government.
> We believe in standing and knowing before Almighty God and no other.[4]

The Church of the Universe was especially interested in Revelation, chapter 22, verses 1, 2, 14, and 16 as they applied to the Tree of Life.

1. Verse 1: And he showed me a river of the Water of Life, clear as crystal, coming from the throne of God and of the Lamb,
2. Verse 2: In the middle of its street of the city, and on either side of the river was the Tree of Life, bearing twelve kinds of fruit, yielding its fruit every month; and the leaves of the Tree were for the healing of the nations.
3. Verse 14: Blessed are they who wash their robes, that they may have right to the Tree of Life and may enter by the gates into the city.
4. Verse 16: I Jesus have sent my angel to testify to you these things for the Churches. I am the root and the offspring of David, the bright morning star.[5]

And just as the cannabis forerunners put their primary sacrament front and center, so did the Church of the Universe. We have the following stated in church literature:

> The Sacred Herb, God's Tree of Life, Marijuana of the Assembly of the Church of the Universe is considered Kosher which is to say that God's

> Tree of Life is a Holy Sacrament in the Church and as such it is imperative that our Holy Church Sacrament, God's Tree of Life, Marijuana, by all its names and terms of endearment, be grown by our own Herbalists/Farmers, and distributed by our own Church Clergy.[6]

The members of the Church of the Universe also believed in an ultimate divine power and used Exodus 13–15 to describe this Godhead.

1. Verse 13: Then Moses said to God, "Behold, I am going to the children of Israel and I shall say to them, 'The God of your Ancestors has sent me to you.' Now they say to me, 'What is God's name? What shall I say to them?'"
2. Verse 14: And God said to Moses, "I AM WHO I AM" and God said, "Thus you shall say to the children of Israel, 'I AM has sent me to you.'"
3. Verse 15: This is My name forever, and this is My memorial name to all generations.[7]

While relying on the verses in Revelation to equate the Tree of Life with cannabis, and accepting the Godhead as described in Exodus—a God who contains all of creation—the Church of the Universe did not see itself as a Christian-centered church. The church "also accepts as valid sources of inspiration ancient and modern sources such as the culture of Sumer, pagan holidays of the solstices, Canada Day, the Knights Templar, Chaldeans, Gnostic Gospels, and Desiderata."[8]

In their church literature, the Church of the Universe described worship as being particular to the individual. "We worship God. However, the way in which we approach, see, encounter, experience and/or worship God is personal, inviolate and inviolable as are our souls."[9] While Walter Tucker and Michael Baldasaro, the registrar for the Church of the Universe, have become familiar faces due to the media's attention on church activities, the church was nonhierarchical and all members were equal and were instructed to call each other "brother" and "sister." Moreover, they did not proselytize. Anyone could become a member and stay a member as long as they demonstrated the "no harm to self or others" rule. According to Peter Small of the *Toronto Star*, the church had as of April 2010, 35 active members and approximately 4,000 more people who identified themselves as members of the church across Canada.[10]

In terms of the cannabis ministries and temples under review here, with the exception of the Ethiopian Zion Coptic Church, their gatherings were not structured or confined to a particular day or time. This does not mean that they did not have a set meeting place, which most of them did, or special occasions for the communal celebration of the sacrament, which all of them did. Matt Mernagh notes: "The Church of the Universe's core belief is cannabis, the tree of life. Therefore, they don't place limits on cannabis use. [Styrsky, a Church member] provided some instruction on marijuana as a religious sacrament, but they didn't reserve their marijuana for time of the day or when or where."[11]

At this point, it is useful to revisit the last two lines of the Church of the Universe's Creed: "First God, then Humanity, then Government. We believe in standing and knowing before Almighty God and no other."[12] These lines are compelling, as they point out the political stance this church took, from its inception, in relation to the Canadian judiciary—this church did not acknowledge the man-made laws of the land.

THE CONSEQUENCES OF SMOKING THE TREE OF LIFE

When Reverend Walter Tucker and Reverend Michael Baldasaro appeared before Judge Scime in the Ontario Court of Justice in 1995, they "appeared in court wearing . . . underpants on [their] head[s]. . . ."[13] Covering one's head in the presence of the sacred is a practice seen in a variety of religions across history and culture. However, by choosing to wear underpants on their heads, the members of this church were demonstrating their contempt for a government that did not recognize religious freedom; or, as noted by Foucault, their actions constituted "an irruption of speech."[14]

A Canadian reporter wrote that "The 47-year old Brother Michael cut an imposing figure with his long hair and massive bushy beard. He was somehow able to maintain his dignity with underwear on his head, just as he could marshal seemingly logical arguments to support legal positions so far out in left field as to be out of sight in the eyes of the law."[15] The statement that this religion was "out of sight in the eyes of the law" is a wonderful metaphor for all of these cannabis-based religions, as it points out that they were truly outside the contextual frame used by the judiciary to legitimate religious practices; they were iconoclastic and eccentric in the true sense of these words.

As we will see with several of these cannabis religions, various members often ran for public office. Michael Baldasaro ran for the office of Mayor of Hamilton, Ontario, as recently as 2014. "This isn't the first time brother Michael has thrown his hat into the political ring. He has run for mayor at every municipal election since 1985, finishing fourth in the last municipal election with almost three thousand votes."[16]

While Brother Baldasaro is still a cannabis activist, Walter Tucker died in 2012. Both Tucker and Baldasaro were convicted of drug trafficking in 2007, when they sold cannabis to an undercover police officer. Tucker was sentenced to one year in prison and Baldasaro was sentenced to two years in prison. They attempted to have these convictions overturned in 2010, but their efforts were thwarted by the judiciary and the 2007 convictions stood. I will return to the Church of the Universe in chapter 5 as their battles with the Canadian judiciary yield some interesting results.

THE CHURCH OF COGNIZANCE FOUNDED BY DAN AND MARY QUAINTANCE

In 1991, Dan and Mary Quaintance founded the CoC in Pima, Arizona. In 1994, they filed a 16-page "Declaration of Religious Sentiment" with the Graham County Recorder's office. This demonstrates that, from the beginning, the couple wanted their church on public record. The introduction to this document states the following:

> Danuel D. Quaintance and Mary Quaintance Do Declare Hemp/Marijuana to be Essential to the practice of Our Religious Beliefs and Sentiments: and do hereby declare ourselves to be an Individual Orthodox Member Monastery of the Church of Cognizance to be Known as dan & mary's Monastery of the Church of Cognizance.[17]

Dan Quaintance is originally from Iowa. He is a Vietnam era veteran and had been a welder until he retired. Mary met Dan when she worked as a nurse's aide in Chico, California, and rented a room from Dan's parents. Both Dan and Mary smoked cannabis before they met and they speak with conviction when they talk about cannabis: Mary had experienced cannabis as something that "makes you better at what you do, enhances who you are. It is the most beautiful plant on Earth."[18]

Dan Quaintance grew up in the United Methodist faith and once was president of his church youth group. In the early 1990s, Dan suffered from a severe attack of pancreatitis and it was during his illness that he would wake in the middle of the night with specific books and verses from the Bible on his mind. He would then get up and turn to those verses, which in turn led him to discover the religious and healing uses of cannabis among ancient cultures, and, from this discovery, which he shared with Mary, they were called to found the CoC.

The *Phoenix New Times* said the following in relation to the CoC: "Quaintance's theology is a lot more involved than you might anticipate. And he comes across as a very thoughtful individual who has done a great deal of personal research into the history of religion."[19]

HAOMA AND COMMUNITY PRACTICES

While the Bible and other sacred texts contributed to the practices of the CoC, the Zoroastrian Scriptures, the *Avesta*—"The Hymns of Zarathushtra," and the *Hom Yasht*, chapters 9–11 of the *Avesta*—were given pride of place. As stated by Dan, "Zoroastrian scripture, namely the *Avesta*, and in particular the *Hom Yasht*, repeatedly finds Zoroaster praising Haoma/ Marijuana as the averter of death"; and Dan interpreted the *Avesta* as confirming not only that haoma signifies marijuana but also "that the energy and spirit that is in marijuana is God. You consume the plant and you consume God. You are sacrificing your body to the deity."[20]

The CoC's open and interpretive approach to Zoroastrianism, as well as their complex membership structure, renders them one of the most interesting churches among a coterie of interesting churches. They relied on the *Avesta* for the following reasons:

> Of all the sacred text[s] translated to date the *Avesta* most openly reveals the sacredness of marijuana, as displayed in *Yasna* 9–11 of the *Hom Yasht*. All later religious text[s] do reveal the same information, however, it is in a fashion that a person must solve the riddle to reveal the Mystery.[21]

In conflating haoma with cannabis, the CoC was engaging in the same process of textual interpretation that occurs within all of these cannabis-based religions. In fact, all religious groups engage in textual interpretation and this selective focus is a familiar process within the history of religions. Moreover, the way in which a religious group interprets a text will often be the primary factor that differentiates one religious group from another. Looking at just the Christian denominations, one finds interpretations ranging from the fundamental to the feminist, from the liberationist to the evangelical, and each of these denominations will apply their own interpretive process to the Bible and focus on particular chapters and verses within this text.

Haoma from the *Avesta* and soma from the *Rig Veda*—the first of the Indian scriptures believed to be divine revelation—are terms that have puzzled scholars for years as to what plant or plants each represents. Some of the possibilities that have been raised include hallucinogenic mushrooms, fermented juice from the ephedra plant, unfermented juice from the ephedra plant, and juice from the cannabis plant. While the identity of each plant is still a mystery, one thing seems certain: each plant was/is experienced as an entheogenic. And, in the Zoroastrian *Zend-Avesta*—the *Avesta* plus commentary—bhang (cannabis) is referred to as a "good narcotic."[22] As far as Danuel and Mary Quaintance are concerned, haoma refers to cannabis.

Like all of these other ministries, the CoC's ritual and belief system rested on their experience of cannabis. This is especially clear in the CoC's "Declaration of Religious Sentiment," which states that "I do honor marijuana; as the Teacher, the Provider, the Protector. Praise be to Holy Marijuana; the Righteous Teacher of my faith!"[23]

Members of the CoC believe:

1. That Marijuana [aka Haoma], when raised and used properly, aids the mind, body, and soul.
2. That Haoma is the ancient teacher of wisdom, compassion, and the way to the kingdom of glory in heaven on earth, while humans let ego block their own, and others, path to this kingdom of glory.

3. That Haoma is the capable provider of all substance required to accommodate a comfortable, healthy, productive, full-bearing life.
4. That Haoma is the righteous Protector of our health and longevity, by way of receptors in the human body that Haoma connects with to heal.[24]

From the perspective of medical researchers, point 4 is well accepted, as cannabis has been scientifically proven to amplify the effects of our endogenously produced cannabinoids as it binds to the body's cannabinoid receptors. And point 2 is reminiscent of statements by Stephen Gaskin, when he described the unified nature of reality, a reality that empowers each of us to create a divine experience on earth. Having read these core beliefs, I asked Danuel Quaintance if he would further elaborate on his understanding of haoma.

> *Quaintance*: Haoma is the name of a plant in which the deity named Haoma resides, and is also the name of a sacred drink made from that plant. The word religion comes from the word "reliant" and Haoma, for us, is what we rely on most.[25]

So, for the CoC, haoma is the plant, haoma is the drink made from the plant that allows access to the divine, and haoma is the divine, a divinity that is imbibed in ritual practice through the drinking of haoma. The CoC's scripture goes on to state: "For this we declare Marijuana the teacher, the protector, the provider. We further believe that the proper religious use promotes Good Thoughts, Good Words, Good Deeds, none of which is harmful to the health, safety, welfare, or morals of society in general."[26] In terms of how they used their sacrament, the Quaintances smoked, ate, or drank marijuana daily as a way of becoming more spiritually enlightened. Sometimes they blended it into a milk-like drink, which they referred to by its ancient name, haoma, saying it helped them to become more enlightened and in tune with the universe. "And, [n]ormally on Christmas we would have shared the herb with our friends and Church members."[27]

In relation to the CoC's Neo-Zorastrian roots and cannabis, Eliade states that "shamanic ecstasy induced by hemp smoke was known in Ancient Iran. Bangha (hemp) is not referred to in the *Gathas*—the hymns of the *Avesta*, but the *Fravasi Yast*, [the 13th of the *Yast* hymns] mention[s] a certain Pouru-bangha, 'possessor of much hemp.' In the *Yast*, Ahura-Mazda is said to be 'without trance and without hemp.'"[28] And Eliade goes on to say that "there is no doubt that the most elementary technique of ecstasy, intoxication by hemp, was known to the ancient Iranians."[29] In fact, after reviewing the Iranian term for hemp, bangha, and enlisting linguistic comparison to other cultures in Central Asia, Eliade notes that "[t]hese facts prove that the magico-religious value of intoxication for achieving ecstasy is of Iranian origin."[30]

According to Quaintance, the Church has 40–50 members in Arizona and additional registered and unregistered members worldwide, making it hard to estimate how many there are nationwide. The CoC membership application requires a person to be 18 to join. This is because 18 is the commonly required age for entering into a legally binding agreement or pledge, such as the one that registered members of the CoC are required to sign. The average age of worshippers registered with the Church is 35.[31] Dan, who officiates at weddings and funerals for the church, states that he does not sell its sacrament or proselytize.

Like other cannabis religions, the CoC believes all of their members to be equal and thus the sacrament is imbibed without recourse to a mediator. And just as the ritual taking of the sacrament is particular to the individual, so, too, is the effect produced by the sacrament on the individual. Eliade makes an interesting point when looking at the *sui generis* nature of enlightened experience. When examining "the legendary descents of Pythagoras and Zoroaster, [they] have no shamanic structure whatever."[32] As this demonstrates, enlightenment is particular to each and every citizen and is not brokered by any religious official.

The CoC, more than any of the other cannabis religions discussed here, is inclusive of other people's ideas and beliefs and encourages their membership "to expand their knowledge through the study of all sacred texts, of all religions, and through the study of information revealed through Archaeological, Scientific, and Linguistic discovery."[33] They have compiled their own sacred text, but it is to be used in conjunction with other sacred texts. Moreover, their own text is dynamic, as it is constantly updated by their membership's contributions. In updating their scripture, "Cogniscenti" play an especially important role. While all members have the same rights and privileges, one can become ordained as a Cogniscenti of the church by studying other religions, especially the role of haoma in other religions, and by becoming deeply familiar with Zoroastrian texts. The idea here is that the church encourages each member to become knowledgeable about the history of Zoroastrianism and other religions so as to be able to contribute to the CoC's open scriptural practice. Any member of the CoC is eligible to become ordained as a Cogniscenti and a majority of all CoC members, whether Cogniscenti or not, must agree on any additions to the CoC's scripture.

> Initiate Cogniscenti are directed to the Church of Cognizance Cultural Information Center to begin their study; Ordained, and Enlightened Cogniscenti are directed to the same to submit any discoveries they have made, for other members' enlightenment; and to be kept aware of the latest discoveries others have submitted. Upon sufficient proof, or upon acceptance by a majority of [members], the new information

> should be incorporated into the CoC text as part of the Church of Cognizance's unique scripture.[34]

This is an inventive approach to scripture, as it allows for new developments and discoveries to update the practices of their belief system as they are revealed. Moreover, while many religious believers think that there may have been some degree of human interpolation when compiling God's directives, what comes to constitute the canon of religious authority is not open to suggestion. This last point demonstrates that there is a continuum of sorts in the degree to which orthodox believers perceive their texts. For fundamentalists in the Christian traditions, for example, the divine word was passed down from the divine to human beings unsullied by human interpolation. For more liberal Christians, there are varying degrees in terms of how much recognition they give to the human redactors of the Old and New Testaments in compiling the final product. To my knowledge, however, only the current Dalai Lama, the highest being in the Tibetan Buddhist tradition, has said explicitly that as science makes new discoveries in the field of neuroscience, these ideas will further open up the Tibetan Buddhist tradition—a religious tradition focused on perception and the workings of the human mind. "If science proves some belief of Buddhism wrong, then Buddhism will have to change."[35]

The Quaintances welcome any and all newcomers into the church and, while very decentralized, there is a definite membership structure underlying the CoC system. The CoC is made up of individual family units, paying dues to the church and adhering and contributing to the ideological and social growth of the church. Dan and Mary Quaintance exemplified this ideal. They were married for almost 40 years and had 2 children and 5 grandchildren, all of whom live in close proximity to each other in Pima, Arizona.

> Their home sits on a four-acre property that's dotted with old vehicles. Alongside their house is a wall made out of tires, which the Quaintances say eventually will form the boundary of an outdoor chapel. . . . Their home bears no resemblance to a traditional Church, inside or out. Yet the Quaintances call it a monastery and are adamant that the Church they founded together is a religious organization based in a sincere, legitimate, faith—on par with any mainstream religious denomination. A tapestry of Bob Marley smoking a spliff decorates the front hallway, and inside, the couple has a few handmade pipes, some of which have won ribbons in the glazing division of the Graham County Fair.[36]

Each member of the CoC pledges the promotion of "the health, safety, welfare, culture, and tradition of the family."[37] These family units are called IOMMs, which is an acronym for Individual Orthodox Member

Monastery. I was very interested in how the CoC was defining family, so I asked Quaintance the following.

> *Author*: Dan, in terms of how you think of family units, is it fairly inclusive or exclusive? In other words, might it be a family of close friends or a family unit composed of a gay couple?
>
> *Quaintance*: I guess we're not real particular about how your family is united. We wouldn't want to interfere with a family. One thing we used to focus on was that the middle folks took care of the senior folks who took care of the very senior folks and the kids. We have members that are Christian, Judaic, and Zoroastrian.
>
> *Author*: Can you tell me about what values your Church holds as a community?
>
> *Quaintance*: First of all, we are a Church; we are a Church with a goal of uniting like-minded individuals regardless of the denomination they claim as their religion. . . . A church is an assemblage of people, a group that comes together through like-minded views. But we don't need to have the same religion to have individuals with like-minded views to come together in the religious organization of a church.[38]

In further analyzing these IOMMs, I discovered the following: First, these "individual" family units are free to use cannabis whenever and wherever they see fit to do so. In this and in other decisions, these individual units are "unique within their own structure from other member monasteries."[39] Second, they interpret the term "orthodox," etymologically, to mean "understanding right from wrong."[40] In this their highest membership intention is very similar to the Golden Rule highlighted by the Church of the Universe. "In living with this understanding, that good thoughts, promote good words, promote good deeds, a monastery may be considered orthodox."[41] Third, to be a "member," one is "to promote the Family Oriented lifestyle, and traditions of the Church of Cognizance; and wherefrom these IOMMs united, the Church of Cognizance Cultural Information Centers are the Church of Cognizance."[42] This "Family Oriented lifestyle," moreover, is necessary not only in life but also in death as, according to Zoroastrianism, your ancestors help you to achieve heaven.[43] Fourth, "monastery" refers to the fact that all IOMMs are sovereign unto themselves and "their actions are not dictated by any other individual whom themselves are mere humans."[44]

While the CoC Cultural Information Center is the primary means of providing a social nexus for this church, this center is also designed to provide an important component shared by all of our cannabis religions; in all cases, these groups are not merely *in* society, they are also *of* society and want their message of social justice situated within the political landscape. That is why they publicly registered their "Declaration of Religious Sentiment" and maintain a dynamic website at danmary.org. For sustaining a connection among the IOMMs, the Cultural Information Center links IOMMs together: "wherein by consensus we may have 'One Loud Voice in worldly matters'; and wherefrom promote a better world for all."[45] Moreover, in their "Declaration of Religious Sentiment," the founders state that it is "their intent to unite the world's Ethnic Minorities, that utilize and rely upon the cannabis plant into an Ethno-Socio-Religious Institution, following Neo-Zoroastrian tenets."[46]

The CoC also has a process for excommunication, although only one member has been excommunicated as of this writing; he was excommunicated for violating his pledge of loyalty to the church when he testified as a state witness against the church and the Quaintances. All dues-paying IOMMs are allowed one vote in this process and a two-thirds vote will initiate excommunication.

Like the other cannabis religions, the CoC does not engage in proselytizing. Rather, they state, toward the end of their materials, the following: "If all of the above sounds like it fits within your beliefs we encourage you to join us as an IOMM of the Church of Cognizance by submitting a Membership Application through the Church of Cognizance Cultural Information Center website on the internet at http://enlightener.net/enroll. Or by mailing your completed application/pledge to the Church of Cognizance Cultural Information Center, Hc 1 box 4352 Pima, AZ." There are no donations required to become a member.

If you want to visit a Cultural Information Center, you can either go to Pima, Arizona or Puna, Hawai'i. If you choose Puna, you can meet there with Enlightened Cognoscenti Daniel Jeffrey. Jeffrey has known Dan and Mary for years and has said that "Dan and Mary are two of the most beautiful, wholesome people. We're not involved with herb for any kind of profit gain. If you tell people that, their mind just can't grasp it."[47] One of the days I spoke with Danuel Quaintance, Daniel Jeffrey was in Pima at Danuel's house and agreed to talk with me.

Author: So is the Church in Puna still in operation out there?

Jeffrey: Yes, yes. It's called the Universal Ohana Aloha Earth, Church of Cognizance Cultural Information Center. Ohana means family.

Author: How many families do you have involved in Puna?

Jeffrey: Probably about five or six. We're not interested in converting anyone. We just want to increase people's knowledge of the herb, because we believe it is the provider and our future.

Author: How did you meet Danuel and Mary?

Jeffrey: In 1997 we were in Arizona on a vision quest—we went to Sedona and then the winds kind of blew us to Dan and Mary's doorstep and we found a [spiritual] fortune there. It changed my life forever.

Author: Is your Church of Cognizance set up along the same lines as the Pima Church?

Jeffrey: Yes, it's set up in just the same way; we have an Information Center like Dan. The only difference is we eat more coconuts.[48]

Danuel Quaintance is passionate when it comes to both the freedom to use cannabis as a sacrament and the way in which cannabis is categorized.

Quaintance: I think what is going on now, with legalizing marijuana for medical or recreational purposes—that's still controlling marijuana—who can use it and when. Even under recreational use, it is controlled. Haoma needs to be decriminalized across the board. You know it's the lawyers running the dispensaries, now, because they know they are not going to make the kind of money they used to in representing people charged with possession.

Dan makes an excellent point here when he talks about how the discourse surrounding both medical and recreational marijuana is still a means of controlling this substance. And he is in good company with all of our postmodern thinkers in terms of how the categorization of something, in this case cannabis, is based on a discourse controlled by those in power; especially those in power within the legislative and judicial arms of the government. In the states where medical marijuana is legal, only those designated by a doctor as being sick can use this substance. Because of this, the discourse around medical marijuana conflates cannabis with sickness and characterizes those who use it for other purposes as deviants. In much the same way, recreational marijuana, as it has been legalized in Alaska, California, Colorado, Maine, Massachusetts, Nevada, Oregon, Washington, and Washington, D.C., has also been categorized and controlled. It is only legal for those over 21; you can only grow cannabis in Colorado, Alaska, Massachusetts, and Oregon, but must limit that growth in Oregon to 4 plants, in Colorado and Alaska to 6 plants, and in Massachusetts to 12 plants. Moreover, Oregon stipulates that the plants must not be visible to the general public. Possession of marijuana is legal in all 8 states plus the District of Columbia with the following caveats: "You can't drive while stoned. You can't sell pot. You can't consume marijuana in public."[49] Moreover, no employer is bound by these rules and, as a result, you can be fired even if you are adhering to state mandates. You cannot possess more than 1 ounce of cannabis in Alaska, California, Colorado, Washington, Massachusetts, Nevada, and Oregon, with the exception of Washington, D.C., where you can possess 2 ounces and Maine, where you can possess 2.5 ounces. And you cannot transport more than 1 ounce of cannabis anywhere.

> *Quaintance*: So if you want to bring marijuana to a family reunion, you better make sure that you have either a small family or light smokers—an ounce doesn't go that far. If you want to grow marijuana and barter it for the vegetables your neighbor grows, you can't grow more than [six] plants in Colorado and none without a medical marijuana license in Washington.

And those who deviate from these rules are criminalized and segregated from the rest of society.

> *Author*: Why do you think that cannabis is seen as such a threat by the government?

> *Quaintance*: Because cannabis gives you everything you need—food for humans and animals, clothing, building materials, medicine, and sacrament for religion. It provides for everything you need in life. So in order to control people, you need to control what they need. You know Mary [Dan's wife] got sentenced to two years and I got five. Mary wasn't sick at all until she had to stop smoking Haoma after our arrest. That's when she developed her heart problems and everything else. And since I served almost my whole term, when I got out, we weren't able to celebrate an anniversary or anything because she passed that year. But it doesn't serve to dwell on sad things. We believe in good thoughts, good words, good deeds. Heaven is here on earth. We all have a conscience and from your thoughts and deeds, you can make a heaven or a hell here on this earth. One evolves through a homeostatic balance.

As noted above, the "Quaintances did not grow their sacrament but, rather, say they relied on donations of it, which they picked up from Church "couriers."[50]

> *Author*: What role did the couriers play and how did they get paid?

> *Quaintance*: We had this monastery in Mexico, and we were able to bring cannabis from Mexico to Arizona. It was very cheap, about $300 per pound. Couriers were paid in herb for their efforts.

Each courier was provided with a Certified Courier License from the CoC that named the courier and stated that he/she was "a Special Courier for the transporting of religious instruments, properties, and sacrament for and between Member Monasteries of the Church of Cognizance."[51]

> *Quaintance*: Then the weed went to Wellness Centers—those people running the Wellness Centers came to study the history and uses of Haoma here in Pima before they went to work at the Wellness Centers. When we or our licensed Wellness Centers provided Haoma/Marijuana to others, we would sometimes take money for it, sometimes it was gifted, but it was purely a non-profit deal.[52]

According to Quaintance, the purpose of the Wellness Centers was to train members of the CoC "to use the Nutritious Haoma Sacrament as a healing herb to nurse sick and dying persons back to health or at the least give some relief to their suffering."[53]

THE CONSEQUENCES OF MAINTAINING A HOMEOSTATIC BALANCE

Transporting more than one ounce of cannabis across the street, much less across state lines, was and continues to be a serious offense and one that caught up with the CoC in 2006, when the Quaintances were arrested in New Mexico along with Timothy Kripner for carrying 172 pounds of marijuana in their car. Joseph Butts, a courier for the CoC, had also been arrested on the charge of distributing marijuana, and as these two cases were related, the Quaintances as well as Butts filed a Motion to Dismiss using the Religious Freedom defense spelled out in the Religious Freedom Restoration Act.

Dan Quaintance, who at that time of his arrest was 56 years old, was sentenced by federal court to five years in prison. Mary Quaintance, 53, was sentenced to two to three years, but was allowed to seek treatment for heart problems prior to serving her sentence. At the time of their arrest, Graham County Sheriff Richard Mack said that "in his 10 years on the job, he's never had a complaint about the Quaintances."[54] Moreover, according to Mary Quaintance's lawyer, they did not distribute to anyone outside of the Church and they never profited from it."[55]

But when the time came for his incarceration, what was really on Dan's mind was his family: "They've assigned us so far away, it's doubtful our family will be able to make that many trips to visit us during our incarceration."[56] And, of course, this would be a great sadness to someone who has built their religion around family. He went on to say "I personally can't think of any greater hardship that a person might face than being taken to such great distances away from loved ones. . . . I don't worry about the toll on me; I worry about the punishment being inflicted on our family as a whole." And for someone who has built his religion around cannabis and smoked cannabis daily, he and Mary were both without cannabis for the duration of their sentence and had to take drug tests for three years after being released to make sure they were cannabis-free. When asked about his conviction, Dan stated, "I am absolutely being persecuted for my religious beliefs. But then every religion has its martyrs."[57]

Author: How is the church now? Are you free to use your sacrament?

Quaintance: Yes, I am free to use my sacrament. Every now and again I'll get hassled. I got pulled over because my insurance on the car wasn't up to date, and the police, as I flipped through my wallet looking for insurance papers, noticed a card with a marijuana leaf and then asked if I was driving under the influence. And I said I thought you pulled me over for my insurance. And the officer asked me to tell him when 30 seconds were up—because you know when you're high you're supposed to lose all sense of time—and I got it right on the button. Then he told me to stand on one foot and he tried to show me and almost fell over, and then I did it and he made me do it for like 2 and 1/2 minutes—and then he was like, I guess you're fine. Then, another time, that same policeman came over and smelled the truck, and then said, "Well I guess this is the wrong one," and just got into his car and drove away.

Author: What are your future plans?

Quaintance: Well, I want to travel around and spread the word a bit for the Monasteries—go to D.C. and go up and down the halls of Congress. I can bring recognition of the fact that we have customs and traditions. Our Zoroastrian religious beliefs and practices are not like many other mainstream religions, so we shouldn't be judged by those standards. I don't know if I realized it, at first, when I started smoking, but cannabis is held in high spiritual regard by an awful lot of people. And when you use it sufficiently, it is the spirit Haoma within the plant that converts the ordinary user into a religious adherent. For us, Haoma holds a higher position than anything else. Cannabis is the element that brought us together . . . we do have customs and traditions and we want to open up to the light of day that cannabis is something that brings [people from all over] together.

CRAIG RUBIN AND THE FOUNDING OF TEMPLE 420

Just like a weed will push itself up through a crack in a sidewalk, when cracks appear in the dominant discourse about cannabis, from either judicial or medical arenas, new cannabis organizations spring up. And as we know from chapter 1, which examined the forerunners of these cannabis ministries, these organizations do not spring up *ex nihilo*. Rather, they have been existing underground, ready to emerge when the timing indicates that they will not be immediately squashed. For example, when the Supreme Court decided unanimously that the church O'Centro Espirita Beneficente Uniao do Vegetal (UDV) should have a religious exemption for using a Schedule 1 drug, dimethyltryptamine (DMT), as a sacrament, cannabis-based religions paid attention and acted to gain judicial legitimacy for their sacrament. As noted by Dan Quaintance, "Everybody followed the UDV case and filed their briefs accordingly."[58]

Craig Rubin, the founder of Temple 420, was especially focused on the UDV case because, like these other ministries, Rubin expected that in allowing a Schedule 1 drug to be used religiously, other drugs such as cannabis would be eligible for a religious exemption.[59] When the decision came down favorably for the UDV, Rubin felt that the time was right, and, on April 20, 2006, in Los Angeles, he founded Temple 420 on the corner of Hollywood and La Brea.

Craig Rubin is one of the more famous ministry founders, as he played the proprietor of a medical marijuana club on the first season of the television show *Weeds*. And his history with religion and cannabis is wide-ranging. He grew up in Beverly Hills in a Jewish family but was interested in Jesus and Christian teachings from an early age. He self-describes as a "curious Jew." As a child, he asked his father who Jesus was, and his father said, "He was the second most famous Jew after Moses." Craig continued to study both the Old and New Testaments of the Bible and "what I understood from my studies was that the New Testament was all about the Ten Commandments helping people."[60]

He connects cannabis and religion because he has felt that, when smoking cannabis with others, there emerges a type of shared transcendent experience. "In terms of cannabis and spirituality—I think that you know, it's hard to quantify. But I found in high school that it forged a camaraderie, it created a spiritual bond. Also, the people who smoke pot are more in touch with their feelings."[61] The experiential realization that smoking cannabis forges a spiritual bond between people is a motif that we have seen throughout all of the cannabis-based religions. Rubin also felt a kinship with the entheogenic practices of Native Americans.

> I got involved with the Havasu Indians and did their sweats and went to their weddings and funerals and they would burn cannabis, or sage, or sweet grass and I would think that this is the way it should be. But it

> also felt like someone else's religion, like I was participating in their religion. I also found that people who were spiritually dissatisfied used cannabis—and Bob Marley for me, he's the person who made me realize that cannabis and the Bible were not contradictory. He got me back into the Bible. I thought, if Bob Marley is doing this, there must be something to it.[62]

POTHEADS AND COMMUNITY PRACTICES

Right out of college, Rubin opened a hemp store. When medical marijuana began receiving a lot of attention, Rubin felt that cannabis should be completely legalized. But what he found was that so many of the marijuana clinics were run by gangsters or police officers.

> You'd go in to get marijuana and some guy without a shirt, and pierced all over with tattoos would be, "what kind of medicine do you want?" So, I decided to open a Church dispensary to help people out, professionalize the industry, and spread the word. Even when I portrayed the medical marijuana club owner on the TV show *Weeds*, I asked to wear a suit to elevate the industry. Because the bottom line is that most pot smokers, they don't feel welcome in church, so we tried to make our dispensary accessible to them.[63]

The part of this quote I want to draw attention to is the last one: "most pot smokers, they don't feel welcome in church." And it is not the church part that is striking, it is the fact that Craig saw people self-identifying as "pot smokers." And he identifies himself and his Temple members in much the same way when he states his motivation for creating Temple 420. "When I decided to open the Temple, I wanted to cater to my people, to potheads, and most of them had never been to a church or a temple. We were the Pot Church and people felt welcome."[64] Whether in the church or out, a closet pot smoker or out, for those who gravitate toward smoking cannabis as a sacramental ritual, "these [r]itual actions are not only performed by people, but, because they evoke a certain kind of response, in an important sense, they 'perform' people."[65] In other words, their ritual actions propel them into a new mode of self-identification; and in signifying Temple members as well as himself as potheads, he has elevated that signification as one for whom cannabis is of "ultimate concern."

As stated in Temple literature, members of Temple 420 understand themselves to fit into the Abrahamic religious traditions. We "sincerely believe we are part of The Church the G-D of the Bible established through his son and disciples.[66] We believe the Bible and the Holy Spirit are the Authority. We believe we're established and brought into G-D's family through Christ as a Judeo-Christian Church."[67]

Their belief system focuses on examining both the Jewish and Christian traditions, and, as noted by Rubin, one of his favorite couples to join Temple 420 were a Jewish woman and her Christian boyfriend—both were 420 friendly.

> They became members, and when they first walked in the Temple, she actually broke down crying she was so happy to find a spiritual home. They drove over one hour, three times a week, to go to our services. . . . On Sundays, we would have this cantor, music director, from another Temple come to our Temple because they had services on Saturdays and he was curious to know about the New Testament too.[68]

All of our previously discussed cannabis religions reinterpreted orthodox texts so as to be relevant to their belief systems. In the case of Temple 420, they chose passages that particularly focused on "compassion," as they believed that G-d wants all people to be loving to their neighbors and that G-d gave people cannabis out of G-d's compassion to heal his people both physically and spiritually.

> Our #1 Mission is Compassion, to be kind and compassionate to our brethren. Even when they disagree with our views, G-d is Love (1 John 4:8). We are provided for and taken care of as his children, if we read Genesis 1:12. In Isaiah 5:20, we are reminded not to call what he made good "evil" and that's what many "religious" [p]eople are doing. . . . In Exodus 30:24 and throughout the Bible . . . [w]e have the right under the Constitution and law to use the gift G-d gave us. We should all be free to burn G-d's herbs as he finds them appeasing as incense and created them for mankind's use (Psalm 104:14).[69]

One of the most pragmatic ways that Temple 420 practiced compassion was to sell pot at an affordable price. "We were also a low cost provider of marijuana. We sold 3.5 grams for $35.00. We had this one guy, he had been shot at Columbine and was in a wheel chair, and he said before he started coming to us, he was paying all his money for medicine—but now, he could get it from us for $35.00."[70]

Their Temple, like all of the other cannabis religions, was inclusive. At the same time, they believed that all faiths would come to know their "Truth," a "Truth" that rests on the primacy of a single male creator God who provides the world with cannabis. So it would seem from the following quote that there is a bit of hedging in their inclusive tenets, as not all of our cannabis religions recognize the primacy of a male creator god. According to Rubin:

> One other thing you'll notice is that we ARE NOT out to deny other faiths. We don't participate in the rituals of other faiths but we do respect them and share in them the Truth. For many are aware that there is a Creator, and he provides Cannabis. If we share the Truth with our fellow man of all faiths it will be revealed. For the Truth, Knowledge and Love of the Almighty Creator will reveal itself. When it

> comes to cannabis all faiths know a Creator has given [Cannabis] to us as a gift.[71]

There is no "hedging" when it comes to their ritualized use of cannabis. As stated in their literature, "G-d also gives us abundant wisdom, science is now here that shows that Cannabis promotes healing. . . . Cannabis ends up making a lot of things for the good of mankind, and that soothe him from the sins he has committed—from shelter, to super-food, it can replace our deathly petroleum need with life."[72] And, moreover, "Cannabis is an amazing representation of how G-D provides, from a pure fiber to incense, medicine, tools for shelter, nutrition you can live on, and more! G-D the Almighty Creator gave us amazing things and this just shows that more. G-D provides!"[73] However, unlike other cannabis-based religions such as the CoC, cannabis itself is not a deity. Rather, "[c]annabis is not to be elevated above Christ or G-D but recognized as an amazing gift."[74] An "amazing gift" that must be fought for as the Temple's literature highlights:

> [Cannabis] is not the only provision and gift of salvation he's given us, but it's important, with the war on "Drugs" innocent families are being destroyed when they could help grow the nation. We were made one nation under G-d. We need to regain that and use what he's given to us [namely] wisdom and in the green flesh. [R]each out to all of our "Stoner" brethren that have been condemned for their practice, especially when it comes to medical and spiritual uses. The "Stoners" and those who use cannabis know G-d's love, they need to be free to express their faith without ridicule, especially in their Church.[75]

According to Rubin, every Wednesday night they had a Bible study and every Friday night they had a Bible study. They kept the Jewish Sabbath; as Rubin notes, "it is God's Sabbath."[76] On Saturday they studied the Old Testament at 4:20 and on Sunday they studied the New Testament, at 4:20. That's a lot of Bible study. Therefore, in stating that Temple 420 engaged in four nights of Bible study per week may be an example of the politics of respectability: a means by which unorthodox practices are made to seem legitimate by framing them within the arena of familiar religious behavior. We will see this issue come up again in chapter 3, in relation to the Hawai'i Cannabis Ministry, when Roger Christie positions his church practices within a frame that closely resembles the Presbyterian services I attended growing up, complete with a coffee hour. One might say that "the politics of respectability" is merely a cover for dissembling about what one is actually doing. At the same time, when one is dunned with the mantle of illegitimacy from the get-go, it provides a means for hiding in plain sight to live another day. As we saw in relation to the CoC, and will see again in chapter 3 with Roger Christie, these founders of cannabis religions, for the most part, were very vocal about what they were doing, as was Craig Rubin, who ran for public office and extolled the virtues of cannabis on YouTube. And he publicly promoted the injustices done to those who claimed membership in cannabis-based religions for the same reason that, Stephen Gaskin, Walter Tucker, and Danuel Quaintance did—they believed that what they were doing was not only right but also constitutionally valid.

In a similar fashion to the Church of the Universe and the CoC, Temple 420 has off-shoots of their ministries and, as Rubin states, "These Temples are in every state—people know me." According to Rubin, there are 420 Temples all across the country, "everywhere I go—in Virginia, in Kansas. I tell them to stay private, though, don't become public. Start with a Bible Study and invite your stoner friends. People still call me up and ask me Bible questions."[77]

THE CONSEQUENCES OF BEING STONED IN THE TEMPLE

The first time Rubin was arrested was in November of 2006, when he was told by the LAPD that his church was not protected under religious law because a Judeo-Christian church is made up and not a real religion. The trial did not happen for a year, but, in the meantime, prior to any conviction, the government seized his life's savings, even though Rubin proclaimed that "[w]e never smoked weed in the Temple because smoking inside is illegal, but plenty of people would come high to the Temple."[78] Maintaining a space where people can both be stoned and participate in a religious service is an explicit example of the ways in which these cannabis-based religions provide metaphysical and physical space for their members to redefine who they are and how they perceive their use of cannabis. But it was not only his stance on cannabis that got him into trouble; it was also his understanding that Judaism and Christianity should be brought together into the same sacred space.

> I'm Jewish, I love being Jewish, but Jewish people tend not to be into Jesus, and, in fact, the wife of the Rabbi of the Temple down the street made us repaint the wall of the Temple that said "Jesus is Lord" because she called it hate speech. My lawyers told me not to fight it, so we repainted it. They actually called the FBI on me and the FBI guy followed up on the hate speech complaint. My lawyer, Brett Rubin, was the one who advised me to paint over it or potentially get arrested for hate speech—whether I was convicted or not the trial would be costly.[79]

To live one's life "oriented" around cannabis forces our founders to take immense risks to "spread the word." They run hemp stores when cannabis paraphernalia is illegal; they protest at rallies; they attend public gatherings where they are targeted as those who would challenge the power structure that controls the discourse around cannabis; and they build ministries, churches, and temples that bring like-minded people together to celebrate what they have experienced as a sacrament. In the face of this reality, the counterargument that these ministers are out to make a quick buck seems tenuous. For one thing, the government has segregated all of our "deviant" cannabis founders from the rest of society by putting them in prison or on probation. They all have had their possessions and savings confiscated. And, even after that, they come back to the frontline willing to "[g]o to D.C. [and] go up and down the halls of Congress" for their religious rights as guaranteed by the Constitution.

Rubin sees himself as a warrior in the war against drugs, as noted by Cindy Holden of the *California Newswire*:

> "Churches and Temples are no longer safe in America," says Reverend Craig X Rubin of Temple 420, who was arrested November 8, 2006, at his religious establishment by over one dozen heavily armed officers of the LAPD. Rubin continues, "If they can do this to us, they can do it to any church that the government disagrees with."[80]

Holden goes on to say that "Reverend Rubin has taken to calling himself "General Pharmer" and is distributing images of himself wearing an army cap emblazoned with a cannabis leaf, while making clear his Church is not about war but peace. Still, he is gearing up for battle with those trying to shut him down."[81]

After the arrest in November of 2006, six months after the Temple opening, the Temple was still able to operate, but could no longer provide low-cost cannabis to people. Prior to his 2007 trial, Rubin employed 17 people and noted that "one of the employees who cleaned up at the Temple, this homeless guy who agreed to be a witness for the defense, ended up committing suicide because he was so threatened [by the authorities telling him] you will spend years in prison if you cooperate with the defense."[82]

Craig Rubin also paid a big price for following his religious convictions. And the word "convictions" is very interesting in this context, for if your convictions challenge those held by the majority, you are likely to face legal conviction and eventually become a convict.

> I tried to do everything right, by the book. Got the permits, got counsel from lawyers, but I still ended up with 13 years of probation. I no longer had a home, I no longer had a job—no one wants to hire somebody with a felony conviction. I was all set to get a job with this TV station as an editor for $80,000 per year, and when one of the bosses found out I was a convicted felon the day before I was supposed to start work they told me not to come in. I had been upfront about it because the woman who hired me was a member of the Temple. There are a lot of things convicted felons can't do. My goal has always been to reach my people, stoners, with the Word.[83]

As one considers the narrative of these founders of cannabis-based religions, their collective stories demonstrate both an acute sadness over all that they have lost and a deep resilience in the battle to have their religious freedom recognized. Chapter 3, which focuses on Roger Christie, the founder of the Hawai'i Cannabis Ministry, proves no exception; Christie was an activist for religious freedom prior to the founding of his ministry, while he was acting as a minister, and during the time of his incarceration. I am devoting an entire chapter to the Hawai'i Cannabis Ministry because they were shut down later than any of the other groups and, as a result, I was able to gain access to ministry members much more easily than with any of the other religious groups. For this reason, I will save the analysis of the Church of the Universe, the CoC, and Temple 420 until the end of chapter 3. In using this approach, not only will we be able to judge if these four cannabis-based religions share the structural template provided by their forerunners but also we will be able to discuss their founders' respective motivations for doing what they do.

NOTES

1. "Church Credo," *Assembly of the Church of the Universe*, http://www.iamm.com/man-cu.htm, accessed October 5, 2017.
2. Michael Pollan, *The Botany of Desire: A Plant's-Eye View of the World* (New York: Random House, 2001), 144.
3. Genesis 2:8–9, 2:9–17, 3:1–24; Revelation 2:7, 22:1–2, 22:14–15; Proverbs 3:13–18, 11:30, 13:12, 15:4.
4. Based on the Book of Genesis 2:8 and the Book of Revelation 22:2.
5. "Tree of Life," *The Assembly of the Church of the Universe*, accessed September, 17, 2015, http://www. iamm.com/69.htm.
6. "Terms of Endearment," *Assembly of the Church of the Universe*, accessed September 17, 2015, http://www.iamm.com/faq.htm#Endearments.
7. "God Is God," *The Assembly of the Church of the Universe*, accessed September, 17, 2015, http://www. iamm.com/69.htm.
8. The Assembly of the Church of the Universe, accessed September 17, 2015, http://www.iamm.com/templar.htm.
9. "Nine Pointed Star," *The Assembly of the Church of the Universe*, accessed September 21, 2015, http://www.iamm.com/star.html.
10. Peter Small, "Smoking Cannabis Is a Religious Right, Court Told," *Toronto Star*, April 8, 2010.
11. Matt Mernaugh, "Church of the Universe Cannabis Court Ruling Fails," *Pot.tv*, February 7, 2011, available at http://www.pot.tv/video/2011/02/07/church-universe-cannabis-court-ruling-fails/.
12. "Church Credo," *Assembly of the Church of the Universe*, http://www.iamm.com/man-cu.htm, accessed October 5, 2017.
13. Kevin Marron, "Counsel to the Damned," *Canadian Lawyer Magazine*, September 1996.
14. Michel Foucault, *The History of Sexuality*, vol. 1 (New York: Vintage Books, 1978), 5.
15. Marron, "Counsel to the Damned."
16. "Baldasaro back in the race," *CHCH*, July 11, 2014, http://www.chch.com/baldasaro-back-race.
17. Certified copy of instrument recorded in Docket 481, pages 81–96, date: 8–12–1994, Time 1:20PM, Wendy John, Graham County Recorder.

18. Stephanie Innes, "Church of Cognizance: Pot Church Takes a Hit," *Arizona Daily Star*, July 9, 2006.

19. Stephen Lemons, "Arizona's Marijuana-Worshipping Church of Cognizance Seeks a Legal, Spiritual High," *Phoenix New Times*, March 6, 2009, available at http://www.phoenixnewtimes.com/blogs/arizonas-marijuana-worshipping-church-of-cognizance-seeks-a-legal-spiritual-high-6501014.

20. Innes (referencing *Avesta* at Yasna 11:10 and 14:2).

21. "Scripture of the Church of Cognizance," *Church of Cognizance Introduced*, http://www.coc.enlightener.net, accessed August 4, 2015.

22. The *Vendidad*, Fargard 22. "Of the 21 books of the Sasanian canon of the *Avesta* . . . this is the only one which has survived in its entirety." J. Peterson, 1995, (Avesta.org).

23. "Declaration of Religious Belief," in coc.enlightener.net, accessed on April 9, 2016, http://haoma.org/coc/documents/dclrtn1.htm.

24. "Scripture of the Church of Cognizance," *Church of Cognizance Introduced*, accessed August 4, 2015, http://www.coc.enlightener.net.

25. Danuel Quaintance, telephone discussion with the author, September 23, 2015.

26. "Scripture of the Church of Cognizance," *Church of Cognizance Introduced*, accessed August 4, 2015, http://www.coc.enlightener.net.

27. Danuel Quaintance, telephone discussion with the author, September 23, 2015.

28. Mircea Eliade, *Shamanism: Archaic Techniques of Ecstasy* (Princeton: Princeton University Press, 1964), 399.

29. Eliade, 400

30. Eliade, 401.

31. Dan Quaintance, telephone discussion with the author, September 23, 2015.

32. Eliade, 393.

33. "Scripture of the Church of Cognizance," *Church of Cognizance Introduced*, accessed August 4, 2015, http://www.coc.enlightener.net.

34. Ibid.

35. Tenzin Gyatso, *The Universe in a Single Atom: The Convergence of Science and Spirituality* (New York: Broadway Books, 2005), Kindle Books Location 49.

36. Innes.

37. "Family Oriented Monastic Orders Promoting Family," *Church of Cognizance Introduced*, accessed August 4, 2015, http://www.coc.enlightener.net.

38. Danuel Quaintance, telephone discussion with the author, September 23, 2015.

39. "Individual Orthodox Member Monastery," *Church of Cognizance Introduced*, accessed August 4, 2015, http://www.coc.enlightener.net.

40. Ibid.

41. Ibid.

42. Ibid.

43. Eliade, 397.

44. "Individual Orthodox Member Monastery," *Church of Cognizance Introduced*, http://www.coc.enlightener.net, accessed August 4, 2015.

45. Ibid.

46. "Declaration of Religious Sentiment," *Church of Cognizance*, accessed August 12, 2015, in coc.enlightener.net.

47. Innes.

48. The Universal Ohana Aloha Earth, Church of Cognizance Cultural Information Center has a website at: http://www.haoma.info.

49. Laurel Andrews, "Highly Informed: 13 Pressing questions about Alaska's marijuana legalization day," *Alaska Dispatch News*, February 24, 2015, accessed August 22, 2016, https://www.adn.com/highly-informed/article/legalization-day-13-most-pressing-questions/2015/02/24/.

50. Innes.

51. "Certified Couriers of the CoC," Church of Cognizance, accessed on August 22, 2016, http://danmary.org/tiki/tiki-index.php?page=Certified+Couriers+of+the+COC

52. Danuel Quaintance, telephone discussion with the author, September 22, 2015.
53. "Greetings and Welcome to Dan & Mary's Monastery-HEMPorium," Church of Cognizance, accessed on August 22, 2016, http://danmary.org/tiki/tiki-index.php.
54. Innes.
55. Ibid.
56. Lemons.
57. Ibid.
58. Danuel Quaintance, telephone discussion with the author, September 22, 2015.
59. DMT is the component of Hoasca that is a Schedule 1 substance.
60. Craig Rubin, telephone discussion with the author, February 18, 2012.
61. Ibid.
62. Ibid.
63. Ibid.
64. Craig Rubin, telephone discussion with the author, September 1, 2015.
65. William LaFleur, *Liquid Life: Abortion and Buddhism in Japan* (Princeton: Princeton University Press, 1992), 155.
66. G-D is used in the Jewish tradition in order to signify that G-D cannot be contained by a single word and that G-D has many names throughout the *New Testament* of the Bible.
67. "The Temple 420 (Mission)—Cannabis and Christianity," Temple 420 Literature, received January 15, 2012.
68. Ibid.
69. "Temple 420 Your Salvation Is Here," Temple 420 Literature, received January 15, 2012.
70. Craig Rubin, telephone discussion with the author, September 1, 2015.
71. "The Temple 420 (Mission)—Cannabis and Christianity," Temple 420 Literature, received January 15, 2012.
72. "Temple 420 Your Salvation Is Here," Temple 420 Literature, received January 15, 2012.
73. "The Temple 420 (Mission)—Cannabis and Christianity," Temple 420 Literature, received January 15, 2012.
74. Ibid.
75. Ibid.
76. Craig Rubin, telephone discussion with the author, February 18, 2012.
77. Ibid.
78. Ibid.
79. Ibid.
80. Cindy Holden, "Hollywood Judeo-Christian Cannabis Church Forced to Close—Arrested Reverend Claims Civil and Religious Rights Violated," *California-Newswire*, December 11, 2006.
81. Ibid.
82. Craig Rubin, telephone discussion with the author, September 1, 2015.
83. Ibid.

THREE

Roger Christie and the Hawai'i Cannabis Ministry

> I am zero afraid of prison. I am committed to the sacrament of Cannabis because it's every citizen's God-given right to partake of the herbs of this earth.
>
> —Christie[1]

Reverend Roger Christie was held in a prison cell without bail in the Honolulu Federal Detention Center from July 8, 2010, when he was taken into custody as a "danger to society" until September 11, 2014, when he was released to a half-way house. Also charged but released on bail were the other members of the Green 14—namely, Christie's wife Share Christie and 12 members of the Hawai'i Cannabis Ministry. As far as the federal government was concerned, the "danger" 63-year-old Christie posed consisted of the manufacture, possession, and distribution of cannabis. Christie does not deny these charges. He does, however, frame these acts not as a "danger" to society but rather as a "benefit" to society, as well as the defining components of the Hawai'i Cannabis Ministry, hereafter to be denoted as the THC Ministry—an intentionally playful acronym used by its members.[2] The other defining components of the THC Ministry mirror their cannabis-based forerunners, but do so in a manner particular to the THC Ministry. These include providing access to sacramental cannabis, highlighting the transformative experience of sacramental cannabis, reinterpreting Biblical passages to support their use of cannabis-infused holy anointing oil, bringing together a community in which to celebrate this sacrament, and providing access to the latest news, state and federal initiatives, and political opportunities to make cannabis legal for sacramental use.

In the same manner as the previous two chapters, this chapter will comprise three sections. First, who were the founders and what was the early development of the group? Second, in what ways did the THC Ministry use cannabis as part of its communal practices? And, third, what have been the legal consequences for using cannabis as a sacrament? In the last segment of this chapter, I will undertake an analysis of the four cannabis-based religions found in chapters 2 and 3 not only to find out if they conform to the structural template provided by their forerunners but also to further answer the question of why these groups do what they do.

ROGER CHRISTIE: THE MAN AND HIS MINISTRY

Born in 1949 in Colorado, Christie has a long history of social activism. After enlisting in the U.S. Army during the Vietnam era, he sought and won an honorable discharge as he was "galvanized into action by the wrongful nature of the war."[3] For many years, he worked to stamp-out the methamphetamine epidemic in his home state of Hawai'i, and, in 2000, was honored with the Ho'omaluhia Peacemaker Award for his efforts. This award is given by the Drug Policy Forum of Hawai'i for "achievement in the development and advancement of rational and humane drug policies."[4] He is described by his supporters as "a crusader" and "[a] spiritual and political pioneer [who] has heroically broken trail at the evolutionary forefront of the world's most ancient global culture."[5] The "global culture" referred to here is one that utilizes cannabis and hemp in their myriad applications, including not only medical and spiritual applications but also product applications such as textiles, paper, biofuel, and food for humans, animals, and birds.

In describing his spiritual sojourn, Christie states: "I was a happy member of the Religious Science Church of Hilo from late 1986 until 1993." (The Religious Science Church was developed in the early 1920s and focuses on the science of the mind, or, alternatively stated, the ways in which the mind creates reality.) Christie continues: "When the Church declined my offer to talk about Cannabis spirituality at a future Sunday service I was disappointed at their lack of courage in exploring the truth."[6] As noted by a member of the THC Ministry who knew of Christie's involvement in the Religious Science Church of Hilo,

> His attitude was always so positive. He doesn't use words like no, or not, or never, cuz he thinks that they will cause you to attract negative energy—instead he would always say "zero," zero this and zero that. He spent a long time in that Religion and Science Church—10 years—and he always looked at the bright side.[7]

In 1993, Christie moved on to the Religion of Jesus Church, founded by James Kimmel, and was ordained as a minister there seven years later, in June of 2000. According to its literature,

> The Religion of Jesus Church is a group of like-minded individuals who believe: That God is Our Father and that we are all, the entire human race, one spiritual family that [comprise] as many paths to God as there are people to walk them. That Cannabis is a Holy Sacrament from times of antiquity. That our main religious text is the *Urantia Book*. . . . We draw upon many religious texts, including the *Holy Bible*, and many others to establish and verify our religious practices.[8]

These religious practices as experienced by members consisted of getting together on Sundays and smoking cannabis as a sacrament, thus opening the door for an enlightened discussion of the *Urantia Book*.[9] At the end of the service, some members would give a donation in order to get a bit of the cannabis sacrament to take home. According to Christie, "[i]t was simple and sincere and it worked well for everyone. I value their teachings every day of my life."[10]

While the Religion of Jesus Church centralized the teachings of the *Urantia Book*, Christie focused on the Bible when he opened the THC Ministry.

> I sought to carry on the Religion of Jesus Church tradition, but with a direction more in line with my personality and more of a full-time commitment. . . . So I sought to do something with science of mind spiritual principles plus Cannabis as the healing sacrament from my home in Hilo. I gravitated more to the Bible than the *Urantia Book*, but the spirit of service to my community was somewhat like Pastor Jim modeled.[11]

After Roger Christie's ordination in the Religion of Jesus Church, he applied to the State of Hawai'i Department of Health for a license granting him the authority to perform marriages. In his application to the Department of Health, Christie clearly noted that he was seeking a license as a cannabis sacrament minister.

> My application to the Dept. of Health included all my basic information, plus the words "Cannabis sacrament" in the space where it asked for my "denomination or sect," as that was our/my truthful specialty. . . . A few weeks later my license arrived in the mail and it was a very happy day as it dawned on me that the State of Hawai'i had just licensed me (for life!) to marry people specifically as a "Cannabis sacrament" Minister.[12]

Christie received his ordination in June of 2000 and opened the THC Ministry three months later. The timing of his actions is significant, for Hawai'i signed into law Senate Bill 862 in June of 2000, legalizing medical marijuana and declaring that they would not be opening any dispensaries in September of 2000. While the legalization of medical marijuana seemed like a positive step toward easing the restrictions around the use of marijuana, the bill promised more than it delivered as it did not authorize any type of "collective cultivation, instructing patients and their caregivers to grow their own cannabis."[13] Two additional facts demonstrate that the state of Hawai'i was not going to make it easy for cannabis to be obtained even by those with a medical marijuana license. First, the patient registry was situated within the Narcotics Enforcement Division rather than the Department of Health, in contrast to other states; and second, the Hawai'i Police Department received almost a quarter of a million dollars annually "to eradicate cannabis and enforce prohibition."[14]

When these governmental decisions were passed, Christie realized that the state's tight control over access to cannabis as well as its continuing prosecution of those seeking access (even those granted a medical marijuana license) necessitated the creation of a space that would provide sanctuary for those in need of cannabis. As Share Christie, Roger's wife as of January 2012, and a coadministrator of the THC Ministry, noted, "Roger likes to put people under his Church to protect them."[15] Moreover, Christie fervently believed in the Constitution's promise of religious freedom, so Hawai'i's strict restrictions around access to cannabis was a further slap in the face, curbing an individual's right to practice his or her own religion. "Roger was always up front about what he was doing because he felt he had a legal right to be doing it. He was very candid and open about his beliefs in these rights—he was planning on growing marijuana in the Church."[16] According to many ministry members, Roger fundamentally did not see himself as a violator of the law.

SACRAMENTAL CANNABIS AND COMMUNITY PRACTICES

When speaking of cannabis, Christie uses exalted terms and biblical references. He describes cannabis as a "botanical savior," one that is capable of saving people from hunger, stress, disease, spiritual and social loneliness, ecological extinction, and poverty.[17] One of the most significant biblical references for the THC Ministry occurs in Exodus 30:23, in which God tells Moses to make sacred anointing oil using *kaneh bosem*, which Christie argues is cannabis. As noted in chapter 1, the translation of *kaneh bosem* as cannabis is a minority opinion among scholars. Christie, however, maintains his position that *kaneh bosem* is cannabis and puts forth the following argument.

> OK, *kaneh bosem*. As you know it's translated into English in King James directly as calamus, or in all other editions it appears vaguely as "fragrant cane," "aromatic cane," "sweet cane," "or spicy rods." From what I know of calamus it's a ROOT, NOT a *cane* or a *rod* at all. If

> we can't yet ADVANCE Cannabis as the mystery ingredient in the holy anointing oil, maybe we can at least ELIMINATE calamus root? Am I correct in remembering that Jews were supposed to be buried in "Kaneh" shirts, or burial clothes? If so, that leaves calamus root OUT of the definition and puts us back into Cannabis hemp as a likely solution.[18]

I would argue that Christie's insistence on *kaneh bosem* being cannabis comes from his desire to find biblical back-up for his religious use of cannabis. In so doing, he not only attempts to legitimate the ministry's ritual use of cannabis but also attempts to position the ministry as a legitimate religious organization. That does not mean to say that Christie is selling snake oil here or is insincere in using cannabis as a primary component of holy anointing oil. In fact, the reinterpretation of orthodox scripture to support and structure ritual activities is one of the five elements common to all of these cannabis-based religions, a reinterpretive process that we will further examine at the end of this chapter.

Christie points to a number of passages in the Old and New Testaments as referring to Cannabis, such as in Genesis 1:29, wherein God gives to Adam and Eve "every plant yielding seed," and in Revelations 22:2 describing the "tree of life," whose leaves were to be used for the "healing of the nations." Share Christie credits Roger's biblical framing of cannabis for her own spiritual awakening.

> When I had gotten Lyme disease when I was working in Mexico, I found that edible cannabis and a Volcano (a cannabis vaporizer) helped my sleeping. But it wasn't until I heard Roger talk about cannabis as the "tree of life" that I really got it. My friends "snobbed" cannabis and hemp seed, but this plant can save our planet, and the healing properties of the "tree of life" make sense to me.[19]

Christie also uses the biblical term "man of the cloth" to refer to hemp, while the "burning bush" refers to cannabis.

Beyond the ritual use of sacramental cannabis in the form of holy anointing oil, Christie and others testify as to the efficacy of this substance in effecting cures for everything from chronic migraines to gangrene. And it is not only in holistic medicine circles that one hears of such cures. When I asked Dr. Mahmoud ElSohly, who runs the only federally legal cannabis field in the country, if oil made with cannabis could heal open wounds on the skin, he replied that "[y]es, it would be effective when used in that manner."[20]

In another testimonial related by Christie, holy anointing oil was said to have cured multiple sclerosis:

> Jeff suffered from a long-term, but slight speech impediment, and a recent diagnosis of multiple sclerosis, hence his self-prescribed need for "medical marijuana." I asked Jeff if he would be interested in being anointed with the holy anointing oil of Moses and the christening oil of Jesus with a personal prayer. He said yes. In addition to smoking a

> little bit of Cannabis daily, Jeff took drops of our tincture and re-anointed himself on a daily basis. About 90 days after he had arrived in town Jeff called me and announced that he was completely healed of the speech impediment and the M.S., and he was going back to his native Florida with a newfound "lease on life." He told me that he was so grateful to me for assisting him in his healing process with Cannabis and prayer that he was giving me the keys to his office, a copy of the remaining lease, and an antique U.S. silver dollar for good luck. Wow! God, that's great! [21]

The office that Christie was given was located within the Moses Building in Hilo, Hawai'i; whether a coincidence or, as Christie might say, an act of grace, it was a fitting home for his ministry. As with most seemingly miraculous cures, such stories are met with skepticism by nonbelievers. However, on March 1, 2012, in Madrid, Spain, researchers reported that "[t]he administration of a cannabinoid agonist halts the advancement of multiple sclerosis, according to preclinical data to be published in the journal *Neuropharmacology*." [22]

Christie is quick to emphasize the healing characteristics of cannabis, but he sees the laws surrounding medical marijuana as being an obstacle to its sacramental use.

> It's obvious that Cannabis use reduces stress and helps to prevent disease. "Medical marijuana" does not allow for that fundamental use; people need to get sick first in order to qualify. Sacramental use provides for preventative health care, and it's backed by the First Amendment to the Constitution, known as the "first freedom." . . . We need to use Cannabis FIRST in order to develop our thoughts, feelings and ideas of spirituality/religion; like Moses met God in the smoke and fire of the "burning bush," THEN he had a notion of what/who he was dealing with. Cannabis use helped to develop my personal spirituality. The good people of the USA need the freedom to use Cannabis, or not, to have religious freedom. [23]

In the same manner as Danuel Quaintance, Christie wants to separate the medical discourse around cannabis from the religious discourse around cannabis, for while the majority of states now protects those who would use cannabis for medical purposes, those who use it in the context of religion are still considered deviants—those who deviate from dominant discourse. Moreover, while believing in the medical effectiveness of cannabis, Christie sees its sacramental use as the essential first step in developing a cannabis practice, a practice through which one is first gifted with a spiritual epiphany that then leads one toward a realization of the physical benefits to be enjoyed. In describing the sacramental use of cannabis, Christie states the following:

> We call Cannabis a "sacrament." Saint Augustine described a sacrament as "the visible form of an invisible grace," my favorite definition for it. In our tradition, budding Cannabis flowers, leaves and fully

developed seeds are "sacraments." Each one can deliver invisible graces by reducing stress and allowing for happiness, gladness, joy and optimum health to occur. . . . It's a description of the spirit not the body.[24]

Christie is a meticulous person, and, when he writes of cannabis, he always capitalizes it as he does the word *god.* His years in the Religious Science Church also show up in his writings, as he always ends an affirmation, wish, or desire with the words "and so it is," which in his belief system works to draw positive energy to that wish. His writing also displays a feminist sensibility, as he always uses gender inclusive terms, decries the immorality of patriarchy, and often refers to the divine as God/ess.

Christie never uses the word "marijuana," as he sees this word as part of the federal government's plan to undermine cannabis. "Even using the very word 'marijuana' should be enough to prove something 'fishy' has been going on as it's a 'mongrel word' made up to be a Mexican-sounding 'false flag' to distract people from the commonly available and historic 'Cannabis hemp.'"[25] In jail, Christie's request for "religious rights for the THC Ministry [including a] hemp diet, hemp soap, holy anointing oil (without Cannabis), hemp cloth prayer shawl, Cannabis literature, and counseling others" was refused. In response to his request, he received the following reply from the warden. "This is in response to your Inmate Request to staff dated August 16, 2011. You requested a 'new or unusual religion' be officially recognized. . . . Your request for the above items was disapproved based on safety and security concerns of the institution."[26] Given that Christie did not ask for cannabis but rather for the ritual items connected to his religious practice, the warden's response serves as a metaphor for how the government views unfamiliar religions—namely, as something perceived to threaten the "safety and security concerns" of those in power.

Christie's writings demonstrate that it was not easy to be incarcerated for so long. For one thing he and his partner Share were forced apart. They worked hard to bridge this gap, and on Friday, January 6, 2012, they were married at the prison:

Share and I had a terrific wedding ceremony on Friday. Who knew? The location disappeared for us as we gazed at each other, held hands, kissed and shared words of love, acknowledgment and mutual support. We "hand-fasted" and "tied the knot" with a hemp cloth prayer shawl. The Minister was brave and did a fine job.[27]

Christie equates his cannabis advocacy with a religious vocation, one in which he shares the good news that in smoking cannabis one can achieve communion with the divine. In fact, he feels that his birth name pointed him toward his vocation.

What's in a name? (Or is it just my ego talking?)

It was interesting to me when I was told by a visitor to the THC Ministry many years ago what my name translated to. I had always known that my last name broke down to Christ ie, as in "Christ example," but that's about it. . . . This visitor told me that the name "Roger" comes from Europe and means "spear-man," "point-man," or leader, and Christie translates to "anointed example." It made me think that the holy spirit was personally guiding me along this path to return the anointing to common usage.[28]

And in order to carry out that spiritual mandate, Christie wanted to gather people together into a ministry so that "'the yoke shall be destroyed because of the anointing.' And so it is."[29]

"the Hawai'i Cannabis Ministry—We Use Cannabis Religiously and You Can Too," was the promotional slogan for the THC Ministry and one of many publicly distributed pieces of literature used by Christie and other ministry members to publicize the ministry and to attract new members.[30] The THC Ministry operated for more than ten years in the Moses Building on Main Street in Hilo, Hawai'i, and services were offered throughout that time, openly celebrating cannabis as a sacrament. Cannabis was provided to members and to medical marijuana patients for a donation; a suggested donation for an ounce of cannabis was $400, which was equal to the street value of cannabis at that time.[31] For a donation of $50, members could receive ID cards, seven plant tags for marking cannabis plants as sacramental-use-only, and, included for an additional donation of $200, the *THC Ministry Guide to Cannabis Spirituality*. The ministry also offered counseling and guidance, medical cannabis education through their Cannabis College, and cannabis advocacy for those faced with "the problems associated with Cannabis prohibition and discrimination."[32]

Christie talks a lot about God, the Holy Spirit, and Jesus, and one of the things he particularly likes about Jesus Christ, the anointed one, is that Jesus revealed the secret of the anointing oil to the masses and, as Christie saw it, empowered people to anoint each other. Christie deeply believes in a nonhierarchical model, in which laypeople are empowered both to effect their own salvation and to take responsibility for leading others, a common membership structure that mirrors the Rastas, The Farm, and the other three contemporary cannabis-based religions.

Over the years, Christie has ordained many other people as THC ministers, and this is one of the places he has run into problems.

I have ordained many THC Ministry ministers, a few who have gone on to open a THC Ministry of their own. It was a well-intentioned, but flawed plan on my part. For instance, Ferre van Beveren of Amsterdam developed a second THC Ministry website with my approval many years ago to give us an international reach online from Europe. It

> worked pretty well until our relationship soured and Ferre evolved away from the THC Ministry mission. Unfortunately for me he has ownership of the website and I have zero influence over what he posts and what he allows to be posted there. We mutually agreed that he would drop the use of the name THC Ministry many years ago, but last I checked . . . he was still using it without my permission.[33]

Christie's ideas for changing the ways in which the ministry ordained people included requiring applicants to spend a training week in person with him. He would also mandate that any offshoot ministries allow for his control over their website. Moreover, he would provide a "letter of good standing" for newly ordained ministers, and he would issue a "letter of bad standing" if it became necessary.

During the time that their headquarter church in Hilo was in operation, Christie officiated at numerous cannabis ceremonies, such as weddings, funerals, and baptisms. Share Christie describes these ceremonies: "Big events, weddings—Roger was so good at that and they were always my favorite part. We would throw hemp seeds and tie their hands with hemp material, a hemp shawl. We had funerals and baptisms—so beautiful, and we always had music."[34] In order to protect themselves, Share Christie said, they always had a door person who would check to make sure that people coming in had either a THC Ministry membership card or a medical card identifying them as eligible to use cannabis for medical purposes. She notes:

> We asked people to give a donation if they wanted to partake; half the people didn't have the money, and we'd give them shake [the cannabis left at the bottom of one's receptacle that contains mostly leaves, seeds and stems]. . . . We gave thousands of dollars to people in cannabis. And while we never turned people away we used lavender to clean the benches. You know, Roger is a clean-conscious person and serious street people came in. . . . But one of the things that I find so endearing about Roger is his love of people; he acknowledges them and hears their whole story. Because Roger didn't have kids, the Ministry was his baby.[35]

Christie concluded a number of his group emails with the THC Ministry Creed: "God that's great! Show me the blessings in this situation . . . and hurry! We are safe, we are loved and all is well."[36] THC Ministry materials proclaimed that cannabis is a great gift to be used in achieving communion with the divine as well as with those around you. They also described the efficacy and sacred nature of cannabis-infused holy anointing oil and exhorted others to "bless their challenges, find the good in any situation . . . honor all of God's creation [and] strive to live with modesty, good manners, and humbleness." Finally, the THC Ministry called on its members to engage in the practice of "making and providing Cannabis sacramental for those in need . . . [as] an important part of the THC Ministry's mission."[37]

The rules of the ministry required that members must be over 21-years-old and "must affirm that they will use Cannabis sincerely as part of their religious practice and method of worship."[38] In fact, if you were to become a member of the THC Ministry, ingesting cannabis in one form or another was a required ritual act. "At the THC Ministry it has always been mandatory to use Cannabis in order to receive the benefits of all its many complex components. We have also used the words 'essential' and 'necessary' when describing our need for this natural herb."[39] Christie's statement here reveals two things about the ministry. First, that cannabis was the centerpiece of the THC's ritual practice. And, second, that Christie was well aware of the court cases waged around cannabis and religious freedom that required that one was "sincere" in their ritual practices and that the illegal substance for which a religious group sought an exemption was "essential" to their religion.[40] These court cases and others will be further addressed in chapter 5.

Early on in our correspondence, I asked Christie what services looked like at the THC Ministry, and he sent me a lengthy description of Sunday services.

> THC Ministry services included a welcome period where we made a circle and offered introductions. Everyone had to speak-up and introduce themselves and say why they were there. Part of my purpose was to weed-out, so to speak, any visitors or members who seemed insincere, or had bad manners as sometimes was the case.[41]

In a structure similar to Christian Protestant services, Christie would then make announcements, including any new information on cannabis, medical marijuana, or the legal status of cannabis, and then would proceed with "a history story of Cannabis sacrament use around the world, a group prayer, and the lesson of the week."[42] Then it was time for communion. But rather than passing out the cubed bread and tiny cups of juice used in Protestant communion rituals, or the wine and bread transmogrified into the body and blood of Christ, as in Catholic mass, Christie distributed holy anointing oil infused with cannabis:

> I explained what the sacraments were made with, and how they were made and blessed. I went around the circle with my two bottles of tincture. . . . I would offer literally just one drop of tincture on the tongue to each participant. . . . Then I would go around the circle one more time with holy anointing oil. I applied a few drops to both inner wrist "pulse points" and asked people to rub their wrists together slowly. . . . Then I would apply about one-third of an eye-dropper of holy anointing oil to their crown chakra and ask them to gently rub it in. As I did this I would say, "May all of your very best dreams come true," a purposefully generic blessing. Once everyone had been tinc-

tured and anointed we would sit in meditation for a few minutes to enjoy the experience and feel the feelings that developed.[43]

Music would accompany this period of meditation, something soothing, and sometimes the congregants would sing together, chant, or focus on their breathing. Christie notes, "I soon had to limit the synchronized breathing as it made some people way too high."[44] Sacramental communion at the THC Ministry had one more component to it.

> The last sacrament of the service was the volcano vaporizer with Cannabis flowers (buds) heated with a pinch of calamus root powder. We passed the large clear inhalation bag around the circle and I would refill it as needed. We would sit in silence for a while, and then go around the circle offering prayers, good wishes, or songs. After a few minutes we would stand, hold hands and I would offer a final blessing for the group.[45]

The concluding portion of the service duplicated Christian Protestant traditions all over the world; people would gather to drink coffee, enjoy pot luck casseroles, eat cookies, and chat. The whole weekly service, held on Sundays, lasted for approximately two hours.

Upon reading that a cannabis ministry duplicated the services held at the neighborhood Protestant Church, one might be inclined toward skepticism. And in fact, in speaking with former members of the THC Ministry, it was clear that more often than not, "services" consisted of Roger sitting down with one or two people at a time, anointing them, talking to them about what was going on with their lives, and supplying them with cannabis. "If people had a problem with their family or something, Roger would give them moral support."[46] And, according to Share Christie: "Most of our gatherings were informal with a handful of people. Roger felt much more comfortable in small groups."[47] Like the equating of *kaneh bosem* with cannabis, I would argue that Christie's desire to describe his church in such orthodox terms was guided by his desire to present it as a "legitimate" religious organization. In other words, he felt bound by a politics of respectability, a discourse that only recognizes a religion as being legitimate if it conforms to dominant Western beliefs and practices. An unfamiliar religious group, even if above reproach, is perceived "as a product of . . . social and cultural marginality and, as a result, [is] likely to enlist few allies but [is] likely to generate determined opponents."[48] Therefore, like Caesar's wife, Christie wanted to present his church to me as being "above suspicion."[49]

Christie loosened up a bit when it came to advertising ministry services in the *Hawai'i Tribune-Herald* in Hilo. The first ad, placed on Friday, February 2, 2007, reads as follows.

> *Cannabis Ministry*
>
> *Date*: Sunday

> *Time*: 6 p.m.
>
> *Details*: The Hawai'i Cannabis (THC) Ministry celebrates cannabis liberation daily, giving thanks to "those who protect our religious freedom to practice our culture." We also seek a political end to the 69-year-old prohibition of "marijuana" which we consider to be "extinctionistic and anti-Christ."
>
> *Location*: Moses Building at 94 Kamehameha Ave., upstairs in suite No. 2, downtown Hilo.
>
> *Contact*: Roger Christie, 961-[XXXX][50]

And on Friday, January 4, 2008, an advertisement was placed for a more elaborate service to be held on Sunday, at the same time and place:

> *Details*: The Hawai'i Cannabis (THC) Ministry celebrates "cannabis liberty" daily, providing the services and sacraments of our ministry with sincere members over 21 years old. Newcomers are welcomed to join by making a private appointment with Roger Christie by calling 217-[XXXX]. This week the ministry welcomes the Rev. Robert Tanner of Louisiana. He is a Canna-Baptist minister visiting Hilo and offering ionic hydro-therapy, a modern version of Jesus washing his disciples' feet. After this high-tech foot washing, anointing of the feet with holy anointing oil and prayer is available upon request, by donation. Sunday's gathering will include a potluck meal followed by "Plenty 4–20." Please bring a healthy dish to share with others. Entertainment will be provided by Heather and Holly, the "Ganja Sisters," with Jean on guitar and vocals."[51]

When I asked Share Christie about these ads she said: "Yes, Roger had some in the newspaper. Oh, he used to laugh so hard when he was writing those."[52] The presentation of a cannabis sacrament service alongside the usual Sunday offerings is funny, for in juxtaposition to mainline churches, there would be quite a "respectability" gap. Thus, while people came to Roger's ministry for a variety of reasons, one of them was certainly the laughter and high spirits offered there. As stated by THC Ministry member, Les, "I enjoyed the spiritual levity and fun at the Ministry."[53]

In speaking with former members of the THC Ministry, it is clear that they occupy very diverse positions in their identification with institutionalized religion; some retain their affiliation with orthodox forms of religion, such as Catholicism and Protestantism, some are ardent atheists, some believe in a broader idea of "spirit," but all speak to the sacramental power of the cannabis plant and the transformative experience that it delivers.

For Patricia, just being around the cannabis plant energized her, as she experienced a connection with the plant.

> Cannabis—there's no other plant like it, no other plant with the same energetic signature. Cannabis makes sense—it makes food, medicine, building supplies, and connects you to the divine. Somebody gave me these orphan plants—really sickly. But I took care of them and these plants were amazing to be around, I had so much fun. And I had an epiphany—a spiritual epiphany where I could connect and feel their energy.[54]

Joe, an artist, experienced cannabis as something that expanded his creativity and allowed him to respond to art more deeply and directly.

> Using cannabis was a revelation to me—a personal, religious revelation—it made me know I was an artist. Cannabis helped him [Roger] come to Jesus. It helped me come to Picasso.[55]

Mark and Les spoke of the power of cannabis to bring one to enlightened experience.

> *Mark*: Cannabis expands the unconscious mind.[56]
>
> *Les*: Cannabis is important and necessary—it's natural. . . . Baudelaire spoke of it, the beauty of cannabis—it makes reality alive—Hello God, Hello life. . . . We discovered cannabis—the enlightenment, the awareness of something beautiful going on.[57]

And Nan, a cannabis minister herself, found that it was cannabis that brought together a disparate group of people into community with each other.

> Cannabis Churches are not exclusive—they are open. I think it's tied to the herb, because of this beautiful plant. It's a locus through which the community comes together. . . . Cannabis expands the unconscious mind.[58]

Nan's statement focuses on the power of cannabis to transform both an individual and a community. In other words, the sacramental ritual of taking cannabis into one's body is experienced as a transcendent event that allows a very diverse group of people to come into community with each other.

In addition to their reverence for cannabis, these ministry members have something else in common: they all love Roger and still regard him as their minister. Tom spoke of Roger as a good friend and guide during hard times.

> Roger used to give me pot all the time. I would burn CDs for him and he would give me pot in exchange. To say Roger is a drug dealer is totally ridiculous. No Way! That is the farthest thing from the truth. The medicine they give me makes me feel like crap, but marijuana wipes all that away. It helps my appetite and takes away my nausea. I'm on three medications; the drugs work good, but they have tough

> side effects. Marijuana is the only thing that alleviates it. A couple of times a week he [Roger] had sit downs with groups of people—usually a pretty small group—and we'd have an open discussion. When people came in, Roger would give them anointing oil, and some literature—tell them what the place was all about. A lot of homeless people came in and Roger wanted to open a food kitchen—he was planning to do it and then he was arrested. Roger is one of the kindest, sweetest, non-violent people I have ever met. The government must really be scared of him to keep him locked up. Don't use my real name or anything. I've got federal housing and my yearly inspection is coming up.[59]

Susan emphasized the community service that Roger was providing in supplying cannabis in a state where no dispensaries were allowed.

> In my experience, people lined up to enter his premises, and it was a one-on-one situation where people would partake of what he had to offer. You would be lined up or sitting in chairs and you'd have a one on one encounter with Roger or one of his staff. Roger would come down the line and he would anoint people. There was no distribution there. What Roger did was provide a service, and there was never any problem; he was always up front. He would say "I have a legal reason, a right to practice my religion."[60]

Nan, Ike, and Mark spoke with me en masse.

> *Nan*: We're going to file a suit—a writ of *habeas corpus* that you can't deny us our pastor. The THC Ministry was much larger than my church. They were righteous. They counseled people. He would do this ritual of washing your hands with hemp soap—and you'd get rich people all the way across the spectrum to street people.
>
> *Ike*: He had this Creed—"Lord, tell me the blessings in this situation and hurry." I got busted and I was looking at some serious time. And Roger prayed and we said the Creed, and the charges got thrown out. One time there was this guy who ended up at 3:00 a.m. in the Emergency Room cuz of rat-lung disease. Roger was at his bedside. When Roger had a church member who got into trouble in Colorado, he helped defend him. He was an activist. And Roger believed.
>
> *Nan*: Roger ministered to his community, cuz he believed in it. Cannabis prohibition puts us all in fear.
>
> *Ike*: He had these aloha bags of organically grown cannabis that he gave to street people. He gave them out to keep people from being desperate. Cannabis keeps people from Meth, helps AIDs people to recover. What does a meth addict need? Sleep and food; cannabis gives them rest—it makes them eat. He gave me that movie *The Secret*.

> I lost it. But Roger always believed that if you believed in a bright future you would get it, he was always so positive.
>
> *Ike*: People who came to him, they always got something—they got help that wasn't available anywhere else.
>
> *Nan*: Roger wanted to help all those around him and express his love for spirit.
>
> *Mark*: Roger is following his dream—it's a nice place—that's what ministers do. They bring you into their warp field with them. I'm way too high to explain what a warp field is so don't ask.[61]

Patricia, the next member that I interviewed, made two significant statements regarding both her self-identification and the need to make space for religious freedom.

> When I first went to the Ministry, up those two big flights of stairs, Roger invited me into his office. Spent an hour talking about his cannabis religion, his Ministry. Not very many people would have the nerve—or the calling. Roger helped me forgive myself for being an addict—he gave me room to expand my thinking. How cannabis is connected to the divine—it's all right there. I was raised Catholic, but I went there [to the Ministry] for six years. . . . There are no dispensaries here. No way to grow plants. No one can legally sell it to me. But Roger would do that—he put himself outside of the law. And it was life-changing for me. I went there a couple of times on Tuesdays, and we would sit around and talk. Roger would give you information, the history of cannabis and how it became illegal. He'd talk about the medical part of it. I remember one time Roger was talking about Christmas carols, "Angels We Have Heard On High," and that you could see it all over the Bible—people getting high. I called Roger twice: Once when my dog died and once when my dad died. I'm pretty turned off by religion. But when you're in that hallway, sitting there—you feel some sort of whisper—it was a religious fellowship. We were all putting ourselves out there. Misfit people. A lot of homeless people—people who were disenfranchised. There was this one guy, a homeless guy, and he would come by the Ministry every day, and Roger would keep his suitcase for him. He did great things for the disenfranchised. It was empowering. What he wanted to do was empower people.[62]

In giving room for Patricia "to expand" her thinking, Christie enabled her to reassign herself from being an "addict" to being someone who used cannabis to be "connected to the divine." This process of shifting one's identity from something negative to something "empowering" is a familiar motif in the history of religions, for it allows one who is socially oppressed to claim a higher authority in defining themselves and their practices. For instance, some of those who suffered under Apartheid in

South Africa chose to self-identify as "children of Zion," rather than accept their Afrikaner-imposed identity as those to be exiled both physically and socially from society. Moreover, when Mahatma Gandhi recontextualized the social position of the untouchable castes by resignifying their status as *harijans*, literally "children of God," he was using religion to empower these castes.[63] In chapter 2, we saw that this process also occurred when Rubin elevated the term "pothead" to signify one who understood the significance of using pot to unite with the divine.

One sees the word "sincere" in conjunction with Roger in almost all of the above narratives. And every time one of these members of the THC Ministry used the term "sincere," they were participating in a fight with the judiciary to get Roger out of prison; for one of the ground rules that the federal judiciary uses to establish whether or not a church is legitimate is to discover whether or not the founders and membership are sincere in maintaining their religious beliefs and practices. That is why both the promotional materials for the ministry and the ministry's membership used the term "sincere" so often.

Adelle spoke about her bond with Roger and Share Christie, a bond that felt like being part of a family in a place where she had no family.

> I lived about 30 minutes away, so I didn't go to Church services. I have a physical condition that cannabis helps. The times I went, there would be a ceremony—well, more of a ritual with the holy anointing oil. There'd be a discussion first. Both of them [Share and Roger] were always so open—they had open arms. I don't have family anymore, and they felt like family. It was so comforting to get some herbal medicine. I felt real support there—connecting with like-minded people. Knowing I could spend the night there if I got into trouble—sleep there at the Ministry. I have night blindness, so it was nice to know that I could stay there. Saying that Roger is a danger to society is ludicrous—they need a sharp attorney. They are dedicated to the cause—I see that and I feel more helpless. They are just warm, wonderful people—no prejudice. I'm in the catering business, and at one point we were looking to collaborate in holding ethical/green events. He did these green weddings, so we thought we could collaborate—do things through the Ministry, and I was about to put up something about our partnership on the Internet when he was arrested. He's just a genuine, sincere, spiritual, kind person. Everybody would have the ritual, where Roger would put a drop of holy anointing oil on their forehead. He would tell you what kind of legislation had passed, events going on, and we would pray. Sometimes there would be ten people at a time waiting to go in—it could be quite a wait. But you could look at posters or literature; nobody minded waiting. Some people were obviously homeless, some were sick, some looked affluent, all ages. They did have a room set up as a chapel, a chapel room. That room wasn't finished until a few months before his arrest. That place took all of his time.[64]

Joe focused on Roger's "religious bent," and the way in which Roger made people feel welcome at the ministry.

> Roger's devotion to this was so strong—he made it into a religious calling. Roger would occasionally quote scripture, he would anoint you. His sincerity was evident, and he made people feel secure, comfortable, and reassured. He'd talk and encourage people to live a good life. Sometimes there'd be a little gathering and people would sit down. Roger is a gentle soul, candid, open about his feelings, he had a picture of his mother in his office. He provided a community service. All artists smoke, but Roger had a religious bent in this work. He believed in the power of cannabis, the spiritual uplift if used properly—and the way that the environment wraps around it.[65]

Les spoke to what he saw as the evolution of Roger's conflation of cannabis and spirituality, and the fact that it troubled Roger that not everyone who came to the ministry saw that connection between cannabis and the divine.

> Roger and I were writing a screenplay together—but he was very busy all the time. The Ministry was a place of communication—a place, you know, where you could tell your story. If Roger felt there was a need, he'd put a $20 bill into someone's hand. In 1982 or '83, I heard Roger on the radio talking about cannabis—and it was great to hear him talking out loud about it. . . . Roger has great sincerity. The sadness is that we are in fear. He provided medicine for the people—nature, herb. It was known by the street people that you could get an aloha bag.[66] Roger was a strong opponent of meth. I remember a kid got grabbed at the airport one time with drugs, and Roger went out there to help him. I saw him as a minister, a helper, a guide. He was sincerely involved with people. If someone came by, he would speak with them. Even when he broke his leg—and you know Roger had polio as a child—but even when he broke his leg, he was a counselor to people. . . . He saw cannabis as a product that would help people. He had the guts. Then he took a spiritual turn and realized that spirituality was the most important thing. He knew that some people were not there, not in that space—and that was on his mind. When you see him, tell him from Les, may the gift of liquid sunshine rain down on him.[67]

After talking with these THC members, I gained insight into how this ministry worked and what Roger Christie provided for these people. I learned that more often than not, the meetings with Roger were informal; that there were structured ceremonies and formal events, such as weddings, but regular services were not on the roster. What was on the roster was a sense of belonging that transcended social status; a place set up to protect those who would partake of an illegal substance; a deep respect for Roger as a person, who cared about others; a proclamation that social justice needed to be delivered, as promised by the Constitution; and a shared sensibility that cannabis matters—physically, socially, and spiritually.

THE CONSEQUENCES OF ESTABLISHING A CANNABIS MINISTRY

The charges against Christie and other members of the THC Ministry all focused on the manufacture, possession, and distribution of cannabis, which the federal government framed as "operating a marijuana distribution ring."[68] Christie framed these charges as being both erroneous and political. And he was particularly maddened by the fact that he had "provided Cannabis sacramentals" in a very open and transparent way and had felt that he had the tacit approval of both federal Drug Enforcement Administration (DEA) agents and local law enforcement. As he described it,

> Soon after my license was granted I was the subject of a front page (above the fold) story in the *Honolulu Advertiser*, the largest circulation paper in the state of Hawai'i. Associated Press picked-up the story and ran it on their newswire around the USA. Talk radio shows from the "continent" soon called me and asked for interviews: Phoenix, Detroit, Pittsburg, etc., etc. . . . My legitimacy seemed totally credible, provable and unique. I felt well protected by law enforcement. Life was good. From the start of my ordainment I stated clearly to anyone that asked me (publically or privately) that I provided Ministry services (weddings, funerals, counseling, fellowship, etc.) and Cannabis sacraments (live plants, flowers, seeds, holy anointing oil, tinctures, etc.) to members only. I placed weekly ads in the local newspaper on the religion page to detail our meeting times, dates, ceremonies and our mission statement.[69]

Things went along smoothly for several years, with no complaints regarding either Roger Christie or his ministry. In order to ascertain that he was protected under the First Amendment, Christie, on occasion, would visit local police and make sure that there had been no complaints filed against him. When George Bush appointed a new U.S. Attorney for Hawai'i in 2004, Christie introduced himself and gave the U.S. Attorney his ministry business card with a fresh cannabis leaf laminated on the back. "He happily shook my hand and told me that I had nothing to worry about as he was focused on the meth epidemic and not on marijuana. . . ."[70] Christie was very smart in attempting to make his unfamiliar religion intelligible to local law enforcement, for in so doing, he was successful for several years in creating a context for his ministry that allowed law enforcement to make sense of what he was doing. Bruce Lincoln notes:

> Within any society, nonetheless, there exist counter taxonomic discourses as well. . . . Alternative models whereby members of subordi-

> nate strata and others marginalized under the existing social order are able to agitate for the deconstruction of that order and the reconstruction of society on a novel pattern.[71]

And one of the most powerful ways to counter dominant, taxonomic discourse is through a claim to divine knowledge. However, when it comes to small groups simply wishing to exist side by side with established religions, I would temper Lincoln's language as it is not necessary to deconstruct society in order to bring an alternative model of religion into the light of day. In fact, the reality is much more prosaic. It requires that, within one's social environment, there occur small but continuous shifts in discourse that allow one's religious practices to be contextualized in a new light, a topic that we will discuss in detail in chapter 4. On the part of practitioners, this act of promoting a counter discourse around cannabis requires tenacity, courage and a deep conviction that what one is doing is worth doing for one may end up having to face the consequences of illegal actions.

In fact, if we look at the means by which Christie attempted to legitimize his ministry, they were peaceful yet strategic. One of the earliest things that he did was to reach out to other ministers in the hope that they would also support the cause of religious freedom. He wrote to Rick Warren of Saddleback Church, Joel Osteen of Lakewood Church, Chuck Misler of Koinonia House, and Richard Stearns of World Vision, sending each of them a mission statement:

> The purpose of this letter is to build a bridge of understanding from Cannabis hemp to Christianity in order to benefit humanity. . . . I thank you for allowing me the courtesy of presenting my case to you. Once you check the facts presented, can I ask you to join me in prayer and action to help save billions of people on this planet from hunger, poverty, disease, weather, pain, spiritual disconnection, false imprisonment and much more? . . . "The spirit of the Lord is upon me because he has anointed me to preach good news to the poor. He has sent me to proclaim freedom for the prisoners and recovery of sight to the blind, to release the oppressed and to declare that this is the Lord's most favored year." Luke 4:18.[72]

Unfortunately for the THC Ministry, Christie "had zero response from any of them."[73]

Christie did, however, have his own version of a professional association, and, in October of 2005, he attended a cannabis minister's conference in Laytonville, California. It was hosted by Reverend Les Crane and included Reverend Jeff Brown from Florida, author of *Marijuana and the Bible*, Reverend Jack Herer, author of *The Emperor Wears No Clothes*, Reverend Eddy Lepp, Reverends Dan Quaintance, Mary Quaintance and Daniel Jeffrey of the Church of Cognizance (CoC), Reverend Ed Forcion—the "New Jersey Weedman," and about 30 others, approximately

10 of whom were women. According to Christie, "he [Lepp] rented an entire motel to house us for a weekend and an event center called "Area 101" complete with catered meals so we all gathered together for two full days. What a time we had!"[74] The gathered reverends created and signed a Statement of Purpose to guide their future collective actions. The ten elements contained in the statement read as follows.

1. To spread the knowledge of the most useful plant of the world.
2. To cover the world with this plant.
3. To be sure everyone can have Marijuana.
4. To stop the persecution.
5. To promote and protect the religious and spiritual uses of cannabis.
6. To form a Body Politic so we can have a voice.
7. To create sustainable world economy thru the legalization and proliferation of hemp cultivation.
8. To bring Truth to the world.
9. To redeem what it is to be human together thru cannabis as a sacrament and hemp as a sustainable resource.
10. To heal the sick and restore the planet.[75]

Christie took other measures to help legitimize and safeguard his ministry. Whenever there were peaceful protests of any kind, he would show up holding a stick with a cannabis leaf flag.[76] As noted above, he made the acquaintance of those in local law enforcement. He publicized his ministry in local papers. He provided his ministry members with the information both to fight for religious freedom and to use language understood by the judiciary to describe their ministry. Moreover, he established rules for the ministry that went a long way toward managing law enforcement's biggest problem with any of the cannabis-based religions: the dispersion of cannabis to the general public. Christie's rules narrowed membership rights to those who met the following requirements: those who were 21 and over, those who had a medical marijuana license or had formally joined the ministry, and those who were sincere in their usage. Again, a "sincere" nod to the judiciary, as only those "sincere" in their unorthodox practices pass the judiciary's religious legitimacy litmus test. Moreover, if you wished to join the ministry, you had to make an initial appointment to speak with Roger: "Roger was always pretty open, but you had to make an appointment where Roger would explain the Ministry, give a person a chance to join, and give them a chance to learn."[77]

In an attempt to join those who contribute to shaping societal law, Christie ran for mayor of Hawai'i County in 2004 and in 2008, and Share Christie ran for the same office in 2012, pledging to support "HONEST LEADERSHIP [and] to declare an end to the disastrous war on drugs."[78] According to THC member, Adelle, Roger's "candidacy was well-received."[79] Adelle also noted that she had worked in government and "was pretty astute" as to the duties of a mayor.

> So, I asked Roger if he thought he would enjoy being mayor. He didn't answer me, he just got a strange look on his face. He only wanted to work toward the legalization of cannabis. So, I told him, do the work you love. Don't concern yourself with all the other stuff that concerns politicians.[80]

Other ministry members spoke of Christie's commitment to religious freedom. Les, a longtime member of THC, said that "Roger had copies of the Constitution, and he felt blessed because of his belief in the First Amendment. . . . I don't feel politically drawn, but Roger was a warrior, that's how I saw him."[81] And THC member Patricia said of Roger and the ministry: "Someone has to be there to hold the parameter, to hold the door open."[82] In other words, someone has to guard that liminal space to prevent the government from doing more to restrict religious freedom.

According to Christie, over the next several years the ministry had two visits by local police. During the first, Hawai'i County police warned Christie to keep his practices quiet. During the second, when the police showed up at Christie's behest to remove a belligerent visitor, the police told him that they understood he had a ministry and, for that reason, it was ok to distribute marijuana. Christie noted, "It should be crystal clear to anyone that I had zero 'criminal (evil or guilty) intent' and I operated in the light of day from the beginning of my ordainment onward."[83]

The Obama-appointed U.S. Attorney for Hawai'i, however, dealt differently with the ministry than the Bush-appointed attorney; on March 10, 2010, Christie's Hilo ministry office was raided by federal law enforcement.[84] However, as noted in the *Honolulu Weekly*:

> In the March search warrant, Special Agent Brian Kon stated, "I recognize that the THC Ministry and its affiliated Hawaii Cannabis College . . . is arguably a functioning entity with employees, and that a seizure of the Ministry's computers may have the unintended effect of limiting the Ministry's ability to provide certain arguably legitimate services to its customers. . . ."[85]

Given the wording of the March warrant, Christie mistakenly assumed that his ministry was recognized as a legitimate religion in the eyes of the law, and that he could therefore continue to provide cannabis to ministry members and medical marijuana patients. The prosecuting attorney, however, took Christie's continued cannabis dispensation as a sign that he was flaunting the law and was in fact "a danger to the community." Share Christie stated that when they were arrested, law enforcement seized not only their condo and all of their financial assets but also "took my social security money—nine $100 bills."[86] These statements are confirmed by local and national news stories that reported that federal investigators appropriated approximately $21,000 through their arrest of

Christie.[87] As stated by one of the members of the THC, "not a lot of money for either a drug kingpin or one's life's work."[88]

The Christie's trial was rescheduled six times and, in September of 2013, both Share and Roger Christie accepted plea deals that would require both to change their not guilty pleas to the following: "Roger Christie pled guilty . . . to 'conspiring to manufacture, distribute, and possess with intent to distribute marijuana, involving 100 or more marijuana plants and two separate tax counts for failure to file federal income tax returns" for two years. Share Christie "pled guilty to 'conspiring to manufacture, distribute, and possess with intent to distribute marijuana, involving 50 or more marijuana plants.'"[89] On April 28, 2014, both Roger and Share Christie were sentenced. Roger received 5 years in federal prison, but as he had already served 4 years, he was released to a halfway house on September 11, 2014. Share Christie was sentenced to 27 months in prison. The Christies decided to accept a plea deal because they felt that the judicial discourse around cannabis had not shifted far enough to ensure a fair trial, a trial in which the spiritual benefits of cannabis would be recognized.

HAVE THE CANNABIS-BASED FORERUNNERS PROVIDED A CLEAR PATH TO UNDERSTANDING?

In his analysis of Jonestown, J. Z. Smith concludes that the process of understanding a religious movement like that of Peoples Temple requires an act of translation: translation to a language that incorporates the words, symbols, and concepts that make translation possible. By using sacramental cannabis as our trigger point,[90] we have found three *exempli gratia*, that work well for the purposes of translation: the Rastafari Religion, the Ethiopian Zion Coptic Church, and The Farm. Each of these groups consistently highlight five elements that form a pattern that helps us to make sense of our contemporary cannabis-based religions: First, the ritual use of cannabis as a sacrament; second, the experiential nature of cannabis precluding a shared doctrinal tradition; third, the reinterpretation of orthodox scripture; fourth, the engagement of a community of like-minded people; and fifth, their immersion in the political process.

As we superimpose this template over the Church of the Universe, the CoC, Temple 420, and the THC Ministry, we succeed, I would argue, in rendering these cannabis-based religions translatable and thus intelligible. In summarizing these contemporary versions of cannabis-based religions, I will first look at the ways in which these groups match up to the template created by their forerunners. Next, I will look at the motivations driving the founders and members of each respective group as I turn from the question of "what" to the question of "why."

The Church of the Universe was the first of our contemporary churches to name their religion as entheogenic: one that draws sacred energy from a plant, and in this case, exclusively a cannabis plant. They surrounded themselves with homemade hemp products and grew cannabis at Clearwater Abbey, their communal home. They used the Bible and the pervasive symbol of the Tree of Life to conceptualize their understanding of the power in this plant. However, unlike either Temple 420 or the THC Ministry, they also drew on other sacred texts and cultural models such as the *Desiderata* and the culture of Sumer and did not consider themselves to be a part of the Christian tradition. Moreover, they did not believe that cannabis itself was divine, but rather was a divine substance given to humanity by God. Their ritual use of cannabis was the most informal of all of our groups, meaning that it had no rules pertaining to when, where, or with whom cannabis was to be smoked. In fact, the use of cannabis was the only repetitive act performed in their rituals. However, it was not merely an everyday act—it was an act replete with meaning and purpose and, as such, conforms to other ritual actions designed to touch the transcendent. They performed this ritual in solitude or in community, but believed that the experience achieved was "personal, inviolate and inviolable as our souls," and that it was the nature of this experience that tied their community together rather than a shared doctrinal tradition.

Their community was nonhierarchical, nonproselytizing and open to anyone who consistently demonstrated their commitment to the church's rule: "Do not hurt yourself. Do not hurt anyone else." In terms of politics, their Church Creed mandated that they recognize "First God, then Humanity, then Government." Believing that cannabis was a plant designed by God to be used sacramentally, they often found themselves in political battles with the Canadian judiciary over their right to use an illegal substance as part of their religious activities. Thus, as we will remember, they wore underpants on their heads in court in order to demonstrate that, in their religious taxonomy, the government lagged far behind both God and humanity. Like the THC Ministry and Temple 420, one of their members, Michael Baldasaro, ran for the office of Mayor of Hamilton, Ontario, in every municipal election from 1985 to 2014 in order to influence from the inside the laws around religious freedom.

The CoC also smoked cannabis as their central ritual experience, but they called it haoma, following the Zorastrian texts they consulted to contextualize their practice. They believed that haoma itself allowed one to achieve an internal homeostatic balance (a dynamic equilibrium that adjusts to outside variants) and that it was possible for haoma to do this because haoma was God. Mary Quaintance, one of the founders of the church, defined haoma as something that "makes you better at what you do, enhances who you are. It is the most beautiful plant on earth."[91]

Family was their primary unit of social organization and they set up IOMMs, or Individual Orthodox Member Monastery[ies], made of up families wherein "the middle folks took care of the senior folks who took care of the very senior folks and the kids."[92] There were no rules governing where or when members smoked cannabis as each IOMM was seen as a sovereign unit. In addition to these IOMMs, there was a Cultural Information Center for each geographically grouped set of IOMMs. These centers served as central spaces for communication whereby members could share with each other their understanding of Zoroastrian scripture, haoma, or enlightenment. Of all of these groups, the CoC was the most experientially driven, as they refused to call themselves a "religion," because the term religion implies a shared set of beliefs. Rather, they called themselves a "church," defining a church as the coming together of like-minded people. These like-minded people, moreover, were encouraged to become Cogniscenti, those not only familiar with the Zoroastrian texts and other religions, but also those who had a deep understanding of their own experience of haoma. The Cogniscenti were also encouraged to add to the church's dynamic scriptural base, as long as their ideas were approved by a majority of church members. Any member of the CoC could become a Cogniscenti, and while recognized as having a unique depth of knowledge, the Cogniscenti were equal in status to all other members. While they did not proselytize, anyone was welcome to join the CoC and they were invited to draw on church materials at Cultural Information Centers or on their website. Politically, the church founders stated that they believed in promoting a better world for all, one that embraces religious freedom and tolerance, and Danuel Quaintance was prepared to walk up and down the halls of Congress in order to influence those who could influence the laws pertaining to religious freedom.

Temple 420, as noted by founder Craig Rubin, was designed to provide a religious gathering place for "potheads," a term elevated to indicate that those self-identifying as potheads experienced their smoking of cannabis as a religious "orientation." Cannabis created a "spiritual bond" among the members of Temple 420, and while cannabis was not smoked in the Temple building, members would usually come to services high. In other words, members would perform their cannabis rituals in order to prepare themselves for the experience of being high in community. "God gave people cannabis out of G-d's compassion to heal his people both physically and spiritually."[93] And Temple 420 members were encouraged to emulate G-d's example as described in the Gospel of John, and highlighted both cannabis and compassion during their Bible studies and services.

When looking at Temple 420, one of the stranger aspects of community resistance to the Temple was not merely cannabis but the fact that they were combining Judaism and Christianity—creating a hybrid religion where, according to their neighboring temple, no hybrid should exist.

But inside the Temple's walls, Judaism and Christianity *were* combined, bringing together people who resonated with both the Old and New Testaments. For Rubin, his favorite couple to join the Temple was a Jewish woman and her Christian boyfriend. In my conversations with Rubin, he emphasized this couple, as he felt that he had opened a space for those who identified with both religions and found that smoking cannabis worked to elevate their understanding of both.

Rubin was defined by Cindy Holden in the *California News Wire* as a "warrior," and in his battles to keep his Temple in operation he had a lot taken from him: his Temple, his daytime job, and his life-savings—twice. However, as we have seen, you cannot keep a good cannabis religion founder down and, in 2009, Rubin ran for mayor of Los Angeles and received 4,158 votes. Prior to that, he organized rallies, such as the one designed to help pass Proposition 215 in California. And, if you look on YouTube, you can find part of a documentary distributed by 21st Century Artists that demonstrates Rubin's ability to galvanize the public to get things done. In it he states: "We've got everybody here. We've got all the potheads in the world here. We're all bud smokers, black, white, red, or yellow. Smoke the bud. We're not afraid. Bill Clinton, you can kiss my ass."[94]

Turning to our last example, the THC Ministry, provided us with many examples of how the founders and members experienced cannabis. For Roger Christie, his ritual practices were all about anointing members with holy anointing oil, cannabis-infused oil that he believed was the exact recipe given to Moses by God. And he believed in the Augustinian definition of this sacrament as being "the visible form of an invisible grace." Members of the ministry recognized this grace and experienced cannabis as a means to transcend mundane reality.

The THC Ministry held events where cannabis was smoked communally, but both founders and members alike found that while cannabis brought them into community with each other, the experience of smoking cannabis is ineffable and particular. As stated by Christie, "Cannabis use helped to develop my personal spirituality."[95]

As far as the ministry's membership was concerned, Christie was thought of as a hero for taking a huge risk in putting himself out there before the eyes of the law, not only to help his membership but also to demand religious freedom. "Whenever there were peaceful protests of any kind, Roger would show up holding a stick with a cannabis leaf flag."[96] He made the acquaintance of those in local law enforcement; he publicized his ministry in local papers; he provided his membership with the information necessary not only to fight for religious freedom but also to use language understood by the judiciary to describe the ministry. As noted, in order to join those who contributed to shaping laws around religious freedom, both Christies ran for public office.[97]

What Roger Christie did, according to his members, was to "hold the door open," guarding that liminal space that protects an individual's freedom to practice religion in one's own way. One might argue that by holding the door open, you open the door to all kinds of religious activities—some of which might be found to be deeply harmful to its practitioners. The Branch Davidians, Heaven's Gate, and Peoples Temple, serve as examples. However, the alternative, as I see it—slamming the door on religious freedom—is far more dangerous.

One element that seems particularly tragic about the government's destruction of these religious groups is that their members expressed how important their community had been to them and how much they missed it when it was gone. So, when denied their ritual usage of cannabis, they lost their fellowship, because cannabis had provided the "locus through which the community [came] together."[98]

The Church of the Universe, the CoC, Temple 420, and the THC Ministry share the five major elements that provided the structure for their cannabis based predecessors: (1) The sacramental use of cannabis; (2) the highlighting of transcendent experience over a collective doctrinal tradition; (3) the reinterpretation of orthodox scripture; (4) the engagement of a community of like-minded people; and (5) The undertaking of political battles to fight for religious freedom.

I expect that there are a number of readers still skeptical about these cannabis-based religions, and that their skepticism takes two forms: First, did these founders dress up their activities in church clothes just to make money? And, second, did these founders and members join these groups just so they could smoke illegal cannabis whenever they wanted to do so and with whomever they wanted to do so?

In answering the second question, I would say yes they did; but they were taking enormous risks in relation to life, liberty, and happiness to do so. For this reason, they had to be motivated by something, and I believe that their motivations arose from what Stephen Gaskin and many members of the THC Ministry spoke to: "Grass is an ally. It naturally engenders spirituality in the people that do it."[99] For those who ingest cannabis and feel an experiential connection to the divine, there is no going back, they cannot unring that bell. Why cannabis evokes this connection is as mysterious as the *mysterium tremendum*.[100] And why cannabis provokes this reaction in some, but not others, is also a mystery. But the members of the THC Ministry, as well as members of The Farm, were particularly articulate in their descriptions of the experience of cannabis: this plant has a unique energy signature that prompts a religious response; it opens one's mind to the unconscious; and it allows one to see the connections between all things. While those who have never ingested cannabis; for those for whom it did not call forth a transcendent disposition, these answers might seem specious; for those who do experience the responses listed above, cannabis is a marvel.

In addressing the first question—did the founders of these churches, temples, and ministries do it for money?—I can only ask, what money? The Ethiopian Zion Coptic Church is the exception to this rule. As stated by Carl Hiaasen: "There is no doubt that Reilly and the other Coptic leaders [are] devoutly religious about marijuana. There is also no doubt, authorities say, that the Coptics are big-time dope smugglers. . . ."[101] However, the rest of the founders and members reviewed here lost not only their money but also their possessions and their liberty when they were arrested. But that did not stop them from going back to their temple, as did Craig Rubin, or from pacing up and down the halls of Congress to petition for a fair reading of the religion clauses, as promised by Danuel Quaintance.

As discussed in the introduction to this book, each of the founders of these cannabis-based religions are contemporary *bricoleurs*; drawing on the cannabis-based religions that went before them to pick up pieces of the communal structure, scriptural passages, and sacramental rituals most relevant to their experiences of the sacred. For example, within the Church of the Universe, cannabis was equated with the biblical "tree of life" in order that members would associate this symbol with the purity, plenty, and nudity of the Garden of Eden. For the CoC, the Zoroastrian *Avesta* provided a better understanding than the Christian scriptures as to why haoma (cannabis) was so important, and how it worked in the human body. For Temple 420, the Old and New Testaments of the Bible provided both a means through which people could understand the nature of compassion and a model for how Jewish people and Christians could come together, just as both scriptures are bound together in the Bible. For the THC Ministry, the Bible, especially the book of Exodus, had handed humanity the recipe for holy anointing oil, so that all might be uplifted and made holy.

A good analysis moves from the question of "what" to the question of "why," and while the members and founders within each of our seven respective groups, as seen in chapters 1, 2, and 3, have implicitly demonstrated their motivations for engaging in various activities, some questions remain unanswered or need further elaboration. As such, do the examples stated above fully answer the question of why the founders and members of these cannabis-based religions felt the need to encapsulate their cannabis-based religions within orthodox scripture? I would say no, and argue that the use of orthodox scripture runs along a continuum between two categories: The first category deals with the fact that by using orthodox scripture, their churches/temples/ministries might appear more legitimate, both to the general public and to law makers. In fact, after many conversations with Roger Christie—during which I expressed my opinion that *kaneh bosem* does not have to equal cannabis for a cannabis-based religion to be both meaningful and legitimate—he stuck to his guns. And he may have been right in doing so, for, as we will see in chapter 5, the judiciary very often needs to see aspects of orthodox practices within these cannabis-based groups to be able to familiarize themselves and thus treat these cannabis-based religions as religions. I will call this use of orthodox scripture "pragmatic use." The second category of those using orthodox scripture as part of their unorthodox practices were those employing scriptural texts to help contextualize their practices. I will call this use of orthodox scripture "germane use." Stephen Gaskin comes to mind here, as he had used a multiplicity of scriptures and practices to form the foundation of The Farm's way of life, with the image of the Hindu household yogi helping to frame his vision. Therefore, in looking at their use of orthodox scripture, each respective group, I would argue, lies somewhere on the continuum between these two categories.

We next move to the question of why it was so important to be in community with others. When I first smoked cannabis, I experienced it as a joy to behold, and a joy which achieved mammoth proportions when I celebrated smoking cannabis with others. While it did not motivate me to change my career objectives, it did realign my value system in one important way. It caused me to divide my family, friends, and acquaintances into two groups—those who smoked cannabis and those who did not. This act of bifurcation was not a conscious decision, and it did not measurably change my relational connections to family, friends, and acquaintances. However, it did cause me to rule out, on a certain level, ever achieving a like-mindedness with those who had not experienced the path to the transcendent as provided by cannabis. Danuel Quaintance used the word "like-minded" to describe the mindset of members of the CoC and it is an important word as it describes a kind of deep fellowship, a kindred feeling, a meeting of minds between practitioners. Thus, I would argue that members of these seven groups sought out others in order to commune with those who had experienced similar spiritual epiphanies.

Answering the question of why these groups involved themselves in the political process is simple: their religions and their personal freedom depended on it. Both founders and members of these religions spent a long time in prison for practicing their religion. However, the founders and members of these traditions did not see their practices as illegal. In fact, they believed in the Constitution nearly as much as they believed in cannabis, and, when they got out of prison, they were poised to fight the good fight for freedom of religion once again, either through election to a political office or by lobbying those in Congress to legalize cannabis across the board. And, whether or not Congress legalizes not only medical cannabis but also recreational cannabis, the religious groups described throughout these chapters would consistently lobby for a third category—that of sacramental cannabis.

As we turn to chapters 4 and 5, we will examine the two discursive modalities that currently serve to shape the setting in which the public perceives cannabis: the voices of the medical/scientific community and those of lawmakers. While neither of these discursive modalities is univocal, at their respective cores they dominate the current parameters around which cannabis is contextualized and thus control the ways in which cannabis can be used. I will begin chapter 4 with an examination of the medical/scientific community and the tremendous advances made within the last few decades in understanding the transformative impact of cannabis.

NOTES

1. Roger Christie, e-mail message to author, November 10, 2012.
2. THC is the active component in cannabis that causes one to feel euphoric.
3. "History, Beliefs, and Practices of the THC Ministry," the Hawai'i Cannabis Ministry, accessed October 22, 2015, http://www.thc-ministry.org/?page_id=362.
4. Drug Policy Forum of Hawai'i, accessed on February 6, 2015, www.dpfhi.org.
5. Paul Von Hartmann, "Aloha Denied: Prosecution or Predation? An Essay in Defense of Roger Christie, Imprisoned Big Island Cannabis Minister." *Honolulu Civil Beat*, last updated May 12, 2012, accessed October 23, 2015, http://www.civilbeat.com/2012/05/15817-aloha-denied-prosecution-or-predation/.
6. Roger Christie, e-mail message to author, November 10, 2012.
7. Nan, THC Ministry member, telephone discussion with the author, November 13, 2012.
8. "Holy Herb Sacrament," The Religion of Jesus Christ, accessed October 22, 2015, http://www.salvationanointed.com/about-the-church/the-holy-herb-cannabis-sacrament-of-the-religion-of-jesus-church/.
9. "The Urantia Book, first published by Urantia Foundation in 1955, presents us with the origin, history, and destiny of humanity. It answers questions about God, life in the inhabited universe, the history and future of this world, and it includes an uplifting narrative of the life and teachings of Jesus." Urantia.org, accessed September 6, 2016.
10. Roger Christie, e-mail message to author, November 10, 2012.
11. Roger Christie, e-mail message to author, November 10, 2012.
12. Roger Christie, e-mail message to author, September 26, 2011.
13. "Hawaii Medical Marijuana Laws," medicalmarijuana.com, accessed 4/29/16.
14. Ibid.
15. Share Christie, telephone discussion with the author, September 12, 2012.
16. Joe, THC Ministry member, telephone discussion with the author, November 12, 2012.
17. Roger Christie, e-mail message to author, November 9, 2011.
18. Roger Christie, e-mail message to author, November 13, 2011.
19. Share Christie, telephone discussion with the author, September 12, 2012.
20. Mahmoud A. ElSohly (The University of Mississippi, National Center for Natural Products Research), in discussion with the author, August 2012, updated May 2015. University, Mississippi.
21. Roger Christie, e-mail message to author, October 9, 2011.
22. "Synthetic Cannabinoid Halts Progression of Multiple Sclerosis," NORML, last updated May 1, 2012, accessed October 24, 2015, http://norml.org/news/2012/03/01/synthetic-cannabinoid-halts-progression-of-multiple-sclerosis-study-says. In chapter 5 we will discuss endocannabinoids, but in sum, a cannabinoid agonist would block the cellular work done by our bodies own cannabinoid receptors.
23. Roger Christie, e-mail message to author, October 31, 2011.
24. Ibid.

25. Roger Christie, e-mail message to author, November 20, 2011.
26. Roger Christie, e-mail message to author, September 12, 2011.
27. Ibid.
28. Roger Christie, e-mail message to author, November 1, 2011.
29. Roger Christie, e-mail message to author, October 9, 2011. Quoting Isaiah 10:27
30. "the Hawai'i Cannabis Ministry," TCH Ministry, accessed October 24, 2015, http://www.thc-ministry.org/images/thcministry.brochure.pdf.
31. Keoki Kerr, "Officials Unveil Big Island Marijuana Case," *KITV4 News*, July 9, 2010, accessed October 24, 2015, http://www.kitv.com/Officials-Unveil-Big-Island-Marijuana-Case/5366164.
32. "the Hawai'i Cannabis Ministry," TCH Ministry, accessed October 24, 2015, http://www.thc-ministry.org/images/thcministry.brochure.pdf.
33. Roger Christie, e-mail message to author, September 12, 2011.
34. Share Christie, telephone discussion with the author, September 12, 2012.
35. Ibid.
36. "Aloha and Welcome—e komo mai," The Hawai'I Cannabis Ministry, TCH Ministry, last updated February 9, 2015, accessed October 24, 2015, http://www.thc-ministry.org/.
37. Ibid.
38. Ibid.
39. Roger Christie, e-mail message to author, January 28, 2012.
40. These court cases included the 1963 Sherbert case and the 1969 Leary case.
41. Roger Christie, e-mail message to author, January 8, 2012.
42. Ibid.
43. Ibid.
44. Ibid.
45. Ibid.
46. Tom, THC Ministry member, telephone discussion with the author, November 6, 2012.
47. Share Christie, telephone discussion with the author, September 12, 2012.
48. David G. Bromley, "Teaching New Religious Movements/Learning from New Religious Movements," in *Teaching New Religious Movements*, ed. David G. Bromley (Oxford: Oxford University Press, 2007), 5.
49. McGraw-Hill, *Dictionary of American Idioms and Phrasal Verbs* (New York: McGraw-Hill, 2005), s.v. "Caesar's wife must be above suspicion."
50. From *Hawai'i Tribune-Herald*, February 2, 2007.
51. From *Hawai'i Tribune-Herald*, January 6, 2007.
52. Share Christie, telephone discussion with the author, September 12, 2012.
53. Les, THC Ministry member, telephone discussion with the author, November 7, 2012.
54. Patricia, THC Ministry member, telephone discussion with the author, November 7, 2012.
55. Joe, THC Ministry member, telephone discussion with the author, November 12, 2012.
56. Mark, THC Ministry member, telephone discussion with the author, November 13, 2012.
57. Les, THC Ministry member, telephone discussion with the author, November 7, 2012.
58. Nan, THC Ministry member, telephone discussion with the author, November 13, 2012.
59. Tom, THC Ministry member, telephone discussion with the author, November 6, 2012.
60. Susan, THC Ministry member, telephone discussion with the author, November 13, 2013.
61. Nan, Mark, and Ike, THC Ministry members, telephone discussion with the author November 13, 2012.

62. Patricia, THC Ministry member, telephone discussion with the author, November 7, 2012.

63. While Gandhi's motivations in this process of resignification were to empower the untouchable castes, sometimes these actions will back-fire when the resignification comes from someone outside those being resignified. For example, some within this caste such as Dr. B. R. Ambedkar thought this term patronizing and not only urged untouchables to convert to Buddhism, but also worked tirelessly to improve the opportunities available to these castes within both the educational system and in the government employment sector.

64. Adelle, THC Ministry member, telephone discussion with the author, November 6, 2012.

65. Joe, THC Ministry member, telephone discussion with the author, November 12, 2012.

66. Aloha Bags were bags of cannabis shake—leaves and seeds that the THC Ministry gave out free.

67. Les, THC Ministry member, telephone discussion with the author, November 7, 2012.

68. John Burnett, "Roger Christie: Deal in Works for Pot Minister?," *Hawaii Tribune Herald*, June 12, 2011.

69. Roger Christie, e-mail message to author, September 26, 2011.

70. Ibid.

71. Bruce Lincoln, *Discourse and the Construction of Society* (Oxford: Oxford University Press, 1989), 8.

72. Roger Christie, written letter to author, September 11, 2011.

73. Ibid.

74. Roger Christie e-mail message to author, November 10, 2012.

75. "First Ever Congress of the United Cannabis Ministries," United Cannabis Ministries, October 28, 2005, accessed on June 30, 2016, http://ucm.enlightener.net/wiki/tiki-index.php?page=First+ever+Congress+of+the+United+Cannabis+Ministries.

76. Nan, Ike, Joe, THC Ministry members, telephone discussions with the author, November 12 and 13, 2012.

77. Les, THC Ministry member, telephone discussion with the author, November 7, 2012.

78. Share Christie, "9 Pillars of the Christie Mayor Campaign 2012," The-Last-Marijuana-Trial.com, last updated September 14, 2012, accessed October 25, 2015, http://the-last-marijuana-trial.com/9-pillars-of-the-christie-mayor-campaign-2012/.

79. Adelle, THC Ministry member, telephone discussion with the author, November 6, 2012.

80. Ibid.

81. Les, THC Ministry member, telephone discussion with the author, November 7, 2012.

82. Patricia, THC Ministry members, telephone discussions with the author November 7, 2012.

83. Ibid.

84. Obama's conservative stance toward cannabis legalization was puzzling given his liberal agenda toward other social issues. Especially in light of a new biography by David Maraniss that depicts Obama as a regular cannabis user in his youth.

85. Cameron Johnson, "Drug Kingpin or Political Prisoner?," *Honolulu Weekly*, April 27, 2011, http://honoluluweekly.com/cover/2011/04/drug-kingpin-or-political-prisoner/.

86. Share Christie, telephone discussion with the author, September 12, 2012.

87. Bonnie King, "DEA Holds THC Minister in Custody after Appeal," Salem-News.com, July 21, 2010, accessed November 11, 2011, http://www.salem-news.com/articles/july212010/roger-christie.php.

88. Nan, THC Ministry member, telephone discussion with the author, November 13, 2012.

89. Malia Zimmerman, "'Marijuana Minister's' Prosecution Invigorates Legalization Fight in Hawaii," *Hawaii Reporter*, April 30 2014, http://watchdog.org/141663/hawaii-marijuana-minister/.

90. A structural component that in some important way reflects a similarity to one's object of analysis. For the sake of ease, I would call this structural component a trigger point.

91. Stephanie Innes, "Church of Cognizance: Pot Church Takes a Hit," *Arizona Daily Star*, July 9, 2006.

92. Danuel Quaintance, telephone discussion with the author, September 23, 2015.

93. Craig Rubin, telephone discussion with the author, September 1, 2015.

94. Mitch Ward, "White People Colored People Los Angeles Craig X Rubin Marijuana Activist," 21stCenturyArtists Hollywood, updated April 20, 2016, accessed November 16, 2016, https://www.youtube.com/watch?v=CUbUEILtpIk.

95. Roger Christie, e-mail message to author, October 31, 2011.

96. Nan, Ike, Joe, THC Ministry members, telephone discussions with the author, November 12 and 13, 2012.

97. Share Christie, "9 Pillars of the Christie Mayor Campaign 2012," The-Last-Marijuana-Trial.com, last updated September 14, 2012, accessed October 25, 2015, http://the-last-marijuana-trial.com/9-pillars-of-the-christie-mayor-campaign-2012/.

98. Nan, THC Ministry member, telephone discussion with the author, November 13, 2012.

99. Stephen Gaskin, *Cannabis Spirituality* (New York: High Times Books, 1996), 74.

100. Rudolf Otto, John W. Harvey trans. (New York: Oxford University Press, 1948), 12.

101. Carl Hiaasen, "Louv Story: Are Brother Louv and His Zion Coptic Church Facing the Last Judgment? *The Miami Herald*, August 2, 1981.

FOUR

The Discourse Shifts

Public Reactions to the Science and Medical Effects of Cannabis

> It's a great plant and it has great potential, has compounds that have such a wide range of biological activities, it's unbelievable.
>
> —Dr. M. ElSohly[1]

Over the last two decades, the findings of medical science have changed the public perception of cannabis more than any other discourse since its vilification by the federal government in 1937. This discursive movement has occurred because many within the medical community have found that cannabis has myriad medical applications. It is important to note, however, that those within the medical community do not speak univocally and that there are dissenting voices as to the medical benefits of cannabis. In fact, discursive clashes around whether or not to legalize medical cannabis are currently taking place between the federal government and state governments; between the federal government and medical/scientific researchers; between those acting at different levels within the federal government; and, finally, between researchers and cannabis adherents within the general public. Thus, the purpose of this chapter is to examine whether or not a new social consensus around medical marijuana is in the offing or if we will remain in a state of discursive disorder. It is impossible to critically examine this debate without some knowledge of the science and medical properties of cannabis, so that is where we will begin.

THE CANNABIS PLANT AND THC'S EFFECT ON THE BODY

To answer many of the scientific, medical, and botanical questions around cannabis, I met with Dr. Mahmoud ElSohly, a research professor at the University of Mississippi and the Director of the Marijuana Project at the National Institute on Drug Abuse (NIDA) for the last 35 years. But, more importantly for our purposes, Dr. Elsohly is in charge of the only federally legal cannabis field in the country. When I asked him how that came about he explained the history of the Center for Natural Products at the University of Mississippi.

> *Author*: Can you give me a short history of the cannabis field at Ole Miss and why it was built here and who it serves?
>
> *ElSohly*: In 1964, the chemical structure [of cannabis] was determined. This is a plant that's been known for thousands of years but everybody was thinking the chemical is something else, so they were going in the wrong direction; but, finally, in 1964, the infrastructure was determined. Once that happened, there was a tremendous interest in doing more research with this drug, and so there was a need for standardized marijuana for research. And, in 1968, we had the Research Institute for Pharmaceutical Sciences and we had the first director of the research institute, Dr. Coy Waller. . . . They [the Federal Drug Administration] were talking about the need for standardized marijuana and this or that, and we have to grow this material because, in the beginning, they said "Well, your research with marijuana, we just use confiscated stuff," and they started using confiscated stuff. Actually, the first batch of extract prepared was made from confiscated material that was very dirty. It had so many other things in there, it was laced with oil, you know, whatever, and so it was contaminated. So that batch was discarded and they realized that they can't just use confiscated material because they don't know the history, they don't know where it's coming from, what kind of variety and all of that, so they decided that there is a need for a place to grow the stuff, harvest it, and process it and standardize it. Well, Dr. Waller was there and he said "Well, we have it in Mississippi, we have the right weather and we have the Institute; we can do it." So, they got the first contract here to do this and the rest is history. From that point on, every three years, the contract comes up for renewal, we apply, we have the infrastructure, we have the know-how, we have the expertise, so we kept getting the contract to grow, harvest, process, and standardize marijuana for research.[2]

ElSohly and his colleagues have the longest continually funded contract in the history of the National Institute of Health (NIH). As ElSohly put it,

"So there's a lot to be said for that."[3] And there *is* a lot being said about that: Evan Halper from the *Los Angeles Times* reports that the Federal Drug Administration's (FDA) sponsored field and research plant in Oxford, Mississippi, "is one of the nation's most impressive stockpiles of marijuana—and probably the most controversial."[4] The controversial nature of the source derives from the perception that ElSohly is seen as holding a monopoly on the only FDA approved cannabis suitable for research. And "[c]urrently, NIDA contracts with the University of Mississippi—and only the University of Mississippi—to produce marijuana for federally-approved studies."[5] ElSohly answers his detractors by saying that anyone with the necessary expertise can apply for this federally funded contract, and the contract procurement protocol is advertised all over the country. ElSohly also notes that he gets a lot of criticism from the "pro-marijuana people."[6] However, he is quick to point out that the cannabis at the center is only produced for research purposes. He is not doing this work for personal gain, the University of Mississippi, or other commercial interests. He highlights the fact that his boss is NIDA and he must follow all of their regulations when sending out the center's cannabis for research purposes.

I would point out, however, that this tension between the federal government and those hospitals, universities, and research centers wanting the Center's cannabis demonstrates the first of many federally implanted obstructions that determine who controls cannabis. As stated by Orrin Devinsky, director of the Comprehensive Epilepsy Center at the New York University Langone Medical Center, "The DEA is acting like this is 1935 and cannabis is this extremely dangerous substance";[7] a substance so dangerous that access to it is almost impossible. And, in addition to this clash occurring between researchers and the federal government, in an even more bizarre fashion, we see the federal government shadow-boxing within its own ranks. In 2007, "a DEA administrative law judge ruled that the University of Massachusetts should also be permitted to grow pot for research. Top officials at the DEA overruled her."[8] So, the perception among medical and scientific researchers who want to work with cannabis is that the federal government has placed "statutory, regulatory, [and] bureaucratic barriers [that] have paralyzed science and threatened the integrity of research freedom in this area."[9] This is also very problematic for those who would want to use cannabis sacramentally, for if drug trials are threatened in the United States, the FDA as well as the Drug Enforcement Administration (DEA) can maintain the illusion that cannabis has no "accepted medical use in treatment in the United States" and thus maintain control of this drug through the Controlled Substances Act.

Author: So why do so many people want to get their hands on cannabis?

ElSohly: Yeah, this is a plant that . . . it belongs to a family, cannabaceae, that only has this one genus—the genus cannabis and that genus only has one species, which is the species sativa, but then has so many varieties, because it's a highly valuable species. So, it's a very, it's a one and only. It really is a great plant; it's a great plant and it has great potential, has compounds that have such a wide range of biological activities, it's unbelievable.[10]

ElSohly's description of the cannabis plant is reminiscent of THC Ministry member Patricia's description: "Cannabis—there's no other plant like it, no other plant with the same energetic signature."

ElSohly: The plant, the cannabis plant is what you call a dioecious plant, dioecious plant meaning it's a plant that has a male and a female. So, if you grow from seeds, for 100 seeds in the ground, you're going to end up with roughly 50 female plants and 50 male plants. The male plants are not traditionally used as a drug, for research, not because they don't have the active constituent [Tetrahycrocannabinol] (THC) but because the level of active constituent is low and the amount of biomass you get out of the male plant is not as good as the female. . . . So, the useful is the female plants. . . . But once they . . . get the female plants, these are the ones that they propagate. Now you can take a female plant, one female plant, and from that one female plant, you make cuttings and you propagate that and all the generations that you get will be female plants and they'll have the same chemical profile, the same genetics as the mother plant.

Author: So the flower is the most important part of the plant?

ElSohly: The flowering buds, which is really . . . the flower is not . . . the flower itself, the part of the flower, then the ovary and the stigma; the stigma, they don't have the THC but the flower for the female plant, the ovary is enclosed within a leaf structure that actually has the highest amount of THC in the whole plant, and then around that small tiny leaf structure, then you have other smaller leaves and it's that . . . so the bud, even though it's the flowering part where the THC is, it's in the leaves, the small leaves around the female flowers.

Author: How many acres make up the field here?

ElSohly: Well, we have . . . right now our field is about 12 acres. Most of the time, really, we'll never grow more than one acre. . . . Yeah, one acre produces a lot of material and the interest in this product comes and goes. There's not that many actually using the material in this year, so the last time we grew was 2007 and we haven't grown any since then. We've had enough, actually had too much. Yeah, we set

> out to grow one acre with the idea we're going to get, like, 400 kilos and we ended up . . . was a good year, so we ended up with over 600 kilos. We had to get rid of some of that because there's a quota. We're only allowed to produce what you have a quota for and, in excess, you have to get rid of. It broke my heart.

THC is certainly the strongest compound within this plant and has attracted the most research activity; however, in addition to THC, researchers have discovered that there are many other active constituents (chemical compounds that have an impact on the body) in the cannabis plant. Second in line to THC is cannabidiol (CBD), which also has healing effects but does not cause much of a psychic change. There are at least 66 more cannabinoids unique to the cannabis plant. Given that smoking or eating cannabis has been recorded throughout the centuries as having a physical, mental, and/or spiritual effect on people, scientists wanted to find out how THC, CBD, and other cannabinoids worked in the body.[11]

From the research into cannabis and its effect on the body, one of the first facts to emerge is the presence of cannabis in our own bodies. In other words, the human body makes an endogenous version of THC known as anandamide—this is a wonderful name as *ananda* means blissful or delightful in Sanskrit. Anandamide is so named because researchers have found that it is able to help in the healing of so many health problems, including flesh wounds, glaucoma, multiple sclerosis (MS), arthritis, inflammation, cancer, and many others. A second endocannabinoid is 2-Arachidonoylycerol (2-AG), which is more abundant in the body than anandamide and "plays a major role in [the] central nervous system and synaptic plasticity."[12]

Anandamide and 2-AG are able to carry out these functions because there are cannabinoid receptors throughout our bodies that activate these compounds. "Cannabinoids bind with the portion of the receptor outside the cell and trigger activity inside. Different cannabinoids bind in different ways, leading to varied amounts of activity within the . . . cell."[13] Then, the cannabinoid is dissolved by enzymes that allow the cell to return to its usual activity. Cannabinoid receptors are also found in animals: rodents, leeches, mollusks, chickens, turtles, trout, fruit flies, and "[e]ven a primitive protozoan, the Hydra, has a cannabinoid receptor that appears to alter its feeding."[14] What THC and CBD (exogenous cannabinoids) do is increase the endogenous cannabinoids' capacity to enhance the body's internal systems in a variety of ways. "Although the receptors are abundant, anandamide and 2-AG are short-acting compounds, so their effects are fleeting."[15] That's where THC and CBD come in; to boost the effect of the body's own endocannabinoids.

The cannabinoid receptors most often activated by our endogenous cannabinoids, namely, anandamide and CBD or their exogenous partners, namely THC or 2-AG, are the CB1 and CB2 receptors. According to

Ananya Mandal, MD, "The CB1 receptors are primarily located on nerve cells in the brain, spinal cord . . . some peripheral organs and tissues such as the spleen, white blood cells, endocrine gland and parts of the reproductive, gastrointestinal and urinary tracts.[16] The CB2 receptors are primarily located "on white blood cells, in the tonsils, and in the spleen."[17]

The body has many cannabinoid receptors. At this time, however, scientists have found that only the CB1 receptors and the CB2 receptors are activated when endogenous cannabinoids (anandamide and 2-AG) and/or exogenous cannabinoids (THC and CBD) find their way to these receptors. They then bind with these receptors and release their chemicals into the receptive cell. So, to break this down into easily digested pieces, when one thinks of the way that the plant works with both endogenous cannabinoids and the body's main cannabinoid receptors, we can simplify the process by remembering that it works in twos: there are two major types of active ingredients in the cannabis plant—THC and CBD; there are two major endogenous cannabinoids in the body—anandamide and 2-AG; and there are two major cannabinoid receptors in the body—CB1 and CB2. However, it is also important to remember that the cannabis plant has 66 more cannabinoids and that the human body has many more receptors than the 2 we know about at present. Thus, another reason why people are attracted to learning about cannabis is not just what we *do* know about it, but also all the potential properties that we know nothing about at present.

When endogenous or exogenous endocannabinoids bind with CB1 receptors, they have an effect on the psyche. However, when the same substances bind with CB2 receptors, they have much less of an effect.[18] The psychoactive effect is further mitigated when CBD, which mainly binds to the CB2 receptor, is used as CBD has only minor amounts of THC in it. When this occurs, the anti-inflammatory and antioxidant effects of CBD work well, especially against MS, Crohn's disease, and other health issues where inflammation is a problem.

While the above statement might be seen as just another scientific fact among the many others facts discussed above, it actually leads to a discursive clash that involves scientists, medical practitioners, and the general public. Some scientists, medical practitioners, and those using cannabis for reasons of their own find the psychoactive component to be an important part of this drug. In fact, some researchers state that the psychoactive high is what drew researchers initially to look seriously at the cannabis plant. "How much longer would it have taken us to figure out the endocannabinoid system if cannabis didn't happen to have these unusual [psychoactive] effects on human physiology?"[19] Others find the psychoactive component of cannabinoids problematic in relation to the business of healing. For example, consider the following statement by those doing a study with CBD. "[A]mong cannabis compounds cannabidiol (CBD), which lacks any unwanted psychotropic effects, may represent a very promising agent with the highest prospect for therapeutic use, particularly in the field of neurodegenerative diseases."[20] Other researchers also categorize the psychoactive components of THC as problematic. Karen Wright, a pharmacologist running trials on Crohn's disease and exogenous cannabinoids, has focused primarily on CBD because it "mitigates the psychoactive effects of THC" while fighting inflammation.[21] Thus, for many researchers who want to prescribe cannabis as a curative, changes in the psyche are regarded as a problematic side-effect

In looking further at the plant's CBD effect versus its THC effect, it is clear that many medical researchers, doctors, and patients want more CBD to be available for study. However, it is difficult to find enough CBD product to carry out medical trials, although this may be changing. As of June of 2015, 16 state governors have signed bills that will make CBD products available to patients under a doctor's care, thus creating a further need for CBD. These states include the following: Alabama, Delaware, Florida, Georgia, Iowa, Kentucky, Mississippi, Missouri, North Carolina, Oklahoma, South Carolina, Tennessee, Texas, Utah, Virginia, and Wisconsin. It is interesting to note that 10 out of 16 of these bills are either named after children or mention children and/or their families as the motivation for the bill. Some examples include Alabama's "Carly's Law," Mississippi's "Harper Grace's Law," and South Carolina's "Julian's Law."[22] This is a wonderful example of discursive spin, as those states most hostile to cannabis legalization of any kind can portray their entrée into the medicalized cannabis arena as a compassionate act necessitated by the suffering of our most vulnerable populace—our children.[23]

ElSohly and his colleagues spent many years in producing a cannabis suppository that would have minimal if any psychoactive effects:

> *Elsohly*: What people don't really understand . . . is, yes, THC has a mind-altering or produces a high at system level, but, then, above that level it will produce the opposite effect. It will produce a paranoia with this and so on. But to get the medical value, you don't really need enough material in your system to cause a mind-altering effect. So you smoke cannabis, then you get the very high level of THC and that goes into the blood stream and it causes all these problems, all these . . . I would call them side-effects and then a half hour, an hour or so after smoking, it goes down into really low level in the blood and that really low level is what's really needed to give the therapeutic effect. So we have developed actually a suppository formulation that contains a pro-drug of THC. THC itself is not absorbed from a suppository, so we have to chemically modify it in such a way that it will be absorbed through the suppository. But, then, once it gets into the bloodstream, it breaks off, producing THC—but at the level that is not high enough to cause psychological activity, but high enough to give the therapeutic value. . . . If anything at all, it was just very mild

> sedation, pleasant feeling but not . . . with high, you don't get the giggles; you don't get the . . . you might get the munchies but not the giggles.

For those partaking in cannabis use as a sacramental ritual, losing the psychoactive aspect of cannabis would rob this plant of its power. Moreover, even in a sacramental setting, the founders and members of these ministries find "the giggles" to be an important part of the experience. As Stephen Gaskin noted: "It is also perfectly fine to get stoned and have fun, which is another kind of prayer."[24] Moreover, for those who use cannabis as a sacrament and value its psychoactive capacity, the potential for more FDA approved drugs containing CBD but not THC is unhelpful. Especially since the only federally approved drugs, like ElSohly's suppository, contain very little THC, as do the other cannabis drugs on the market. Marinol has been on the market in the United States since 1985. It is a capsule containing synthetic THC. Another drug, Cesamet, that is almost exactly the same in its composition and effects as Marinol, is also legal and available in the United States. Additionally, there is a new product made by J. W. Pharmaceuticals in Canada—a mouth spray called Sativex.[25] None of these drugs will give you "the giggles."

CANNABIS AND ITS MEDICAL APPLICATIONS

Another factor pushing researchers to pursue their exploration of the cannabis plant is the fact that this plant has been used across time and across cultures as a home remedy. According to Joan Bello, "Down through the centuries in nearly all kinds of cultures throughout the entire world, Cannabis has been acknowledged as a unique and invaluable regulator, if not a 'gift of the gods.'"[26] And ElSohly mentions that the ancient literature on the healing powers of the cannabis plant has been proven true by contemporary research.

> *Author*: There are all sorts of claims about cannabis and its healing properties. In your experience, what kinds of ailments can it really affect?
>
> *ElSohly*: Well, actually, if you go back to the old literature and you look at the indications for which cannabis was prescribed, it goes all the way from pain, arthritis, pneumonia, of course, analgesic, it goes to diarrhea. It's almost everything which makes it at some point in time. Before the last 15, 20 years you'll say, "You must be going crazy; you must be going nuts. There's no drug that will do all that." And now that we know what we know about the THC and where it affects the body and the receptors in the body—the receptors are everywhere, mainly in the central nervous system, but there are some in the

> peripheral [areas of the body]. [T]hose receptors that are triggered by THC are present everywhere. This, there is a mechanism by which you can explain every one of those indications that were in the old literature. People knew that it will help that but they don't know how. For example, if you have a fever, THC is good for a fever. Well, we know now that THC actually has a hypothermic effect that lowers the body temperature, even the normal body, you take it and if you have a fever, of course it will help. So there are good mechanisms by which you can explain a lot of that old literature. Having said that, the most common things that THC is really good pharmaceutically for is alleviating the nausea and vomiting from a session of chemotherapy, and appetite stimulation, which is used mainly for AIDs and cancer patients that are not eating and have wasting syndrome, and so on, so you give them that and it helps them to open their appetite and they can eat more and they can . . . of course, it makes them feel better, a little bit more healthy. And then pain, different types of pain, and then glaucoma.
>
> *Author*: That's an interesting one.
>
> *ElSohly*: Yeah, it lowers the interocular pressure, the pressure inside the eye. THC will lower that pressure and glaucoma is caused because of the increased pressure inside the eye and putting too much pressure on the optic nerve that eventually will manage to cause blindness. THC lowers the optic pressure.

There is also work being carried out in Israel, the United Kingdom, and Spain respectively on the long-term effects that cannabis may have on MS, Crohn's disease, and cancer. In terms of cancer research, new data suggests that THC may be lethal to tumors themselves. Biochemists Guillermo Velasco and Manuel Guzman of Complutense University in Madrid have spent more than a decade establishing ". . . that THC can kill cancer of the brain, skin and pancreas. THC ignites programmed suicide in some cancerous cells . . . [but] the healthy cells don't die."[27] In fact, all of the following cancers have been found to be responsive to THC in documented trials: lung carcinoma, glioma, thyroid epithelioma, lymphoma/leukemia, skin carcinoma, uterus carcinoma, breast carcinoma, prostate carcinoma, and neuroblastoma.[28]

In looking at MS, a team of researchers in England "compared MS patients who received a placebo with patients receiving either a capsule containing THC or one with THC and CBD. Both of the cannabis-based drugs outperformed a placebo, and the researchers are now working on a multiyear MS trial."[29] This team is led by neurobiologist John Zanicek, who has found that the MS symptoms positively affected by exogenous cannabinoids were such things as "burning pain in the legs and muscle stiffness and spasms that keep them awake at night."[30] According to Earleywine, research is also being done to see the ways in which exogenous cannabinoids affect the following: "seizures, tumors, insomnia, menstrual cramps, premenstrual syndrome . . . tinnitus, schizophrenia, adult attention deficit disorder, and surprisingly, drug addiction."[31] The drug trials that use a substantial amount of THC and result in proving THC's beneficial effect on a variety of health problems cannot help but shift public opinion over time. Moreover, as one drug trial after another confirms the physical benefits of THC, the position of cannabis as a Schedule 1 drug will be increasingly hard to defend.

A TOUR OF THE MARIJUANA FIELD AND FACILITY

During our discussion, ElSohly gave me a tour of the facility. The first thing that awakens one's senses is the smell; this place is saturated with cannabis, and ElSohly said "I love the smell." I then asked him the question that I'm sure every interviewer has asked him, including Evan Halper from the *Los Angeles Times*: "Have you ever smoked it?" "Never ever," he reported both to me and Halper: "It doesn't make sense for me to be working with a controlled substance and be using that controlled substance."[32] Our first stop was the indoor grow room, where hundreds of little plants were being nurtured into maturity. The next process involved the separation of male plants from female plants and the replication of the female plants, so that the center could get more of the THC-rich product only produced by the female plants. Our next stop was the vault. Inside the vault—and only ElSohly's secretary has a key to its door—we found the elixir that ElSohly had referred to earlier in our conversation, the tar-like substance that results from extracting the THC from the plant—and he had a huge vat of this product.

> *ElSohly*: Right now, the only pharmaceutical that you can get out of the plant will be taking that plant, doing an extract, so you extract all the chemicals in there, and then you take that extract . . . looks like tar, and then out of that you subject it to a separation process to get the pure compound, which is the purest THC and the THC is the active constituent.

ElSohly then showed me pictures of some of the huge cannabis bushes he has grown in the field as well as hundreds of baggies of cannabis. These baggies are sent to him from the local police and are analyzed at ElSohly's facility for purity and potency.

Next, we examined one of the most interesting products made at the cannabis processing plant at the University of Mississippi: cannabis cigarette cans. Cannabis cigarette cans were first approved by the federal government stemming from a 1978 court case, *Randall v. United States*, that decided in favor of the defendant's right to have access to cannabis, as cannabis was proven to help his glaucoma better than any FDA-approved drug. However, the government had established three conditional precedents for allowing a "Medical Necessity Defense." In summary, the three conditions were, first, that the defendant did not cause her/his condition; second, FDA-approved medications were proved to be not as effective in relation to nonapproved medications; and, third, that the problems associated with the disease were more dire than allowing the use of a non-FDA approved drug.

So, in 1978, 8 years after the passage of the Controlled Substances Act, the federal government allowed people from all over the country to petition to receive medical marijuana cigarettes. Officially named the Compassionate Investigative New Drug (IND) Program, only 14 people were allowed this option, and, at this point, only four remain. But those four still get monthly cans containing 300 cigarettes courtesy of the federal government, made from the cannabis in ElSohly's field. The senior George Bush's administration then changed the law in 1992, and no other petitions were accepted, but those who had first received marijuana were grandfathered in. In a CBS News interview, ElSohly said that "the four patients are getting pot with about 3 percent THC. He said 3 percent is about the range patients have preferred in blind tests."[33] The four living participants are Barbara Douglass, who has MS; Elvy Musikka, who has glaucoma; George McMahon, who has nail-patella syndrome; and Irving Rosenfeld, who has multiple congenital cartilaginous exostoses. ElSohly framed the program as follows:

> *ElSohly*: Yeah, it's almost like it's a research, so it's not given as a medicine. It's not given as, "Okay, yeah, we know that marijuana is a drug for treating glaucoma, so we're giving you this as a medication." No, we're giving this as a research object for that physician to use this material to see if it will help your glaucoma.
>
> *Author*: Do the physicians keep any kind of papers on this?
>
> *ElSohly*: They're supposed to, but I don't think . . . honestly, once we get it out, I have no feedback. I have asked that question to myself, because there's nobody else to ask. I wonder if those physicians have any records of what happened to this . . . what kind of effect this thing had on those subjects.
>
> *Author*: Interesting; and they [the cannabis cigarettes] come from here?
>
> *ElSohly*: Yeah, but we prepare the material and then we have some contract with a research institute in North Carolina to actually take the

> product and process the cigarettes, because they have to have a cigarette rolling machine to do this and they use this for large collections.

What struck me, upon further reflection about our conversation, was that ElSohly had neatly sidestepped the possible interpretation that the IND Program might be perceived as a policy flip-flop by the federal government. He did this by framing the program as "research," rather than a program that recognized the medical benefits of cannabis. However, no research has ever come out of the program. The second issue that came to mind was the sheer amount of cigarettes in those cans—approximately 300 per can per month. While the White House Office of National Drug Control Policy estimated in a 2014 report "that marijuana's average THC content rose from roughly 5% in 2000 to 8% in 2010," 10 joints a day at 3 percent THC content is still a lot of THC.[34] Third, while the Democratic Carter administration started up the IND Program, the Republican Regan administration left it alone for the duration of its eight-year term. Following the Regan presidency, another Republican president, George H. W. Bush, closed it down, but two Democratic presidents, Bill Clinton and Barak Obama, put myriad obstacles in place to make it more difficult for citizens to obtain medical marijuana. In looking at this list, it does not seem to reflect what one would expect from Democratic administrations versus Republican administrations, and thus shows a deeply founded confusion within the executive branch as to the best way to deal with medical cannabis. Moreover, the elder George Bush closed down the program in 1992, when the AIDS epidemic resulted in over 2,000 applications. I would argue that he did so because he did not want to push the Compassionate IND Program into some degree of legitimacy and longevity. However, while only 14 people ultimately benefited from the Compassionate IND Program, it demonstrates that the Executive Branch of the federal government can do an about-face in terms of legalizing medical marijuana when those in power (either Democrat or Republican) elevate compassion over control.

The IND Program thus demonstrates a major discursive shift around the medical benefits of cannabis. A shift in which the federal government deemed that cannabis could be more effective than FDA drugs in cases involving certain medical conditions. However, this ruling did not trigger a shift in the federal rescheduling of cannabis, which has remained a Schedule 1 drug, one "with no currently accepted medical use. . . ."[35] I would argue that it is precisely this kind of double-talk, where words and actions are not in sync, that has led to the polarized discourse we now have around the subject of medical cannabis, a polarization that has led to a divide between the 29 state governments and the District of Columbia, who have legalized medical cannabis, and the federal government and the 22 states that have not.[36]

While cannabis has polarized American society, the percentage of Americans who would legalize cannabis has risen since 2011. According to a 2015 Harris Poll, 81 percent of adults now support legalizing medical cannabis. "As for who should be making the big legalization decision, 44% favor each state resolving the issue for itself, while 35% favor a single law handed down by the federal government."[37] This is an interesting statistic given that, if the federal government were to legalize cannabis, it would remove the significant problem of having state laws opposing federal laws—so one would think that the above statistic would favor a federal mandate. As we have seen, however, in initiatives such as the IND Program, the federal government is no stranger to taking legal initiatives back to the drawing board and either reconsidering their decisions or reversing them outright; and, given that fact, it is not surprising that the general public would rather keep laws around cannabis in the hands of the states. The federal government has also been dunned for not applying their rules equally to all people—in other words, they have failed the test of general applicability in several cases. We will discuss this issue further in chapter 6, as certain cannabis-based religious groups, such as the Ethiopian Zion Coptic Church, do not feel that they have been treated fairly compared to other groups that use illegal substances sacramentally, such as the Native American Church.

THE ARGUMENTS AGAINST MEDICAL MARIJUANA

Throughout this chapter, we have examined the science and botany of the cannabis plant, the way that cannabinoids react in the body, the various health problems that are deemed by medical researchers to positively react to cannabis, the cannabis products that are either on the market or soon will be, and the various discursive clashes over who controls cannabis and whether or not it should contain a psychoactive component. I will now turn to those voices within both the medical and scientific communities who believe that cannabis is harmful and should not be legalized for medical use.

Without question, doctors, researchers, and many average citizens have a problem with the means by which cannabis is ingested, smoking being the biggest problem. We live in a time when big tobacco companies have been paying out billions of dollars in lawsuits over the carcinogenic effects of smoking. According to the British Lung Foundation, "3–4 [c]annabis cigarettes a day are associated with the same evidence of acute and chronic bronchitis and the same degree of damage to the bronchial mucosa as 20 or more tobacco cigarettes a day."[38] And they go on to say that "[c]annabis smoking is likely to weaken the immune system. Infections of the lung are due to a combination of smoking-related damage to the cells lining the bronchial passage and impairment of the principal immune cells in the small air sacs caused by cannabis."[39] Two previous U.S. Surgeon Generals have also weighed in on the problematic aspects of smoking associated with cannabis. Regina M. Benjamin, who served under President Obama from 2009–2013, states: "There's evidence that shows that it [cannabis] is useful for medicine, but we need to investigate how to avoid the adverse effects of smoking marijuana."[40] Richard Carmona, who served under President George W. Bush from 2002–2006, says: "I cannot recommend to anyone that they smoke, first of all. Smoking is so bad for you."[41]

Mitch Earleywine, a professor of Clinical Psychology who specializes in addictive behaviors, focuses on a different problem of smoking, the fact that dosage is very difficult to regulate when one smokes cannabis.

> Limited absorption may contribute to the minimal effects that novice smokers report the first few times they try cannabis. Many eventually learn to inhale and report more impact from the drug. Some never learn to inhale and subsequently run for public office. The amount of THC an individual assimilates while smoking can vary dramatically.[42]

ElSohly also points to the problems associated with smoking and monitoring dosage.

> [W]hen you talk about making it as a smoke material like people want to . . . you got to go through the . . . and the puffs, how many puffs you're going to get, what's the size of the puff and how you control the puff. I mean, it's a totally different situation and it's not going to be easy to get the right information, the right dosing, the right . . . you and I would be smoking this quite differently. How can we standardize it?

Beyond the problems associated with ingesting cannabis through smoking, two other difficulties attributed to cannabis include the potentially addictive quality of marijuana and the perception that marijuana is a "gateway drug"—in other words, that it leads one to using increasingly dangerous drugs. In relation to the "gateway" hypothesis, the National Center on Addiction and Substance Abuse at Columbia University (CASA) states that "[d]eterring use by teens is important . . . because those who have never used marijuana by age twenty-one will most likely never use any drugs."[43]

In addressing the issues of addiction, Dr. Alan J. Budney, Professor at the Geisel School of Medicine at Dartmouth, states that physical problems result when one attempts to quit smoking cannabis that are similar to the problems encountered with nicotine withdrawal: "withdrawal effects appear similar in type and magnitude to those observed in studies of nicotine withdrawal. . . . Craving for marijuana, decreased appetite, sleep difficulty, and weight loss reliably changed across the smoking and abstinence phases."[44] And according to John P. Walters in *No Surrender: The Drug War Saves Lives*, he states the following:

> The truth is, that there are laws against marijuana because marijuana is harmful. With every year that passes, medical research discovers great dangers from smoking it, from links to serious mental illness to risks of cancer, and even danger from in utero exposure.[45]

And Wenger, Moldrich, and Furst add to this argument by stating that CB1 receptors may be instrumental "in cannabis addiction by acting directly on reward-related structures [in the brain]."[46]

Additionally, many claim that the cannabis of the twenty-first century is much more potent in comparison to that illicitly available in previous decades. According to William J. Bennett,

> While marijuana is more prevalent, it is also more potent. The content of the active ingredient, THC, has increased from an average of less than one percent in 1974 to an average of seven percent today, and in some varieties ranging as high as 14–30%. This dramatic increase creates tolerance for lower doses, causing users to need higher doses to get the same effect.[47]

There are those who argue that marijuana impairs one's ability to drive safely. According to Arran Frood:

> Cannabis significantly affected one criterion, known as tracking ability. Volunteers found it more difficult to hold a constant speed and follow the middle of the road accurately while driving around a figure-of-eight loop. . . . This test requires drivers to hold their concentration for a short time, a task which is particularly badly affected by the intoxicating effect of cannabis.[48]

As far as driving under the influence of cannabis is concerned, I would argue that cannabis will remain a problem for both the states and the federal government until the following occurs: First, a standard is set by law enforcement as to how much cannabis is too much when operating a motor vehicle; and, second, when someone creates a device that allows law enforcement to accurately measure the amount of THC in a driver's system.

COUNTERARGUMENTS

As related earlier in this chapter, a majority of medical and scientific experts' research supports the fact that cannabis has medical usage for treating numerous health issues, from glaucoma to cancer. We have seen, moreover, that cannabis may have long-term benefits for not only easing the symptoms of these diseases, such as wasting disease, but also potentially curing diseases such as MS and cancer. "[C]annabis may someday do more for cancer patients than relieve pain and nausea. New research suggests THC may be lethal to tumors themselves."[49] Currently, "[s]tudies have examined the brain, the immune system, the reproductive system, and the lungs. . . . Observations of marijuana users [in the neurological and neuropsychological tests applied in] the Caribbean [and] Greece . . . reveal little disease or organic pathology associated with the drug."[50] I would argue, then, that the primary catalyst in causing the discursive shift around medical cannabis has been the new scientific evidence that has emerged over the past two decades that corroborates the experiences of those who use cannabis and demonstrates that cannabis has far-reaching medical potential.

In looking at cannabis as an addictive substance, opinions among the medical and scientific community are mixed. But, according to Hall and Babor in the journal, *Addiction*, "Only a small proportion of users adopt the pattern of use that poses the greatest risk of adverse health effects, namely, weekly or more frequent use over months or years. American research on cohorts of adolescents who initiated cannabis use in the mid-1970s suggest that around 1 in 10 cannabis smokers used [cannabis] on a daily basis beyond their mid to late twenties. . . ."[51]

Marijuana and the "gateway hypothesis" have also been scrutinized. Morral, McCaffrey, and Paddock state that "neither use nor opportunity to use marijuana is associated with hard drug initiation. . . ."[52] Finally, "[a]ccording to FDA data obtained by our filing of a Freedom of Information Act (FOIA) request, marijuana was not reported as a primary cause of death at all between June 1 1997 and June 30, 2005 (the time for which data were available.)"[53]

So where does this leave us in terms of the discursive debate among the experts in the field of medical cannabis? I would argue that there are two things about medical cannabis that we can say for certain, one that supports the discourse blocking medical cannabis and one that supports the discourse promoting medical cannabis. First, even though a 2006 UCLA study "found no association between marijuana and lung cancer, and it suggested marijuana may even have 'some protective effect,' the discursive flood around the evils of smoking will be a tough perception to overcome, especially given the number of cancer deaths caused by smoking cigarettes and the putative damages won by smokers against Big Tobacco." As noted by Seppa, "no smoked substance has ever been formally approved by U.S. regulatory agencies."[54] And while there are different ways to ingest cannabis such as cannabis-infused liquids and edibles, smoking is still the norm.

The second thing that can be said about medical cannabis that has undisputedly changed the discourse around this plant is that cannabis has been proven to ameliorate many of the effects of various diseases. Moreover, studies are beginning to show that cannabis has not only a palliative effect, but also might act to stop the progression of diseases such as MS, Crohn's disease, and cancer. As noted by Zajicek, a neurologist at the Peninsula College of Medicine and Dentistry in Plymouth, England, "To me, the really exciting stuff is whether these drugs have a much more fundamental role in changing the course of MS over the longer term."[55] As noted by Mechoulam, the biochemist responsible for discovering "the euphoria-inducing component of cannabis," THC . . . in 1964:

> [W]hen a person consumes cannabis a flood of THC molecules bind to thousands of CB1 and CB2 receptors, with longer-lasting effects. The binding triggers so many internal changes that, decades after the receptors' discovery, scientists are still sorting out the effects. From a biological standpoint, smoking pot is like starting up a semitruck just to listen to the radio. There's a lot more going on.[56]

I would argue that this reality alone is going to drive the scientific community to continue to bring studies to the public that are likely to drive the discourse around the benefits of cannabis from a discursive flood to a discursive tsunami. It may also lead to research that finds that the psychoactive component of THC has medical benefits, as researchers discover more about the interconnections between the body and the mind. As stated above, when it comes to cannabis "there's a lot more going on," and, as we have seen, cannabis-based church founders and members who are attracted to smoking cannabis are well aware of this.

So, what does the future look like for the federal legalization of medical marijuana?

Under federal law, the government classifies marijuana as a more dangerous substance than cocaine, one that has no medical use, even as consumers in 29 states and the District of Columbia can legally light up. Moreover, the DEA guards [ElSohly's] "stockpile here as if it were plutonium."[57] But researchers in other countries have access to a larger "stockpile" than those in the United States have and far fewer restrictions in getting it. So, the research will continue elsewhere even as it faces restrictions in the United States.

Law professor Peter J. Cohen blames the federal government for refusing to acknowledge the clear scientific evidence that proves the medical benefits of cannabis, and thus calls for the rescheduling of this drug. Cohen is right to blame the federal government, because, so far, the government has ignored expert findings and there has been no realistic attempt to change the scheduling of cannabis.[58]

After considering myriad voices calling for the federal government to reconsider the scheduling of cannabis, and seeing the government ignore these voices, decade after decade, one must come to the conclusion that the government has something at stake in keeping cannabis a Schedule 1 drug and is hopeful that the public will continue to ignore the fact that the emperor wears no clothes.[59] According to Alan Bock, the author of *Waiting to Inhale: The Politics of Medical Marijuana*, the federal government is far too invested in their drug control policies to rescind its laws on medical marijuana. The stakes include the billions of dollars the federal government controls to fight the "war on drugs"; the careers of those making drug policy; the money made by privatized prisons; and the loss of face that would occur should the federal government admit "we were wrong."[60]

In chapter 5, we will analyze the second discursive stream that affects the public perception and use of cannabis: the laws dealing with cannabis at both the state and federal levels. And while the court system, historically, has not been a friend to these cannabis-based religions, that might be slowly shifting in the same way that the discourse around medical cannabis has been shifting. We will examine both the ways in which the judiciary defines religion and the ways in which it treats religions that use drugs as part of their ritual observances. Moreover, we will focus on judicial moments in which judges have attempted to work with cannabis-based religions to find the least restrictive ways that church members might carry on their practices.

NOTES

1. Mahmoud A. ElSohly (The University of Mississippi, National Center for Natural Products Research), in discussion with the author, August 2012, updated May 2015. University of Mississippi. All interview quotes with ElSohly are from this discussion.
2. Ibid.
3. Ibid.
4. Evan Halper, "Mississippi, Home to Federal Government's Official Stash of Marijuana," *Los Angeles Times*, May 28, 2014, http://www.latimes.com/nation/la-na-pot-monopoly-20140529-story.html.
5. John Hudak and Grace Wallack, "Ending the U.S. government's war on medical marijuana research," Center for Effective Public Management at Brookings, October 2015, https://www.brookings.edu/wp-content/uploads/2016/06/Ending-the-US-governments-war-on-medical-marijuana-research.pdf.
6. ElSohly. By pro-Marijuana People he means NORML and other groups who are lobbying for the legalization of cannabis.
7. Halper.
8. Ibid.
9. Hudak and Wallack.
10. ElSohly.
11. Mitch Earleywine, *Understanding Marijuana: A New Look at the Scientific Evidence* (New York: Oxford University Press, 2002), 121.
12. N. Murataeva, A. Straiker, and K. Mackie, "Parsing the Players: 2-Arachidonoylglycerol Synthesis and Degradation in the CNS," *British Journal of Pharmacology* 171 (2014): 1379–91.
13. Ibid.
14. Earleywine, 139 and 140.
15. Nathan Seppa, "Not Just a High," *Science News* 177, no. 13 (2010): 16–20.
16. Ananya Mandal, "Cannabinoid Receptors," *News Medical*, June 2, 2014, http://www.news-medical.net/health/Cannabinoid-Receptors.aspx.
17. Ibid.
18. Ibid.
19. Seppa, 17.

20. T. Ijvone, G. Esposito, D. De Fillippis, C. Scuderi, and L. Steardo, "Cannabidiol: A Promising Drug for Neurodgenerative Disorders," *CNS Neuroscience & Therapeutics* 15 (2009): 65–75.
21. Seppa, 17.
22. Ibid.
23. Only 2 of the 16 states listed here have legalized medical cannabis, namely, Delaware and Florida.
24. Stephen Gaskin, *Cannabis Spirituality* (New York: High Times Books, 1996), 70–71.
25. Sativex has just been approved in France in October 2015, but not yet in United States.
26. Joan Bello, *The Benefits of Marijuana: Physical, Psychological and Spiritual* (Susquehanna, PA: Lifeservices Press, 2008).
27. Seppa, 16–20.
28. Ibid.
29. Ibid.
30. Ibid.
31. Earleywine, 171. As to treating drug addiction, Earlywine states that "[a]t least one surprising case shows cannabis has helped end addiction to other drugs," 192.
32. Halper.
33. "4 Americans Get Medical Pot from the Feds," *CBS News*, September 28, 2011, accessed March 11, 2016, http://www.cbsnews.com/news/4-americans-get-medical-pot-from-the-feds/.
34. Niraj Chokshi, "How Much Weed Is in a Joint? Pot Experts Have a New Estimate," *New York Times*, July 14, 2016.
35. "Drugs of Abuse," A DEA Resource Guide, 2015 Edition, accessed March 11, 2016, https://www.dea.gov/pr/multimedia-library/publications/drug_of_abuse.pdf#page=72.
36. Data as of June 2016.
37. "Harris Poll: 81% Support for Legalizing Medical Marijuana In America," The Weed Blog, May 18, 2015, accessed November 13, 2016, https://www.theweedblog.com/harris-poll-81-support-for-legalizing-medical-marijuana-in-america/.
38. "A Smoking Gun? The Impact of Cannabis Smoking on Respiratory Health," British Lung Foundation, November 2002, accessed October 12, 2015, https://www.blf.org.uk/Files/5cbdf46e-8c70-4e75-b135-a06200de58a6/A_Smoking_Gun.pdf.vembe.
39. Ibid.
40. "11 US Surgeons General and Their Views on Medical Marijuana," ProCon.org, updated August 15, 2012, http://medicalmarijuana.procon.org/view.resource.php?resourceID=004872.
41. Ibid.
42. Earleywine, 132.
43. "nonmedical Marijuana II: Rite of Passage or Russian Roulette?," National Center on Addiction and Substance Abuse at Columbia University, April 2004, available at http://www.casacolumbia.org/addiction-research/reports/nonmedical-marijuana-rite-of-passage-or-russian-roulette-2004.
44. A. J. Budney, J. R. Hughes, B. A. Moore, and P. L. Novy, "Marijuana Abstinence Effects in Marijuana Smokers Maintained in Their Home Environment," *Achieves of General Psychiatry* 58 (2001): 917–24.
45. John P. Walters, "No Surrender: The Drug War Saves Lives," *National Review* 56, (September 14, 2004): 41.
46. Tibor Wenger, Gabriella Moldrich, and Susanna Furst, "Neuromorphological Background of Cannabis Addiction," *Brain Research Bulletin* 61 (2003): 125–28.
47. Bennett's estimate of 14–30 percent is a much higher estimate than the 2014 report put out by the White House Office of National Drug Control Policy. In that report, cannabis potency had risen to about 8 percent. 2014 Study: Naraj Chokshi,

"How Much Weed Is in a Joint? Pot Experts Have a New Estimate," *New York Times*, July 14, 2016.

48. Arran Frood, "Dope at the Wheel," *New Scientist* 173 (March 23, 2002): 4.

49. Seppa, 16–20.

50. Lester Grinspoon, James B. Bakalar, and Ethan Russo, "Marihuana: Clinical Aspects," in *Substance Abuse: A Comprehensive Textbook*, ed. Joyce H. Lowinson, Pedro Ruiz, Robert B. Millman, and John G. Langrod, 4th ed. (Philadelphia: Lippincott Williams & Wilkins, 2005), 263–76.

51. Wayne Hall and Thomas F. Babor, "Cannabis Use and Public Health: Assessing the Burden," *Addiction* 95, no. 4 (2000): 485–90.

52. Andrew R. Morral, Daniel F. McCaffrey, and Susan M. Paddock, "Reassessing the Marijuana Gateway Effect," *Addiction* 97, no. 12 (2002): 1493–1504.

53. "Did you know?" ProCon.org, last modified April 19, 2013, accessed October 18, 2015, http://medicalmarijuana.procon.org/view.resource.php?resourceID=000091.

54. Seppa, 19.

55. Ibid., 18.

56. Ibid., 17.

57. Halper.

58. Ibid.

59. Jack Herer, *Hemp and the Marijuana Conspiracy: The Emperor Wears No Clothes* (Van Nuys: Hemp Publishing, 1990).

60. Alan Bock, *Waiting to Exhale: The Politics of Medical Marijuana* (Santa Ana, CA: Seen Locks Press, 2000), 180–83.

FIVE

Religious Freedom, Cannabis, and the Law

> The Law knows no heresy. . . . It embraces the right to maintain theories of life and death and of the hereafter which are rank heresy to followers of the orthodox faiths.
>
> —*United States v. Ballard*[1]

In asking whether or not the judicial branches on both the state and federal levels are going to allow for the existence and potential prosperity of cannabis-based religions, two questions must be asked. First, how does the judiciary define religion? And, second, when it comes to religious freedom, how does the judiciary handle cases based on religion and drug use?

When it comes to the issue of religious freedom, we know that the words one uses to define "religion" have consequences. This is especially true when these definitions are in the hands of the judiciary, for they can either categorize religious practices as legitimate or categorize them as delegitimate and make deviants of those in the latter category. Furthermore, legal discourse is built upon precedents. Each new judicial decision must cite its relationship to the decisions that have been made before; and the Constitution and its Amendments remain the true north from which all judicial decisions should be derived. I use the word "should" here because, at times, the decisions made by both state and federal courts seem to stray very far from the Constitution and its Amendments.

The religion clauses of the First Amendment of the Constitution are very clear about the importance of religious freedom. However, the judicial decisions pertaining to the religious use of cannabis are anything but straightforward, as they are consistently subsumed by the gravitational pull of the dominant discourses around cannabis; especially the discursive streams emanating from the 1937 Marijuana Tax Act that vilify the use of cannabis in any setting. Thus, this chapter examines how the dynamic concept of religious freedom has been shaped by the judiciary over time. However, I am not merely narrating the judicial history around religious freedom. Rather, I am attempting to identify clearly two things: the judicial barriers blocking the survival of cannabis-based religions and the potential judicial openings by which these cannabis-based religions might be recognized as legitimate.

In examining the Amendments, Acts, and legal precedents that govern religious freedom—and, thus, the sacramental use of cannabis—I will be looking at the following. The First Amendment Religion Clauses, dated 1791, and the Religious Freedom Restoration Act (RFRA), dated 1993. Moreover, I will highlight several cases that both pertain to the subject of religious freedom and allow us to examine the following themes: first, the problem of theism; second, the idea of religious "sincerity"; third, the displacement of "God language" with the help of theologians such as Paul Tillich; fourth, the orthodox laundry list; and fifth, the lack of general applicability when it comes to exempting religions from the laws governing the use of illegal drugs.

THE PROBLEM OF THEISM

Starting with the Religion Clauses of the First Amendment, it is clear that our founding fathers believed not only in the separation of church and state but also in the necessity of protecting the development of new and different ways of being religious. Therefore, the ways in which the Religion Clauses convey these beliefs is as follows: "Congress shall make no law respecting an *establishment of religion* [the first Clause] or prohibiting the *free exercise* thereof [the second Clause]."[2] To further elaborate, the Establishment Clause stops the government from promoting state-sponsored churches, and the Free Exercise Clause protects those citizens who participate in unorthodox religions as long as their religious practices do not compromise government interests.

> [T]he framers did indicate, in three distinct approaches, the functional importance of protecting religious belief. Roger Williams maintained that it necessarily sheltered the autonomy of the Church from intrusive governmental action. Thomas Jefferson asserted that it fundamentally safeguarded secular interests from encroaching religious influence. James Madison, however understood that religious and secular interests alike were advanced by diffusing and decentralizing power; both religion and government could reach their independent goals only if each were allowed to flourish in its own sphere.[3]

In theory, this approach welcomes diversity and plurality, but as we will see, the best *de jure* intentions can be derailed by those who favor majoritarianism over pluralism.

Despite the best efforts of the founding fathers to allow space for unorthodox beliefs and practices, theism dominated the judicial decision-making process from approximately 1791 to 1944. Clearly, this is problematic, because not all religions, as we have seen in previous chapters, have an anthropomorphic god at the helm. One sees this bias very explicitly in the Supreme Court's decision in *Davis v. Beason* in 1890, which focused on the Court's upholding of anti-Mormon policies, about which the Justices wrote: "The term 'Religion' has reference to one's views of his relations to his Creator, and to the obligations they impose of reverence for his being and character, and of obedience to his will."[4]

This theistic bias is also found in *United States v. Macintosh* in 1931, wherein the Supreme Court "rejected the naturalization privilege of a foreign citizen refusing to bear arms for religious reasons."[5] In reference to that case, the Justices stated that "we are a Christian people," but "unqualified allegiance to the Nation and submission and obedience to the laws of the land, as well those made for war as those made for peace, are not inconsistent with the will of God."[6]

Clearly, this is a judicial moment when the Justices affirmed their decision through an appeal to divine authority.

SINCERITY AND THE FREE EXERCISE OF RELIGION

Thirteen years later, we find that the Justices are critically examining their reliance on theistically grounded precedents in decisions pertaining to the free exercise of religion; and in the case of *United States v. Ballard* in 1944, they came to the conclusion that they must find better measures to determine issues of religious freedom. "Without directly announcing a definitional standard, the Ballard Court stated that religious freedom incorporates 'the right to maintain theories of life and death and of the hereafter which are rank heresy to followers of the orthodox faiths.'"[7] While this statement forced the courts to expand their thinking about what constitutes religion outside of "orthodox faiths," the defendant also had to meet certain criteria—namely, he or she had to prove the "sincerity" of his/her beliefs. In Justice Jackson's opinion on the Ballard case, he notes the problem of a jury's biases as they attempt to determine what counts as a sincere belief. "I do not see how we can separate an issue as to what is believed from consideration as to what is believable."[8] Regardless, the Supreme Court in the Ballard case did define a new judicial position in relation to evaluating religious freedom. "Religions did not have to be empirically true but only sincerely believed. . . . An immediate implication of this stance is that religion need no longer 'look like' Christianity to be protected."[9]

In 1963, 19 years after examining the Free Exercise Clause through the Ballard case, the Supreme Court again was compelled to look at this clause and analyze whether their decisions really allowed for the free exercise of religious practices. This judicial soul-searching came about as a result of the Sherbert case of 1963, wherein the judiciary attempted to further explicate what counted as "sincere" in a judicial setting. This resulted in a four-pronged test, two prongs applying to the individual seeking religious freedom and two prongs applying to the government. For the individual, the court must determine

1. whether the person has a claim involving a sincere religious belief, and
2. whether the government action is a substantial burden on the person's ability to act on that belief.

If these two elements are established, then the government must prove

3. that it is acting in furtherance of a "compelling state interest," and
4. that it has pursued that interest in the manner least restrictive or least burdensome to religion.[10]

In examining the Sherbert case and the 1972 Yoder case, which is structurally similar to Sherbert, Annelisse Wright states that "[p]rior to these cases, the Supreme Court had adopted a position that the 'freedom to believe' should be protected but the 'freedom to act' should not be."[11] That changed in the wake of these two cases. At the same time, none of our cannabis-based religions have been granted the "freedom to act," a point that will be taken up later in this chapter.

A case that has gained a certain notoriety over the years involved Timothy Leary and the Free Exercise Clause. In short, in 1965 Timothy Leary and his son Jack, daughter Susan, girlfriend Rosemary Woodruff, and friend Charles Jaeger left for a vacation in the Yucatan. As they approached the border, they were stopped and searched, because Leary had been deported from Mexico in 1963. Because they were still on the U.S. side of the border, the group entered the U.S. Customs building and were found to have a small bit of cannabis in a silver case as well as seeds on the floor of the car.

While others in the group pleaded guilty, Leary first affirmed that he was a practicing Hindu and that smoking cannabis was a necessary part of his religion. However, when this defense turned out not to be effective, as Hindus are not "required" to smoke cannabis as part of their religious practices, Leary and his defense team turned to two other legal strategies: the first being that the Native American Church (NAC) and other groups were able to gain an exemption in order to use illegal drugs in their ceremonial practices; and the second being that he was both an American citizen and a scientific scholar and that these points should allow him to exercise his constitutional right to practice his religion. This case highlights an important point in relation to the free exercise of religion: one's religion must necessitate the religious practice in question. If the practice is neither central to nor required by the religion, then the government need not allow the practice to be exempted from generally applicable laws.

Directly after Leary's arrest, he made a statement that members of cannabis-based religions believe fervently: "I wasn't going to submit passively to the role of scapegoat. . . . Liberty was at stake here, freedom of access to your own body and brain, a right I believed was protected by the Constitution. . . ."[12] However, what becomes increasingly evident as one looks at encounters between the law and sacramental drug use is the fact that while the judiciary's reading of the Constitution should be the final arbiter in defining what counts as a religion, current discourse surrounding drug use as well as a foundational conservativism that places the state above individual interests is what most often sets the stage for judicial rulings. The highest court in the land thus directs their rulings toward the "furtherance of a compelling state interest" rather than "whether the government action is a substantial burden on the person's ability to act on [their] belief."[13]

So, Leary was given a 30-year sentence in prison and a $30,000 fine. A huge outcry followed this severe sentencing decision, and while some saw it as a fair and just decision, others regarded it as nothing short of cruel and unusual punishment. Ultimately, the Fifth Amendment, disallowing a defendant to incriminate himself, was the Amendment that turned the tide, and the Supreme Court overturned Leary's 1965 conviction.

The THC Ministry drew strategic knowledge from both the 1963 Sherbert case and the 1965 Leary case, as these court cases demonstrated that one must be "sincere" in one's practices, and that one's practices must be an essential component of one's religion. Ministry literature thus stated that "[a]t the THC Ministry it is MANDATORY to use cannabis." And ministry members understood that the notion of sincerity was driving religious freedom, and thus the word "sincerity" came up in almost every conversation that concerned either Roger Christie or the THC Ministry as a whole.

GOD V. ULTIMATE CONCERN: THE ESTABLISHMENT OF RELIGION

Having focused on the Free Exercise Clause, the Justices were compelled to turn their attention to the Establishment Clause in the 1965 case of *United States v. Seeger*. In this case, Seeger, who sought the status of "conscientious objector" to the Vietnam War due to a "religious faith . . . based upon an ethical creed," required the Court to look at the relationships between religion, ethics, and philosophy as it was stated in the Universal Military Training and Service Act, and determine if the federal government were in some manner establishing a religion through this act.

Drawing on the work of theologian Paul Tillich, the Court reasoned that "religious training and belief" would encompass "all sincere religious beliefs which are based upon a power or being or upon a faith, to which all else is subordinate or upon which all else is ultimately dependent."[14] The Seeger Court thus articulated a "functional test" that examined whether a "sincere and meaningful" belief "occupies a place in the life of its possessor parallel to that filled by the orthodox belief in God."[15] Thus, the term "functional test," as used here, means that "all sincere religious beliefs" will be judged according to how these beliefs play out in the life of the believer. More importantly, the Court, with the help of Paul Tillich, expanded the way in which the judiciary defined religion. In *Shaking the Foundations*, Tillich writes:

> The name of this infinite and inexhaustible depth and ground of all beings is God. That depth is what the word God means. And if that word has not much meaning for you, translate it, and speak of the depths of your life, of the source of your being, of your ultimate concern, of what you take seriously without reservation.[16]

Tillich's contribution to the judicial understanding of religious freedom helps unorthodox religions in a very significant way: it allows explicitly that one's "ultimate concern" might not be served by "God language." One would expect that the Church of Cognizance (CoC) would be well served by this contribution, as Danuel Quaintance experienced the Haoma plant as divine and cited the *Avesta* as affirming his practice. Unfortunately, Tillich's contribution did not aid the judiciary in helping either Danuel or Mary Quaintance, as they were not recognized as having a legitimate religion.

Tillich's focus on the language of "ultimate concern" also played into the Church of the Universe's case. As this was a Canadian church, their case was tried in accordance with the Canadian Charter of Rights and Freedom. The charter not only allows for a broad definition of the divine, along the lines of Tillich's "ultimate concern," but also allows for the fact that, in accessing an unorthodox divine power, one might be dependent upon an unorthodox approach. Walter Tucker stated that: "My religion is about worshipping God, and my communication thereto, and the use of the cannabis marijuana plant, the tree of life for my health and for my spiritual well-being."[17] The Canadian Charter reads as follows:

> Defined broadly, religion typically involves a particular and comprehensive system of faith and worship. Religion also tends to involve the belief in a divine, superhuman or controlling power. In essence, religion is about freely and deeply held personal convictions or beliefs con-

> nected to an individual's spiritual faith and integrally linked to one's self-definition and spiritual fulfilment, the practices of which allowing individuals to foster a connection with the divine or with the subject or object of that spiritual faith.[18]

While Tucker's definition of his religion clearly "involve[d] the belief in a divine . . . power" and held "personal convictions or beliefs connected to an individual's spiritual faith," and, finally, recognized that one's practices allow one "to foster a connection with the divine" through cannabis, the Canadian Supreme Court ruled against him. In his case, one of the Supreme Court Justices, Justice Drake, stated that "a religion which encourages or at least condones the commission of indictable offences, in this case under the Narcotic Control Act and Food and Drugs Act, is no religion at all so far as the Charter of Rights and Freedoms is concerned."[19] As far as the Supreme Court of Canada was concerned, the church's actions in using cannabis constituted a threat to the good citizens of Canada. Basically, the Canadian's and the American's respective Supreme Courts framed religious freedom and its potential connection with harmful practices in very similar ways as they both elevated the government's compelling interest in protecting their citizenry over and above a citizen's right to religious freedom.

PEYOTE, CANNABIS, AND THE RELIGIOUS FREEDOM RESTORATION ACT

The 1990 case of *Smith v. Oregon* has attracted the attention of many judicial scholars, given that Congress decided that the Supreme Court's ruling did not apply "strict scrutiny" as to whether or not they were overburdening an individual's religious practices. *Smith v. Oregon* involved the use of peyote by two Native American drug rehabilitation counselors who were subsequently fired and denied unemployment benefits. The Supreme Court went along with Oregon. "Justice O'Connor stated that the Court could rightfully deny their free exercise claims. Oregon's 'compelling interest' in preventing the distribution of dangerous drugs precluded exempting the use of peyote."[20] However, as noted by Justice Blackmun's dissenting opinion, we have the following:

> He [Blackmun] supported strict scrutiny because, without an exemption, individuals like this would have to make the tragic choice between work and religion. . . . In addition, Blackmun criticized the majority for turning a "blind eye to the severe impact of a State's restrictions on the adherents of a minority religion."[21]

While Blackmun was in the minority in the *Smith v. Oregon* decision, Congress agreed unequivocally with Blackmun. Thus, in 1993, Congress declared that the Supreme Court had failed when they denied Smith a religious exemption and, as a result, passed the 1993 RFRA in a vote of 97–0 in the House and a near unanimous vote in the Senate. In sum, the RFRA requires members of the judiciary to demonstrate explicitly their "compelling interest" in substantially burdening a religion by applying the rigors of "strict scrutiny." As this Act has many complexities, it is worth stating it fully here, in narrative form.

a. *In General*: Government shall not substantially burden a person's exercise of religion even if the burden results from a rule of general applicability, except as provided in subsection b.
b. *Exception*: Government may substantially burden a person's exercise of religion only if it demonstrates that application of the burden to the person—

(1) is in furtherance of a compelling governmental interest; and
(2) is the least restrictive means of furthering that compelling governmental interest.[22]

The RFRA has been much debated recently. In 1997, the Supreme Court ruled that while the RFRA was applicable to federal cases, it was unconstitutional as applied to states, for in creating the Act, Congress had overstepped its powers. However, many states did not take this decision lying down, and since 1997, 22 states have passed their own versions of the RFRA. In speaking about the RFRA with a constitutional law professor, she did not pull her punches in declaring the Act's inadequacies.

Author: In your opinion, what are the good points and bad points of the RFRA?

Professor: RFRA is the stupidest Act ever made by Congress. You can't blame the courts for that.

Author: Why do you feel so strongly about this?

Professor: For many reasons: First, the strongest power that Congress has is in the realm of commerce, and in making the RFRA, they overreached themselves in telling states what they can and cannot do. That's why the Supremes took it down.

Author: Beyond Congress overreaching itself, what other kinds of problems do you see in the application of the RFRA?

Professor: Because the RFRA basically requires religious exemptions, in so doing, it strips protection from those who, under this Act, are to be protected. It also forces the courts to decide what counts as a religion versus what counts as a secular/moral act. Moreover, these religious exemptions are making it so that a person is exempt from generally applicable laws.

Author: Do you feel that the federal circuit courts as well as the Supreme Courts have been treating religious freedom cases fairly without the RFRA?

Professor: Yes, for the most part, the Supreme Court can provide broad protection for those with a sincere belief that occupies the same position that God does in an orthodox tradition. And they have to provide that there is a compelling interest. From my point of view, the courts have moved away from theism. Also, for the most part, the courts do accept that people are asking for sincere religious exemptions—that they demonstrate a comprehensive belief system. Really, one of the few places that a judge might say that a belief system is not sincere is when prisoners are asking for some kind of special privilege.

Author: What do you think of laws that will keep a cannabis user in prison for 20 years? The person I am speaking of is a Missouri citizen who had three strikes against him but was a nonviolent offender.

Professor: The three strikes rule is fine—it's perfectly Constitutional in terms of the Eighth Amendment.

Author: Do you think that medical marijuana will become legal nationwide? And following that, do you believe it will be legal to use cannabis religiously or recreationally at any time in the near future.

Professor: That I don't know. It's all about politics.[23]

While it is a serious mistake to view religion as being "all about politics," religion is a powerful tool for political oppression, political subversion, and political liberation. One sees this as various parties have used the Act to lobby for the protection of orthodox religions as well as for the protection of unorthodox religions. However, given that the RFRA puts an additional burden on the judiciary to prove that the challenged government action is in furtherance of a compelling governmental interest and is implemented by the least restrictive means, one would have to declare it a victory, at least in theory, to the practitioners of unorthodox religions.

IMPEDIMENTS TO RELIGIOUS FREEDOM: ORTHODOX LISTS AND RULES OF EVIDENCE

The "orthodox laundry list" is a method that applies to a list of elements drawn from orthodox religions to test the legitimacy of unorthodox religions; and it can present big problems in the courtroom for those engaged in unorthodox religions. This was certainly the issue in the 1996 case of the *United States v. Meyers.* Meyers attempted to use a Religious Freedom defense and testified that "he is the founder and Reverend of the Church of Marijuana and it is his sincere belief that his religion commands him to use, possess, grow, and distribute marijuana for the good of mankind and the planet earth."[24] The 10th Circuit Court ruled that Meyers's religion lacked the five criteria necessary to constitute a legitimate religion: (1) ultimate ideas, (2) metaphysical beliefs, (3) a moral or ethical system, (4) a comprehensiveness of beliefs, and (5) accoutrements of religion.[25] In lacking these criteria, the Court determined that Meyers's practices did not merit a Religious Freedom defense as he was not seen as engaging in an exercise of religion.

The CoC got caught up in the same net as Meyers when the United States District Court of New Mexico utilized that case to determine whether or not the CoC was a legitimate religion. Now, the fact of the matter is that all five criteria as spelled out in the Meyers's case could be judged to be present in the CoC's activities. They hold ultimate ideas in their understanding of the united nature of reality; they ritually act out their metaphysical beliefs regarding haoma; they have a clear ethical creed listed in their "Declaration of Religious Sentiment"; their beliefs may be unique, but they are certainly cogent and comprehensive; and item five is so broad it could include almost anything.

In the case of the Quaintances, the CoC was perceived as lacking the necessary components of a legitimate religion. The Court based their decision on the fact that the respective members of the CoC did not necessarily hold the same religious beliefs, and as such, could believe in anything and everything and still be a CoCo member. In other words, while they were recognized as a "church," they were not recognized as a "religion." So for the Quaintances, the fact that their membership was like-minded but not bound to a specific doctrinal tradition meant that they did not meet the standards of this orthodox list.

This same issue came up in a case involving another one of the CoC's members, Danny Ray Hardesty. In 2005, Hardesty was arrested for smoking cannabis while driving. At his trial, he was not allowed to use a Religious Freedom defense and was convicted and received 18 months of probation. At trial, Hardesty argued that his "method of worship, according to the ruling, was to 'smoke and eat marijuana without limit as to time or place.'"[26] The Court granted the state's motion to exclude Hardesty's Religious Freedom defense at trial, and Hardesty was convicted.[27]

Both the Meyers Court and the Courts responsible for the CoC rulings lacked the ability to broaden their conception of their own criteria. It is therefore not surprising that neither Meyers nor the founders and members of the CoC were deemed by their respective Courts to have met the above-listed five-point criteria; and as a result, they were not allowed to use a Religious Freedom defense. In fact, in both cases the defendants were said to be engaging in secular, philosophical activities that did not constitute a "religion." Judicial scholar Elizabeth Bergaron explains the secularization of unfamiliar religions as reflecting the fact that "courts may, in their definitional interpretation, inordinately emphasize the practice's 'secular purpose.'" Moreover, "[w]hen confronted with unfamiliar belief systems, courts have looked to external indicia to measure the system's resemblance to recognized religion."[28] Both courses of action unjustly categorize unfamiliar religions as nonreligious.

An important judicial declaration emerged from the Meyers's case when the 10th Circuit admitted that "[i]n applying the Meyers factors . . . a district court cannot rely solely on established or recognized religions to guide it in determining whether a new and unique set of beliefs warrants inclusion."[29] Never was a truer statement made by a judicial body, admitting that they lacked the necessary analytical framework to assess whether or not an unfamiliar religion deserves a Religious Freedom defense. The Meyers's case thus sets a potentially crucial legal precedent in saying that orthodox criteria do not allow district courts to make informed decisions about the merits of unfamiliar religions.

However, more often than not, an unorthodox group such as the CoC will be denied the chance to use a Religious Freedom defense from the get-go as they are not recognized as having a bona fide religion. At that point, there exists no defense to counter the judicial determinative that the defendants not only are not legitimate churches but also are engaging in the use of an illegal substance. As lawyer Alan Young noted in relation to the Church of the Universe members, "they are going to be caught between a rock and a hard place because they don't have an alternative program in mind . . . and as such they can no longer follow their own religious principles."[30]

As we will recall from the Introduction to this book, the Church of the Universe met a similar fate. In 2011, two members of the church of the Universe, Peter Styrsky and Sharooz Kharaghani, went to court in order to have the church recognized as a legitimate religion. Madame Justice Thea Herman "agreed marijuana had spiritual benefit for the two reverend brothers." The prosecution enlisted two scholars of religion to help the Crown decide whether or not the Church of the Universe was a legitimate religion. While I admire these two academicians' understanding that a component of scholarship requires one to educate not only one's students but also the public, their methodology was flawed as it was based on a classificatory system that was derived from orthodox traditions. The following contains these academicians' list of the necessary elements that should appear in all religions as it was submitted to the Crown.

"Religious worldviews have all the characteristic features of every worldview plus the following ten. These ten are listed below."

1. They presuppose either supernatural dimensions or ultimate experience (or both) that transcend but also transform everyday life.
2. They help people live with fundamental paradoxes of the human condition and respond to existential questions that emerge from it.
3. They rely on symbol systems that give coherence to both personal and communal life; apart from doing anything else, religion provides the symbolic glue that holds communities together.
4. They presuppose both sacred time (as distinct from profane, not secular, time) and sacred space (as distinct from profane space).
5. They find primary expression in forms such as myth, scripture, hagiography (sacred biographies), and ritual.
6. They find secondary expression in their interpretations and applications of primary ones; these secondary expressions include kinship, taboo, theology, philosophy, morality, law, the arts, and so on.
7. Considering the characteristic primary and secondary features of religious worldviews together, it becomes clear they are comprehensive or nearly comprehensive ways of life.
8. They sustain groups (defined by birth or choice), not merely isolated individuals; every community has a public dimension, in other words, which involves at least some face-to-face encounters.
9. They claim sources of authority for these ways of life and thus for belonging to the group.
10. Finally, their religious worldview is successful enough to endure for a long time.[31]

Thus, one finds that these scholars of religion have confined an unorthodox religion within the boundaries of familiar, orthodox religions by judging them against the general characteristics of orthodox religions—for instance, dividing the sacred from the profane is certainly an orthodox feature that comes right out of a sociological, dualistic approach.

Madame Justice Thea Herman, as well as another academician, Dr. Lorne Dawson, also found the above approach flawed. Madame Justice writes: "In Dr. Dawson's opinion, the Young-Nathanson approach is problematic for several reasons: it is difficult to apply; it relies on multiple criteria that cannot be measured; it is too restrictive; and it is systemically biased against new religions in favour of long-standing highly institutionalized religions."[32]

I would argue that the Church of the Universe actually does meet several elements from the above list, but the academicians, "on an objective evaluation," have fallen into the trap of populating these structural elements with orthodox features. Because of this approach, they are blind to the likenesses between the Church of the Universe and their system of classification. The Church of the Universe has a "supernatural dimension"; they have guidelines that allow them to "sustain groups not isolated individuals"; they rely on "sources of authority," including the Bible and "ancient and modern sources such as the culture of Sumer, pagan holidays of the solstices, Canada Day, the Knights Templar, Chaldeans, Gnostic Gospels, and Desiderata";[33] and, most importantly for the members of the Church of the Universe, they have "a foundational primary expression in forms such as . . . ritual" in their use of sacramental cannabis. Thus, a second problem with lists such as these may not be that the structural elements listed are wrong, (they may be broad enough to be inclusive of unorthodox religions), rather, it is the way in which the judiciary and some academicians see these structural elements and populate them with familiar, orthodox qualities that is problematic. In other words, the orthodox laundry list implicitly mandates that you cannot be a church unless you look like other churches. Thus, the academicians responsible for this list have failed to recognize the overlap between the Church of the Universe and other "bona fide religious worldviews."[34]

Another potential impediment to religious freedom comes in the form of state and federal Rules of Evidence that limit the kind of evidence that can be brought to trial. The federal Rules of Evidence law states the following:

> The court may exclude relevant evidence if its probative value is substantially outweighed by the danger of one or more of the following: unfair prejudice, confusing issues, misleading the jury, undue delay, wasting time, or needlessly presenting cumulative evidence.[35]

Foucault would have had a field day with Federal Rule of Evidence 403, as it can be used to prohibit any kind of discourse but the dominant one.

The state of California version of this law was imposed on Temple 420 when they attempted to use an RFRA defense at trial. Because they were a Temple that brought together both the Jewish and Christian religious traditions and studied both the Old and New Testament, they were seen as a "made-up" church. Thus when Craig Rubin's trial went forward in 2007, he was tried under state law and was restricted from saying anything about medical marijuana, the Bible, the Bill of Rights, or the Constitution, as all of these things were said to be irrelevant. In other words, he was not able to present a Religious Freedom defense. The Californian court system was able to do this because they invoked Evidence Code 352. It reads as follows:

> The court in its discretion may exclude evidence if its probative value is substantially outweighed by the probability that its admission will (a) necessitate undue consumption of time or (b) create substantial danger of undue prejudice, of confusing the issues, or of misleading the jury.[36]

This statement is an excellent example of the judiciary imposing a vow of silence among those who would attempt to disrupt a dominant discourse. And as we saw with the CoC, this vow of silence can also be imposed when a Religious Freedom defense is denied in order to protect special government interests. When this occurs it puts a roadblock in the way of the testimony necessary to properly contextualize a Religious Freedom case and makes the judge in each case an evidentiary gatekeeper.

In 2007, Rubin was given three years' probation and Temple 420 was closed. After the trial, Rubin met with supporters to demonstrate another use of sacramental cannabis.

> We burned a nice fat bud as a sacrifice, because it was so expensive, and gave people a smudge on their forehead, and this also goes back to the idea that burning marijuana as a sacrament was like the way that Native Americans' prayers turn into smoke, the smoke is a physical manifestation of their prayers.[37]

After the Temple went up in smoke, so to speak, Rubin worked as a pastor at the Family Church in Pasadena. He also taught a course at Union Bible College, "Jewish History of the New Testament."[38] And his advocacy for the religious use of cannabis went beyond his role as pastor and teacher, for, like Mike Baldasaro of the Church of the Universe, Craig Rubin ran for mayor of Los Angeles in 2008.

LAWS—DE FACTO AND DE JURE

When reviewing judicial history as it relates to religious freedom, one sees both negative and positive developments. The laws that have served as impediments to religious freedom include both the state and federal Rules of Evidence and the establishment of definitional lists drawn from orthodox religions. The Rules of Evidence block any attempt to provide a Religious Freedom defense if the religion at hand is deemed unworthy of being signified as a religion. Orthodox list-making encompasses the problem of the judiciary using orthodox elements to judge whether or not a religion is all that it should be. As unorthodox religions, by definition, do not fit within the template of orthodox religions, they are often deemed unworthy of being signified as religions and are barred from using a Religious Freedom defense.

Overall, the major judicial rulings that have had an impact on unorthodox religious practices have been positive when it comes to expanding religious freedom. Both the Establishment and Free Exercise Clauses of the First Amendment function to separate church and state so that each can prosper in their respective realms. And the Canadian Charter of Rights and Freedom is sufficiently broad to be inclusive of unorthodox practices. Furthermore, all of the following actions have resulted in the courts movement away from theism and orthodox belief systems as their primary criteria for what constitutes a religion. First, the courts' focus on "sincerity" rather than on "orthodox beliefs"; second, the replacing of God-centric language by the language of one's "Ultimate Concern"; and third, the potential use of the RFRA that holds the government responsible for demonstrating a compelling state interest toward any action taken that might overburden religious practitioners.

These cannabis-based religions have used various means at their disposal to subvert the laws that would shut them down. They have done this in a number of ways: by engaging in the politics of respectability; by using legal criteria, such as the term "sincerity" and mandating the "essential use" of cannabis in both their written and spoken statements; by building personal relationships with those in power; by advising members of their Constitutional rights as encompassed within the Religion Clauses of the First Amendment; and by scrutinizing the ways in which courts are using legal precedents to make their decisions. These cannabis-based religious groups understand the fact that their ability to use cannabis as a sacrament is directly linked to how the state and federal governments define religion and thus promote or demote religious freedom.

SCHOLARS, DISPERSION, AND A SHIFTING OF JUDICIAL UNDERSTANDING

Given the above analysis of the laws dealing with religious freedom, it is clear that the progressive judicial rulings outnumber those that would impede religious freedom. As such, one must question why it is that these rulings have not benefited the cannabis-based religions under review? To answer this question we must return to the system set up in the Sherbert case and its reflection in the RFRA. As we will recall, both the Sherbert case and the RFRA set up similar systems by which U.S. courts were to abide when adjudicating religious freedom cases.

1. Does the person have a claim involving a sincere exercise of religion?
2. Does judicial action pose a substantial burden on the person's ability to act on their religious beliefs?
3. Does the government have a compelling reason to undertake this judicial action?
4. Has the judiciary determined the least restrictive means for meeting their compelling interest?

First, I would argue emphatically that each one of the cannabis-based religions under review in this book have met the first two requirements as they all demonstrate the sincere exercise of religion, and the actions undertaken by the judiciary pose a substantial burden on the practice of their religious beliefs. Second, unfortunately, each one of these cannabis-based religions has acted in such a way as to provide the judiciary with a compelling reason to take judicial action. In examining the first point, the fact that the Church of the Universe, Temple 420, and the Quaintances of the CoC were judged unworthy to be called legitimate religions, reflects a failure on the part of both the Canadian and the American judiciary to think outside of the orthodox box. That is why religious studies scholars are needed to aid the judiciary in understanding unfamiliar religions. In cases like this, an expert witness must set up a template through which the judiciary can make sense of an unfamiliar religion. And this is not merely to render the scholar of religions a respectable member of academia; this is to allow those practitioners of unfamiliar religions a chance to keep alive those practices which they hold most sacred. This is not a small thing.

In examining the second point, whether or not the government has a compelling reason to undertake judicial action, then the problem sometimes lies with the cannabis-based religions. On April 21, 2013, both Share and Roger Christie filed their joint Motion in Limine to present a RFRA defense.[39] According to the court documents, the Christies had to demonstrate the following: "1) an articulation of the scope of their beliefs; 2) a showing that their beliefs are religious; 3) a showing that their beliefs are sincerely held; and 4) a showing that the Government's practice substantially burdens the exercise of their sincerely held religious beliefs."[40] I acted as an expert witness for the defense of Roger and Share Christie and the THC Ministry, and the Court found that "[b]ased on the uncontested declarations by Defendants' and Dr. Cozad, this Court finds that the Defendants have established that the enforcement of the Controlled Substances Act . . . substantially burdens the exercise of their sincerely held religious beliefs."[41] However, as the deliberations of the Court moved forward, they found that the Christies had not acted to stop the diversion of a Schedule 1 drug to the general public. During various times when Christie was not available, or the ministry had too many members to service, they ignored their own rules of conduct and participated in an "express service" through which one could obtain cannabis without the usual checks and balances and without being anointed. In other words, the ministry's self-imposed rules limiting distribution to those 21 years and over, ministry members, and those licensed to receive medical marijuana were not upheld. Christie spoke of overreaching the fragile pact he had sustained with local law enforcement in the following poem, which he sent out on New Year's Day, 2012.

> Welcome to my poetry, it gets inside my brain
> I want to show you more of me, and hope something you'll gain
> This is one way to frame my thoughts, I'm sharing what is true

> it's free to have a look around, I trust it's fun for you.
> Some say that pot's the "devil's weed"—I'll bet that God's offended.
> we know that hemp's a basic need, and He's to be commended.
> Yes, "they" say I broke the law that got me on this ride,
> but living like I had it made my fall was caused by pride.
> I did my best to follow bliss, smoked pot and smiled a lot
> But I was loose and having fun and this is what I got.[42]

During his incarceration, one can sense the beginning of a judicial shift in attitude as Christie had the support of a great many people including scholars, lawyers, and judges. This should not surprise one as the judiciary is not immune from the pro-cannabis perspective emphasized in chapter 4. An example of this support comes from an Ohio attorney:

> The case [against Christie] boils down to the fact that the Federal Government took umbrage to Christie's THC Ministry. . . . His ministry had started to get legs and people were starting to believe that cannabis could exist in this land of religious freedom.[43]

Christie's supporters used every means available to weigh in on his plight as letters of support reached the internet, print media, and the press, where they appeared in *USA Today*, the *Honolulu Civil Beat*, *The Orange County Register*, and the *Hawaii Reporter*. The following is an example from an editorial in the *Honolulu Civil Beat*:

> Reverend Roger is a true hero, a good friend, and a gentle-hearted man, much appreciated for the wisdom, boldness, humor and humility he brings to the Cannabis debate. His motivations and accomplishments are imbued with Aloha and a courageous, spirited desire to achieve harmony for the Big Island.[44]

Unfortunately for the Christies, upon reviewing their "express service," the Judges ruled that the closing down of the ministry as well as the imprisonment of the founders did represent the least restrictive means of achieving their objective. Thus, the Court was satisfied that they had met the third and fourth conditions of the RFRA.

While these judicial actions were seen as draconian, the punishment was deemed necessary in the eyes of the Court to protect the citizens of Hawai'i. Clearly, the issue of diverting Schedule 1 drugs to the general public is perceived as a substantial problem not just in Hawai'i but throughout the United States. And in fact, it is the one differentiating feature between the cannabis-based religions reviewed here and the other religious groups using Schedule 1 substances sacramentally such as the NAC.

If we compare the judiciary's treatment of the Ethiopian Zion Coptic Church (EZCC) with that of the NAC, this point is abundantly clear. Both religious groups are using Schedule 1 drugs under the Controlled Substances Act (CSA), but the DEA and Congress "have decided to accommodate the religious practices of the NAC, and accord it [a] preferential position by establishing . . . its right to religious drug use" over and above the EZCC.[45] According to legal scholar Cynthia Mazur, in certain ways, the NAC is less cohesive both in terms of membership and practices than the EZCC. "When one tries to solidify a definition of the NAC, it must be remembered that America has 307 Native American tribes living within its borders. There is no majority control of the NAC. . . . [A]nd how the NAC conducts its rituals and celebrates its sacrament is subject to myriad differences."[46]

While different tribes vary in their ceremonial use of peyote, one can point to particular components that are held in common. In its sacramental usage, a peyote ceremony "is a tradition, [a] precisely circumscribed ritual and Peyote itself is an object of worship."[47] For the most part, the chewing and/or ingesting of the peyote button (the top crown of the cactus peyote plant) is done in silence, so that one is not disrupted by interaction with other members. These peyote ceremonies are communal events and are not practiced by individuals alone or outside of a religious ceremonial context. In other words, the NAC's use of peyote is circumscribed by their own rules and is not made accessible to the general public.

In federal government hearings that discussed both the NAC and "a non-Indian Church," the following discussion took place:

> In the first instance . . . the Native American Church did ask us by letter as to whether or not the regulation, exempting them by regulation, would be continued and we assured them that it would because of the history of the Church. We presently are involved in another hearing regarding another Church that is a non-Indian Church that is seeking the exemption and the order is going to be published, I believe either today or tomorrow denying them the same exemption as the Native American Church.[48]

The federal government's decision to allow the NAC to use a Schedule 1 drug as a sacrament while disallowing the same use by the EZCC is not an isolated event. In 2006, the Supreme Court decided that the Brazilian-based church, O Centro Espirita Beneficente Uniao do Vegetal (UDV) could use a Schedule 1 drug, namely hoasca, in their religious ceremonies. In the UDV ruling, the Supreme Court went against previous rulings saying that this church, founded in Brazil with offshoots in the United States, could use hoasca in their religious ceremonies, stating that the government had not met its burden of proof that barring hoasca was of compelling interest to the state. The prime hallucinogenic chemical in hoasca is N,N-dimethyltryptamine (DMT), and, like cannabis, it is produced both endogenously as well as within plants.

Dr. Richard Strassman was among the first psychologists to study the effects of DMT and other psychedelic chemicals. "Dr. Strassman discovered that DMT is released by the pineal gland while a person is approaching death. . . . DMT is also released during the 49th day of fetus development. Dr. Strassman attributes this to be the beginning of the soul. He often referred to the drug as the 'God molecule' or the 'spirit molecule.'"[49] The fact that Dr. Strassman discovered that DMT is endogenously produced and that we will recall that the active compounds in cannabis are also endogenously produced, the Controlled Substances Act of 1970 is basically commanding the members of the human race to control themselves. Or as noted in relation to DMT, "So ironically, it is illegal to possess a compound which is in fact naturally inside of all of us."[50]

In both of these cases, the one concerning the NAC and the one concerning the UDV, the federal judiciary deemed that neither peyote nor hoasca were dangerous to society, and as such, both groups were able to continue as legitimate churches. These respective determinations were reached as a result of the fact that the judges involved in both of these cases believed that neither the NAC nor the UDV allowed for the diversion of Schedule 1 drugs outside of their ceremonial context.

Clearly, the diversion of Schedule 1 drugs to the general populace lies at the heart of judicial opinions, and each of the cannabis-based religions reviewed here have allowed for diversion. Even Temple 420 and the CoC, both of which were denied a Religious Freedom defense as they were regarded as "made up" religions or in the case of the CoC, "a Church but not a religion," were also dunned for allowing for the dispersion of cannabis. As such, each of these cannabis-based religions has been shut down by the judiciary. I would argue, however, that making the judicial argument hinge on the issue of accessibility is flawed thinking; peyote, hoasca, and any other drug is accessible if you try hard enough to get it—especially as peyote, like cannabis, is a free-growing plant. More to the point, controlling the accessibility of cannabis by making it illegal is not working now and has not worked historically. As stated by the government of India in chapter 1, "there is the doubt whether the total prohibition of drugs easily prepared from a wild-growing plant could in practice be made effective."[51] However, whether or not cannabis is accessible is a moot point. If the judiciary believes that the general public can get access to your illegal sacrament, the government will shut your place of worship down.

Is it possible that one might change the outcome of these court cases by changing the laws around the CSA? If cannabis were to be removed from the Schedule of Controlled Substances, using cannabis sacramentally would no longer be a problem. I would argue that this is not going to happen any time soon. Jeffrey Sessions, Trump's Attorney General, has issued new guidelines that reverse "Obama-era policy and gives prosecutors more leeway to enforce federal laws against the drug in states where it is legal."[52] Thus as noted by public policy analysts Hudak and Wallack, the federal government's stance on cannabis is out of step with the general public and state legislatures. Even if one lives in a state where cannabis is legal, medical researchers, doctors, and those citizens who feel they would benefit from cannabis feel themselves on shaky legal ground. In relation to health care, "[t]he resulting legal gray area means that from day to day, state to state, practitioner to practitioner and even case to case the delivery of health care in the U.S. is interrupted and complicated by inconsistent and often contradictory policies."[53] Hudak and Wallack make a further case by looking at the two routes by which the government can remove a substance from the CSA. The first involves the Executive Branch and is enacted by the Attorney General. This route is long and complicated and it certainly will not be initiated by Jeffrey Sessions. The other route relies on a congressional vote to remove a substance from the CSA. While this is a much more straightforward process, Congress has shown no interest in making such a move.[54]

The far easier solution in attempting to keep the cannabis temples, ministries, and church's doors open is for these cannabis-based religions to monitor their own practices and put practices in place that attempt to circumscribe the diversion of cannabis to the general public. If these cannabis-based religions are going to continue to exist, they will not only have to come up with policies for controlling their distribution of cannabis, but also they will have to follow these policies to the letter. For example, the THC Ministry said they would only sell cannabis to members and to medical marijuana patients, but they did not follow their own policies and, as a result, they lost their RFRA defense when they were deemed a threat to public health. Thus, their case failed not because they failed the test of being a religion, but because the state perceived that they had a compelling interest to safeguard the public and felt that the only measure left to them was to close down the ministry. It should be noted, moreover, that "[j]udges, it seems, are uncomfortable with carving religious exceptions out of general laws. The likely reason . . . is that '[b]ehind every . . . claim is a spectral march: grant this one, a voice whispers to each judge, and you will be confronted with an endless chain of exemption demands from religious deviants of every stripe.'"[55] As such, the judiciary tends to overemphasize the meaning of what counts as a "compelling interest."

A SHIFTING IN JUDICIAL DISCOURSE

Unfortunately, the law seems to lumber along behind discursive shifts within society. However, all is not lost. The Court allowed the Christies to put forward a Religious Freedom defense, and two Justices, one working with the Church of the Universe and one working with the CoC, demonstrated a certain sense of openness when reviewing each of these groups. Looking first at the Church of the Universe, Justice Thea Herman stressed the necessity of understanding the principles that guide an unfamiliar, unorthodox religion when she argued that Styrsky's and Kharaghani's use of cannabis had a spiritual benefit. In her written judgment, she states the following:

> I agree with the Crown that something more is needed than a connection to God or to the divine in order to conform to [fundamental freedoms]. The connection must have a relationship with religion, in that it is part of a belief system that provides a person with a sense of purpose and meaning. That system of belief need not be complex and it can be highly individualistic. In my opinion, the applicants' professed beliefs satisfy this definition. They claim that cannabis is their connection to God but they also claim that the connection provides them with meaning and purposes and gives them guidance as to how to live their lives. While the applicants' religious beliefs may seem absurd to some or to many, that is not a basis on which to challenge those beliefs. The fact that a central tenet of the applicants' beliefs involves an illegal substance is also not a basis on which to decide that those beliefs are not religious in nature. I conclude, therefore that the applicants' professed beliefs fall under [the section of the Charter dealing with fundamental freedoms] s. 2(a).[56]

This openness in creating space within which a cannabis-based religion might exist represents a significant judicial moment and may provide the lynchpin that turns the tables for these groups.

We see this judicial flexibility again in the case against Danny Ray Hardesty, a member of the CoC who was first convicted in 2005 for smoking cannabis while driving. When Hardesty's case was heard before the Arizona Supreme Court in 2009, the Justices allowed Hardesty's lawyer to make a Religious Freedom defense. Unfortunately, they maintained Hardesty's conviction saying that "a man cannot claim an unlimited religious freedom right to smoke marijuana."[57] However, the court made a point of conceding that "this ruling does not mean all religious uses of drugs are unacceptable."[58]

Hardesty, however, was not ready to give up. Pertinent to this case is the fact that the Federal Supreme Court in 2006 had ruled in favor of the UDV using the illegal drug hoasca in their religious ceremonies. Given this ruling, William Craig, Hardesty's lawyer, felt emboldened to bring the case to the Arizona Supreme Court. Especially since he was in good company as

> [a] variety of religious groups representing millions of members filed briefs supporting O Centro Espirita Beneficente Uniao Do Vegetal . . . among them the Arizona Civil Liberties Union, the U.S. Conference of Catholic Bishops, The National Association of Evangelicals, and the Union for Reform Judaism.[59]

In front of the Arizona Supreme Court, Hardesty's lawyer argued that the rejection of a Religious Freedom defense by the State of Arizona was contrary to the Arizona Free Exercise of Religion Act (AFERA), and the Supreme Court of Arizona agreed. However, while accepting a religious defense and agreeing that "Hardesty's religious beliefs were sincere, the Supreme Court of Arizona rejected his lawyer's arguments that under the free exercise of religion he had the right to use marijuana as a sacrament."[60]

The Supreme Court of Arizona, however, had agreed to hearing a Religious Freedom defense, and in fact had tried to get Hardesty's lawyer to make a better case for this defense. Unfortunately, Hardesty's lawyer dropped the ball hard when asked what he would deem "the least restrictive means" for dealing with a cannabis-based religion, and Hardesty's lawyer had no answer for this question. At that point, the Arizona Supreme Justices tried to lead Williams "to hypothesize about what outcome he wanted in regards to the 'least restrictive means' test and the Supremes peppered him with questions trying to get Williams to play imaginary ball, but Williams resisted."[61] Why Williams stood in court like a deer caught in the headlights is not clear, but at that point, "Vice Chief Justice Rebecca White Berch even offered up a hypothetical on Williams's behalf asking 'if the government's universal ban would be the least restrictive means of burdening the religion in question if the pot smoker had his altar in his back yard, and only smoked marijuana there during religious ceremonies?'[62] Williams affirmed her argument but he still seemed unprepared to provide a compelling reason for why the state's ban prohibiting the use of cannabis for any reason did not allow for religious exemptions."[63]

Assistant Attorney General Joseph Parkhurst stuck to his guns and rationalized a universal ban on cannabis, arguing that the evidence of marijuana's ill-effects was overwhelming and incontrovertible."[64] In other words, he stood by the *Reefer Madness* argument. The wording of this ruling is ironic given that four years later Arizona passed a proposition allowing for the medical use of cannabis, thus supporting the argument that cannabis had "incontrovertible" beneficial effects.

Just as we saw in the Church of the Universe's case, Hardesty's case was not a victory for religious freedom. However, it does represent another important moment regarding the judicial process, as the Justices involved clearly tried to steer Hardesty's attorney to find a means that would allow for both religious freedom and the protection of the citizenry.

IN SUMMATION

We have seen in this chapter that certain members of the judiciary have acted to police their own decision-making process with respect to religious freedom and drug use. Justice Blackmun in *Smith v. Oregon* stated in his dissenting opinion that

> [h]e supported strict scrutiny because, without an exemption, individuals like this would have to make the tragic choice between work and religion. . . . In addition, Blackmun criticized the majority for turning a "blind eye to the severe impact of a State's restrictions on the adherents of a minority religion."[65]

Moreover, two Justices, Justice Thea Herman in the Church of the Universe case and Justice Rebecca White Berch, in the CoC's Hardesty case, supported some kind of compromise ruling that would allow for the continued existence of cannabis-based religions. This is not a small thing. In each case, the opinions of the above listed Justices looked for a rational balance to be put forward, wherein the religion was recognized as a religion and the closing of the church/ministry was considered not to be the least restrictive way of safeguarding the public. As such, these cases demonstrate that the judiciary might be taking responsibility for the strict scrutiny necessary to allow religious exemptions for cannabis-based religions.

At the same time, these cannabis-based religions have to develop and demonstrate their own commitment to limiting the potential dispersion of cannabis to the general public. In making the effort to adhere to their own rules, these cannabis-based religions will be able to demonstrate their own strict scrutiny, and in so doing, meet the judiciary half-way. Thus, we have seen here that there is a shifting judicial attitude to religions using cannabis sacramentally in both the United States and Canada. And if this shift continues, along with the self-monitoring of cannabis-based religions, we might find that the right case with the right court of judges might work to keep these cannabis-based religions alive.

NOTES

1. *United States v. Ballard*: 322 U.S. 78 (1944).
2. U.S. Const. amend. I.
3. Elisabeth Bergaron, "'New Age' or New Testament?: Toward a More Faithful Interpretation of 'Religion,'" *St. John's Law Review*, 65, no. 1 (Winter 1991): 369.
4. Ibid., 370n37.
5. *United States v. Macintosh*, Legal Information Institute, accessed on September 4, 1915, http://www.law.cornell.edu.
6. Ibid.
7. Bergaron, 371.
8. Tuan Samahon, "The Religion Clauses and Political Asylum: Religious Persecution Claims and the Religious Membership-Conversion Imposter Problem [notes]," Georgetown Law Journal 88 (May 2000): 2220.
9. Sergey Tokarev, "Sincerity of Religious Belief," U.S. Civil Liberties, last modified May 9, 2012, accessed October 9, 2016, http://uscivilliberties.org/dle101_utf8/themes/4488-sincerity-of-religious-belief.html.

10. "What Does 'Free Exercise' of Religion Mean under the First Amendment?," First Amendment Center, accessed August 8, 2015, http://www.firstamendmentcenter.org/faq/frequently-asked-questions-religious-liberty.

11. Annelise M. Wright, "Dude, Which Religion Do I Have to Join to Get Some Drugs? How the Supreme Court Got It Wrong in *Gonzales v. O Centro Espirita Beneficiente Uniao Do Vegetal*, 546 U.S. 418," *Nebraska Law Review* (2006): 990.

12. Timothy Leary, *Politics of PsychoPharmacology* (Berkeley: Ronin Publishing, Inc., 1988), 22.

13. *Sherbert v. Verner*, 374 U.S. 398, 414 (1963).

14. *United States v. Seeger*, 380 U.S. 163 (1965).

15. Bergaron, 371–72.

16. Paul Tillich, *The Shaking of the Foundations* (New York: Palgrave Macmillan, 2015), 9.

17. Jim Young, "Church of the Universe Argues That Marijuana Is a Sacrament Protected by Freedom of Religion," Centre for Constitutional Studies, July 9, 2010, accessed August 15, 2015, https://ualawccsprod.srv.ualberta.ca/index.php/Constitutional-issues/25-other/78-Church-of-the-universe-argues-that-marijuana-is-a-sacrament-protected-by-freedom-of-religion.

18. Canadian Charter of Rights and Freedoms, s 2, Part I of the Constitution Act, 1982, being Schedule B to the Canada Act 1982 (UK), 1982, c 11.

19. Young.

20. In 1994, the Supreme Court decision was reversed when the American Indian Religious Freedom Act was passed.

21. Mark Kende, "Free Exercise of Religion: A Pragmatic and Comparative Assessment," *Drake University Legal Studies Research Paper Series*, Research Paper No. 11–30, March 4, 2010.

22. The Religious Freedom Restoration Act of 1993, Pub. L. No. 103–141, 107 Stat. 1488 (November 16, 1993), codified at 42 U.S.C. § 2000bb through 42 U.S.C. § 2000bb-4.

23. Interview with Constitutional Lawyer on June 6, 2016, who wishes to be anonymous.

24. *United States v. David Meyers*, No. 95–8079, U.S. Court of Appeals (10th Cir., September 6, 1996), available at http://caselaw.findlaw.com/us-10th-circuit/1074566.html.

25. Ibid.

26. *Arizona v. Hardesty*, 214 P.3d 1004 (2009).

27. As stated earlier in this chapter, the Religious Freedom Restoration Act is the basis for a Religious Freedom defense, but a court can refuse to hear this defense if they decide that the religion in question is not a "real" religion.

28. Bergaron, 384.

29. Ibid.

30. Jeremiah Vandermeer, "Canadian Government Will Appeal Court Ruling Striking Down Marijuana Laws," *Cannabis Culture Magazine*, April 18, 2011.

31. Katherine K. Young and Paul Nathanson, "The Church of the Universe: Is It a Religion?," Affidavit filed with the Canadian Federal Court in the case of Christopher Bennet and the Attorney General for Canada, July 20, 2009, available at http://www.cannabisculture.com/files/Young_and_Nathanson_Opinion.pdf.

32. *Citation: R. v. Kharaghani and Styrsky*, 2011, 18.

33. "God Is God," *The Assembly of the Church of the Universe*, accessed September, 17, 2015, http://www. iamm.com/69.htm.

34. Young and Nathanson.

35. Fed. R. Evid 403.

36. California Evidence Code Section 352, available at http://codes.findlaw.com/ca/evidence-code/evid-sect-352.html.

37. Craig Rubin, telephone discussion with the author, February 18, 2012.

38. Ibid.

39. Motions in Limine—literally, at the threshold or prior to a juried trial—are used to proactively include or allow evidence.

40. In the United States District Court for the District of Hawai'i: *United States v. Roger Cusick Christie et al.* "First Preliminary Ruling as to Defendants' Motion in Limine to Present Religious Freedom Restoration Act Defense," available at https://www.scribd.com/document/195062859/US-v-Christie-1.

41. Ibid., 15

42. Roger Christie, e-mail message to author, January 1, 2012.

43. Cameron Johnson, "Drug Kingpin or Political Prisoner?," *Honolulu Weekly*, April 27, 2011, http://honoluluweekly.com/cover/2011/04/drug-kingpin-or-political-prisoner/.

44. Paul Von Hartmann, "Aloha Denied: Prosecution or Predation? An Essay in Defense of Roger Christie, Imprisoned Big Island Cannabis Minister." *Honolulu Civil Beat*, last updated May 12, 2012, accessed October 23, 2015, http://www.civilbeat.com/2012/05/15817-aloha-denied-prosecution-or-predation/.

45. Cynthia Mazur, "Marijuana as a 'Holy Sacrament': Is the Use of Peyote Constitutionally Distinguishable from That of Marijuana in Bona Fide Religious Ceremonies?," *Notre Dame Journal of Law, Ethics, & Public Policy* 5 (1991): 693.

46. Ibid., 694.

47. Ibid., 714.

48. Ibid., 699.

49. "DMT," Treatment 4 Addiction: Online Recovery Resource Directory, accessed September 11, 2015, http://www.treament4addiction.com.

50. "U.S. Federal Law," DMTSite, accessed October 24, 2015, www.dmtsite.com/dmt/information/law.html.

51. Westel Willoughby, *Opium as an International Problem* (Baltimore: Johns Hopkins Press, 1925), 379.

52. *New York Times* Editorial Board,"Jeff Sessions's Endless War on Marijuana," *New York Times*, January 7, 2018.

53. Hudak and Wallack, "Clearing up misconceptions about marijuana rescheduling: What it means for existing state systems," The Brookings Institute, May 27, 2016.

54. Ibid.

55. Ira C. Lupu, "Where Rights Begin: The Problem of Burdens on the Free Exercise of Religion," 102 Harv. L. Rev. 933, 947 (1989) as quoted in *Is O Centro A Sign of Hope for RFRA Claimants?, Virginia Law Review*, Vol. 95:1281, 2009.

56. *R. v. Kharaghani and Styrsky*, 2011.

57. Americans United for Separation of Church and State, "Arizona Court 'Just Says No' to Religious Pot Defense," October 2009, accessed April 9, 2016, https://www.au.org/Church-state/october-2009-Church-state/au-bulletin/arizona-court-%E2%80%98just-says-no%E2%80%99-to-religious-pot.

58. Ibid.

59. Stephanie Innes, "Church of Cognizance: Pot Church Takes a Hit," *Arizona Daily Star*, July 9, 2006.

60. Phillip Smith, "Marijuana: Arizona Court of Appeals Rejects Religious Defense," *Drug War Chronicle*, 546, August 8, 2008, available at http://stopthedrugwar.org/chronicle/2008/aug/08/marijuana_arizona_court_appeals.

61. Stephen Lemons, "Arizona's Marijuana-Worshipping Church of Cognizance Seeks a Legal, Spiritual High," *Phoenix New Times*, March 6, 2009, available at http://www.phoenixnewtimes.com/blogs/arizonas-marijuana-worshipping-Church-of-cognizance-seeks-a-legal-spiritual-high-6501014.

62. Ibid.

63. Ibid.

64. Ibid.

65. Mark Kende, "Free Exercise of Religion: A Pragmatic and Comparative Assessment," *Drake University Legal Studies Research Paper Series*, Research Paper No. 11–30, March 4, 2010.

Conclusion

The Evolution of Religious Freedom?

We believe so much and know so little.

—William Slemons[1]

On February 12, 2016, I was watching the Bill Maher show, one of the only unscripted panel discussions on television dealing with current events. On this episode, Maher went into a riff on cannabis legalization and lit up a joint. Two of his guests joined him, comedian Margaret Cho and rapper Killer Mike. But, for our purposes, the most important part of this segment was what Maher had to say about legalizing cannabis.

> Stop treating [marijuana] like you would never lose it. . . . Everybody seems 100% certain that a completely weed-legal America . . . is right around the corner. . . . Okay, you hippies need to get your head out of your grass. Progress doesn't just automatically snowball. Think of other rights we never thought would be rolled back. Look what's happened with abortion. Since 1991, 81% of abortion clinics have closed. . . . So too with pot. In 2013, L.A. had nearly 700 dispensaries. But since then, over 500 have been shut down. . . . And we still do not have a major politician who will simply say, "Legalize it nationally. Period." President Obama has tried to move the needle a little. He says pot is "not very different from cigarettes and no more dangerous than alcohol. But, it's a bad habit." And this is what passes as supportive? . . . I can't think of another example of a drug that's legal in one state but not in another. It's not a tenable situation. . . . In conclusion, please remember, that legalizing pot is a long way from a done deal.[2]

With the public demand for legal cannabis demonstrated by both state referendums and the medical community, it is not surprising that cannabis advocates would think that the national legalization of cannabis would be a done deal. Especially as new federal banking regulations are already in place that will allow "banks to provide financial services to marijuana-related businesses operating legally under state laws as long as lenders make regular reports to the Treasury Department and watch for suspicious activity."[3] Moreover, "Deputy Attorney General James Cole said in 2013 that federal law enforcement wouldn't seek to prosecute marijuana businesses that comply with state law."[4]

However, as Maher noted, "progress doesn't always snowball," and the current Attorney General, Jeff Sessions, is adamantly opposed to the federal legalization of cannabis. There is also a precedent for closing the door on medical cannabis, which occurred when the senior Bush administration curtailed the 1978 Compassionate Investigative New Drug program (IND) in 1992, a program in which only 14 people were allowed to participate. And even if medical cannabis were to be legalized federally, such an action still makes deviants out of those who would use cannabis for nonmedical reasons.

Over the course of the last five chapters, I have documented broadly divergent opinions about the proper relationship between religion and cannabis. I examined the words of a constitutional lawyer in chapter 5, sanctioning the Three Strikes Rule, which can result in life sentences for pot-related offenses. I heard from the founders of these cannabis religions, Dan Quaintance, Roger Christie, and Craig Rubin, and learned that they came out of their prison cells fighting for the legalization of cannabis and would continue the fight until it was won. And I explored the National Center for Natural Products Research at the University of Mississippi with Dr. Mahmoud ElSoholy, finding that he had serious reservations regarding medical marijuana dispensaries, as only FDA-approved cannabis should be allowed for medical purposes.

Each of our interviewees has come honestly by his or her opinion. What I mean by this is that each opinion comes out of a discursive flow that, in this time and place, has split into myriad tributaries. Part of this split is highlighted by the fact that 29 states have legalized medical marijuana and 8 states have legalized marijuana fully. Each of these states is currently breaking the laws around cannabis upheld by the federal government. And, as Bill Maher noted above, this is not a tenable situation; it is a cold war, a refutation of the centralizing authority of the federal government. Even during alcohol prohibition, which was mandated by the 18th Amendment in 1917 and strengthened by the Volstead Act of 1919, there were no states that opposed prohibition. Of course, during this time, speakeasies were opened where one could obtain illegal alcohol, and, interestingly, doctors could give out prescriptions for alcohol with prescription cards printed up by the Treasury Department. And even the clergy got in on the action, as they also were able to "procure and disseminate liquor under Prohibition."[5] However, between 1917 and 1933 (when the 21st Amendment repealed the laws around the prohibition of alcohol) the states fell into line.

A CBS News Poll conducted April 20, 2015 got the following results:

1. To the Question "Do you think that the use of marijuana should be legal, or not?"

    53 percent Legal; 43 percent Not legal; 5 percent Unsure/No answer

2. To the Question "Do you think doctors should be allowed to prescribe small amounts of marijuana for patients suffering from serious illnesses, or not?"

    84 percent Allowed; 13 percent Not allowed; 3 percent Unsure/No answer

3. To the Question "Do you think laws regarding whether the use of marijuana is legal or not should be determined by the Federal Government, or left to each individual state government to decide?"

    37 percent Federal government; 58 percent State governments; 1 percent Both; 4 percent Unsure/No answer.[6]

Thus, while the positive discourse around medical marijuana has pushed the general public to endorse its use, the legalization of cannabis is split down the middle, and there is merely a rough consensus on whether or not the states or the federal government should be in charge of the laws around legalization.

It is fair to say that, since the Civil War, nothing has pitted the states against the federal government like cannabis—except for one thing: same-sex marriage. And while one can focus on the contestants on either side of that debate, one of the more interesting cases involved the connection that occurred among people who would not sit next to each other on a crowded bus. Such an ideological connection was forged between Kim Davis of Kentucky, a hero/martyr/whipping woman for straight marriage, and Bill Levin of Indiana, the "pied piper of pot."[7] And the tie that bound these two was the Religious Freedom Restoration Act.

As noted in chapter 5, the 1993 act is meant to allow for members of unorthodox religions to assemble and practice their beliefs without government interference, unless the government can demonstrate that their practices cause harm to others. So, both parties (those from an orthodox religion who oppose same-sex marriage and those from an unorthodox religion who would use cannabis religiously) have used this law as a means of protecting their exercise of religion. Kim Davis thus decided to leverage this law into refusing to grant marriage licenses to same-sex couples, because it "forces me to disobey God."[8] And Bill Levin decided to leverage this law to open the First Church of Cannabis in Indiana, stating that "When you're right, you're right."[9]

However, "right is not right" here, because neither Kim Davis nor Bill Levin are getting what they want at this point in time from the Religious Freedom Restoration Act. Bill Levin and members of the First Church of Cannabis cannot smoke their sacrament in church. And Kim Davis spent five days in jail for refusing to issue marriage licenses to same-sex couples in Kentucky. So, there is another thing these two people have in common: "They cannot engage in their religious practices as they would choose to do."[10]

There is, however, an important distinction between same-sex marriage and the legalization of cannabis: billions of dollars are not at stake in the promotion of same-sex marriage, while the legalization of cannabis brings a huge amount of economic baggage to the table. According to the Office of National Drug Control Policy, "[t]he U.S. federal government spent over $15 billion in 2010 on the War on Drugs, at a rate of about $500 per second. State and local governments spend at least another $25 billion . . . these figures account for merely one year of financing 'drug control.'"[11] Additionally, there are other interested parties who would take a hard economic hit if the legalization of cannabis were to occur. These include privatized prisons, big pharmacy, and the liquor industry, all of which have lobbyists in Washington working to ensure that legalization does not happen.

In contrast, there is a great deal of money to be made from the taxation and regulation of legalized cannabis. As noted by economist Jeffrey A. Miron, "[u]sing conservative assumptions that would be likely to bias results downward, [he] estimated that legalizing cannabis would lead to $13.9 billion annually in combined revenue and cost savings."[12] From a purely economic standpoint, these figures underscore the enormous advantages at the federal, state, and local government levels that would accrue from legalizing, taxing, and regulating cannabis. However, even with these financial incentives at hand, the federal government has not budged from its position that cannabis is a danger to society. Moreover, the current Trump administration has authorized federal prosecutors "to more aggressively enforce federal laws against the drug in states that have decriminalized its production and sale, most recently in California."[13]

For those who wish for legalization, it is important to remember the artist and activist Sister Corita Kent's statement on freedom: "One must be both energized and passionate and acutely aware that freedom is not a given that just occurs someday, it must be protected, and someday is now."[14] The founders of these cannabis-based religions and their members have undergone severe deprivations, prison terms, and social ostracism, but they have continued to fight for religious freedom. They have been found wanting, however, each time they have gone to court. The Quaintances were not considered to be a legitimate religion because they did not comprise a defined group that came together around a shared belief system founded on doctrinal tradition. And while Danny Ray Hardesty of the Church of Cognizance was allowed to make a Religious Freedom defense, it crumbled when the prosecutors objected to his "tokin' while driving."[15] The Church of the Universe was made into an "inside joke among people who like to smoke marijuana." Craig Rubin's lips were locked shut when the state of California enforced Statute 352, which stopped him from saying anything at his trial that dealt with religion, cannabis, the Constitution, or the Bill of Rights. And Roger Christie took a plea deal after spending almost four years in prison without bail, because he was waiting for the rescheduling of cannabis to happen; an event that has not happened and will not happen anytime soon. Thus, none of these cannabis-based religions were able to win a Religious Freedom defense.

It is at this point in the judicial process, when the courts are trying to understand what counts as a legitimate religion, that it is crucial to have scholars of religion close at hand. Dr. Winnifred Sullivan notes, "American lawyers and judges are generally poorly educated about religion and they have little capacity to understand religious issues as they pertain to legal questions, to competently present or evaluate them in court. . . ."[16] Without a scholar of religion to act as an expert witness in these cases, two large problems emerge. First, some of the founders of these religions, such as the Quaintances and Rubin, are prosecuted without ever being allowed to defend their religious practices. Second, cases such as these set precedents regarding the treatment of unorthodox religions; precedents mandating that unfamiliar religions equal illegitimate religions.

In the Introduction to this book I stated that I would explore four issues. First, to demonstrate that these cannabis-based religions have not arisen *ex nihilo* but rather are a *bricolage* of beliefs and practices from other times and other places. Second, using J. Z. Smith's methodology, to contextualize these cannabis religions by looking at the patterns demonstrated by earlier renditions including the Rastafari religion, the Ethiopian Zion Coptic Church (EZCC), and The Farm. Third, to assemble case studies of the Church of the Universe, the Hawai'i Cannabis Ministry, the Church of Cognizance, and Temple 420 to understand better both their routine use of cannabis and the ways in which these routine practices reveal a deeper religious significance. And, fourth, to examine the medical science and legal discourses around cannabis to determine the extent to which these cannabis-based religions exceed the boundaries of instantiated definitions of religion and perhaps broaden those definitions.

I answered the first three questions over the course of the previous five chapters. And I would answer the fourth question in the following way: these groups do not exceed the boundaries of instantiated definitions of religion. Moreover, there is no need to broaden the instantiated definitions of religion, for if judicial rule were critically applied in these cases, these groups would fit into the current definitions of religion and thus enjoy the free exercise of their religions. We know that the Constitution, in theory, protects both the establishment and free exercise of religion. We have watched the judicial system displace theism and "God-language" for more inclusive terms. And finally, we have examined not only the Sherbert rules but also the state and federal renditions of the

Religious Freedom Restoration Act, both of which dictate that the judiciary should abide by rules that protect religious practitioners from undue burdens on their religious freedom. As such, there is a judicial system in place that should allow for the cannabis-based religions reviewed here to be recognized as legitimate religions. I use the term "should" here to highlight the fact that the judiciary does not follow their own rules. Instead, they make decrees against unfamiliar religions by building frameworks out of orthodox elements and enforcing evidence codes that silence those who would object to these judicial transgressions.

As such, it is not surprising that the founders and members of these religions see their losses as a constitutional issue. Stephen Gaskin spoke eloquently about the need for judicial redemption through the resurrection of the Constitution.

> I believe in the Constitution. . . . [I]t is one of the most important documents in history. I think it protects freedom of religion for all Americans, and also freedom from religion.[17]

Roger Christie's passion was also fueled by his belief in the Constitution's promise of religious freedom. "He was always up front about what he was doing because he felt he had a legal right to be doing it. He was very candid and open about his beliefs in these rights."[18] Thus, in many ways this is a fight over the Constitution. And while the founders of the Constitution put the necessary elements together to promote religious freedom, they are not being enforced correctly by our own judicial system.

As chapter 5 demonstrated, however, there is a minority of judges acting in accordance with the precedential rules protecting religious freedom. In looking at the Church of the Universe and its relation to the Canadian Charter of Rights and Freedoms, Justice Thea Herman noted that she endorsed a very simple definition of religion, put forth by a sociologist and scholar of religion, Lorne Dawson; one that posited that a legitimate religion need only make "references to the transcendent."[19] Madame Justice was clearly aware that the degree to which religious freedom is allowed depends on how one defines religion. And she liked this definition of religion as she believed it would help the judiciary to frame these unfamiliar religions within a much simpler yet inclusive classificatory grid. In reference to Dawson's definition, Justice Herman states: "Dr. Dawson takes a contextual approach. This, too, is in keeping with the [Canadian] Charter."[20]

I would thus argue that taking a contextual approach, one that focuses on a structural template rather than on a content-based list, is an action that must be undertaken by any judicial system charged with protecting religious freedom. An action, moreover, that is long overdue. If one looks at the contextual framework drawn from our cannabis-based religions, one sees the following: a pattern of religiosity that employs a ritual sacrament to effect a transcendent experience justified both by passages of scripture and pieces of ancient cultures attracting a like-minded community willing to fight for their religious freedom. By drawing out this structural framework from the cannabis-based religions and their forerunners, one sees the ways in which these groups construct a cohesive template, allowing one to fit these groups into a familiar setting. As such, this template provides a classical example from which other religions of this type might be understood.

Once these unfamiliar religions get past the first barricade to religious freedom, namely, being recognized as legitimate religions, it is up to the religious founders and members to find some way to coexist with the laws pertaining to controlled substances. As noted in chapter 5, blocking the dispersion of cannabis to the general public is the necessary next step to get past the rest of the rules governing religious freedom. In fact, as far as the judiciary is concerned, it has been the capacity to block the dispersion of Schedule 1 substances that allowed both the Native American Church and O Centro Espirita Beneficente Uniao do Vegetal to use peyote and hoasca respectively in their sacramental rituals. And if the law is to be generally applicable, then the courts must rule for the rights of these cannabis-based religions to use cannabis in their sacramental rituals as long as these cannabis-based religions are consistent in their efforts to-block the dispersion of cannabis to the general public.

At this point, I can see a savvy reader wondering if the necessity of changing one's practices to coexist with the judiciary does not obviate religious freedom from the get-go. To my way of thinking, it is a practical necessity if these religions are to maintain their practices. In fact, whenever churches, ministries, or temples deal with state and/or federal laws, a prime example being exemptions from certain taxes, they must be pragmatic about their role in the intersection between church and state. Furthermore, it would not surprise me if this same savvy reader might find this pragmatic agenda—one in which these cannabis-based ministries conform to governmental statutes—problematic as it functions as a blueprint for the operation of huckster religions; those who might outwardly conform to this type of religion but are actually out to make a buck or grab the limelight? And the answer to this potential problem is yes; this outward conformity to governmental statutes might open the door to imposter religious groups. In fact, some of the groups highlighted in this book may have opened their ministries, churches, or temples to grab a piece of the cannabis action, rather than provide a place and a space for the sacramental use of cannabis. But what would be worse? To occasionally open the door for imposters, while opening our society to fresh approaches to being religious, or to slam the door shut and let the prevailing discourse around religion protect only the orthodox? I would say that the latter is much worse. And, as noted by Dan Quaintance: "One day, we will look back on the government's harassment of individuals for smoking something other than tobacco and wonder where this mania for punishing people came from."[21]

Having examined the four issues set out at the beginning of this book, I want to revisit these cannabis-based religions with an eye toward both their flaws and their merits. Do I believe that the tremendous amount of money involved in the operations of the EZCC always went back into the church or in some other way contributed to the social good? No. Do I believe that the Christies distributed cannabis always with a word from Roger and an anointing? No. Do I believe that the Quaintances's courier system and wellness centers always worked the way they were supposed to? No. Do I believe that Temple 420 regularly held four Bible study services every week? No. But, looking at the larger picture: Do I believe that any of our cannabis religion founders were motivated by the idea of being drug lords? No. Do I think that all of our cannabis religion founders wanted to make a living doing what they believed in? Yes. Do I believe our cannabis founders took enormous risks to promote an alternative way of practicing religion that might be of great benefit to a large, diverse group of people? Yes. Do I believe that any of these organizations were harmful to the public? No. Do I believe that all of our cannabis religion founders had experienced cannabis as a sacrament? Yes.

The term "experience" has come up a great deal in examining these cannabis-based religions. In highlighting this aspect of these religions I am pointing to the fact that these groups had joined together, not through a shared doctrinal tradition, but rather through their experience of accessing the transcendent through cannabis. This is an important point given that the Church of Cognizance at the Quaintances trial was delegitimized as a religion because their church brought together multiple doctrinal systems that individual members were free to accept or to ignore. In fact, none of our cannabis-based religions had either a shared doctrinal tradition or a required roster of practices to which all must adhere. However, it was not the lack of a shared doctrinal tradition that I found most interesting, rather it was the fact that the smoking of cannabis allowed them the experience of touching the transcendent. To my mind, touching the transcendent is what makes humans crave religion.

I have long been a fan of Wilfred Cantwell Smith's definition of religious life, because it focuses not on one's "belief" in the transcendent, but on one's "response" to the transcendent—"a dynamic response of the person to the living reality of God."[22] For our purposes, we will replace "God" with "the sacred," nevertheless, Cantwell Smith's experience of the divine as being real, dynamic, and experientially accessible resonates for all who have a religious practice. Not the trappings of a cumulative tradition, which Cantwell Smith understands as the other half of orthodox religious life, but the moment outside of human construction, the moment when the sacred becomes tangible.

I saw the sacred become tangible when I was traveling from Banaras to Delhi on a train. There was an Indian man sitting across from me and we discussed our reasons for going to Delhi. I said that I was going to buy a handwoven carpet that was going to look great in my house. When I asked him why he was going to Delhi, he said, "I am going to see God." I wish I had let him go first. Experience is something one can feel in the body, in the heart, and in the mind. Or, in the words of Albert Einstein: "All knowledge comes from [one's own] experience."[23]

This came across clearly when our cannabis religion founders and members spoke of the experience of using cannabis. "Using cannabis was a revelation to me—a personal, religious epiphany. . . ." "Cannabis expands the unconscious mind." "Cannabis is important and necessary—it's natural . . . the beauty of cannabis—it makes reality alive—Hello God, Hello life. . . . We discovered cannabis—the enlightenment, the awareness of something beautiful going on."[24] Charles Long describes this kind of religious experience as providing one with "a self-defined central awareness from which one orients oneself."[25] And, from the Amish to the Zoroastrians, one can rejoice and speak of divine experience, so it is also inclusive. It follows, however, that, in highlighting experience driven ritual over a comprehensive system of belief, one must allow for a potentially new type of church, one which Danuel Quaintance described as follows: "[W]e are a church with a goal of uniting like-minded individuals regardless of the denomination they claim as their religion."[26]

Even when not ingesting cannabis, simply being around the plant seems to yield, for some, a unique sensory experience. "[A]nd I had an epiphany—a spiritual epiphany where I could connect and feel their energy."[27] ElSohly spoke in a similar fashion when he described the scent of cannabis and what cannabis could do. "So, it's a very, it's a one and only. It really is a great plant; it's a great plant and it has great potential, has compounds that have such a wide range of biological activities, it's unbelievable." And "I love the smell."[28]

Throughout this book, we have looked through both a historical and cross-cultural lens to find the *bricolage* and contextual framework through which we can trace the activities of these cannabis-based religions. As a metaphor, one might imagine a pool of water with concentric rings rippling out from the central ritual of ingesting cannabis. Whether it is smoked, eaten, or mixed with oil and anointed, the ritual experience of taking cannabis into one's body transports one from the mundane to the sacred as experienced by those involved in these religious practices. The next ripple reveals that each of these groups takes sacred orthodox texts and/or practices from other cultural traditions and reinterprets them to support their ritual activities. The scriptural texts and practices differ, for Roger Christie and Craig Rubin, it was the *Old and New Testaments*, for James Kimmel it was the *Urantia* book, for Danuel Quaintance it was the *Avesta*, and for the Church of the Universe it was the ancient culture of

Sumer and the "Desiderata." However, none of these texts or practices were taken *in toto*, and all were subject to the reinterpretation of the user. The next ripple involves the energy of a community enjoying this "gentle ritual":[29] Hands touching in the passing of a pipe, eyes meeting over a shared joke, and the ease of settling into a group who know the magic of this sacrament. From there we have the ripples widening out to symbolize the unstructured, nonhierarchical (with the exception of the EZCC), nonproselytizing nature of these groups. As said by E. C. Daniel Jeffrey, "We're not interested in converting anyone. We just want to increase people's knowledge of the herb, because we believe it is the provider and our future."[30] And, for the final wave rippling out to meet the shore, these groups have been and continue to be politically motivated. They are out in the street protesting and waving cannabis leaf flags; they are filing endless lawsuits and keeping track of what politicians are saying about cannabis; they are attempting to inform the public even from their jail cells, and they are running for political office—they are political advocates for cannabis and they know the law.

In the 2017 special edition of *Time* magazine, the topic was cannabis and the edition was entitled, "Marijuana Goes Main Street." Clearly, the public discourse around cannabis is shifting quickly these days. And, to my mind, the unorthodox religions discussed throughout this book deserve every tax exemption given to orthodox churches. Moreover, operating under these conditions, these cannabis religions would be more visible to the public and attract others who have experienced the wonders of cannabis but have yet to find a group of like-minded people.

In conclusion, I want to draw on *The Botany of Desire*, a book by Michael Pollan that speaks eloquently of the wonders of cannabis.

> Indeed, I would venture that more than any other single quality, it is the relentless moment-by-moment forgetting, this draining of the pool of sense impression almost as quickly as it fills, that gives the experience of consciousness under marijuana its peculiar texture. It helps account for the sharpening of sensory perceptions, for the aura of profundity in which cannabis bathes the most ordinary insights, and, perhaps most important of all, for the sense that time has slowed or even stopped. For it is only by forgetting that we ever really drop the thread of time and approach the experience of living in the present moment, so elusive in ordinary hours. And the wonder of that experience, perhaps more than any other, seems to be at the very heart of the human desire to change consciousness, whether by means of drugs or any other technique.[31]

And so it is.

NOTES

1. William Slemons, "Memorial addresses on the life and character of Alpheus S. Williams," Delivered in the House of Representatives and in the Senate (Washington, DC: Government Printing Office, 1880).

2. Bill Maher, *Real Time with Bill Maher*, episode 377, HBO, February 12, 2016.

3. Andrew Grossman, "Banks to be allowed to do business with marijuana dispensaries," *Wall Street Journal*, February 14, 2014, http://www.wsj.com/articles/SB10001424052702304434104579383150782034282.

4. Ibid.

5. Jennie Cohen, "History in the Headlines, Drink Some Whiskey, Call in the Morning: Doctors & Prohibition," A & E Network, January 17, 2012 by Jennie Cohen, accessed March 21, 2016, http://www.history.com/news/drink-some-whiskey-call-in-the-morning-doctors-prohibition.

6. Sarah Dutton, Jennifer De Pinto, Anthony Salvanto, and Fred Buckus, "Poll: Support for legal marijuana use reaches all-time high," *CBS News*, April 20, 2015, accessed on October 25, 2015, http://www.cbsnews.com/news/poll-support-for-legal-marijuana-use-reaches-all-time-high/.

7. Mark Alesia and Tim Evans, "Who Is First Church of Cannabis Founder Bill Levin?" *Indianapolis Star*, June 27, 2015, http://www.indystar.com/story/news/2015/06/27/part-huckster-part-high-priest-pot-indys-counter-culture-icon-sparks-controversy/29287515/.

8. "Kim Davis: I Am Being 'Forced to Disobey God,'" *CBSDC*, September 14, 2015, accessed October 24, 2015, http://washington.cbslocal.com/2015/09/14/kim-davis-i-am-being-forced-to-disobey-god/.

9. Alesia and Evans.

10. Ibid.

11. "Drug War Clock," drugsense.org, accessed on April 20, 2016, http://www.drugsense.org/cms/wodclock.

12. Christopher Glenn Fichtner, *Cannabinomics: the Marijuana Policy Tipping Point* (Northbrook, IL: Well Mind Books, 2010), 182.

13. Charlie Savage and Jack Healy, "Trump Administration Takes Step That Could Threaten Marijuana Legalization Movement," *New York Times*, January 4, 2018.

14. "Corita Kent: Biography," Corita Art Center, accessed August 27, 2016, http://corita.org/about-corita.

15. Stephen Lemons, "Arizona's Marijuana-Worshipping Church of Cognizance Seeks a Legal, Spiritual High," Phoenix New Times, March 6, 2009, http://www.phoenixnewtimes.com/blogs/arizonas-marijuana-worshipping-church-of-cognizance-seeks-a-legal-spiritual-high-6501014.

16. Winnifred Fallers Sullivan, "The Religious Expert in American Courts," *Archives de sciences sociales des religions*, July-September 2011, 6.

17. Jessica Bliss, "Stephen Gaskin, Founder of The Farm, Dies at 79," *The Tennessean*, July 2, 2014.

18. Joe, THC Ministry member, telephone discussion with the author, November 12, 2012.

19. Citation: *R. v. Kharaghani and Styrsky*, 2011, 19

20. Ibid.

21. Stephen Lemons, "Arizona's Marijuana-Worshipping Church of Cognizance Seeks a Legal, Spiritual High," *Phoenix New Times*, March 6, 2009, http://www.phoenixnewtimes.com/blogs/arizonas-marijuana-worshipping-church-of-cognizance-seeks-a-legal-spiritual-high-6501014.

22. Wilfred Cantwell Smith, *The Meaning and End of Religion* (Philadelphia: Fortress Press, 1962), 31.

23. Albert Einstein, *Ideas and Opinions* (New York: Three Rivers Press, 1954), 271.

24. Chapters 3 and 4.

25. Charles H. Long, *Significations: Signs, Symbols, and Images in the Interpretation of Religion* (Aurora, CO: The Davies Group, 1995), 9.
26. Danuel Quaintance, telephone discussion with the author, September 23, 2015.
27. Patricia, THC Ministry member, telephone discussion with the author, November 7, 2012.
28. Mahmoud A. ElSohly (The University of Mississippi, National Center for Natural Products Research), in discussion with the author, August 2012, updated May 2015. University of Mississippi.
29. Stephen Gaskin, *Cannabis Spirituality* (New York: High Times Books, 1996), 40.
30. Daniel Jeffrey, telephone discussion with the author, September 23, 2015.
31. Michael Pollan, *The Botany of Desire: A Plant's-Eye View of the World* (New York: Random House, 2001), 162.

Bibliography

"4 Americans Get Medical Pot from the Feds." *CBS News*, September 28, 2011. http://www.cbsnews.com/news/4-americans-get-medical-pot-from-the-feds/.

"11 US Surgeons General and Their Views on Medical Marijuana." ProCon.org, 2014. http://medicalmarijuana.procon.org/view.resource.php?resourceID=004872.

"23 Legal Medical Marijuana States and DC." ProCon.org. medicalmarijuana.procon.org/view.resource.php?resourceID=000881.

"A Smoking Gun? The Impact of Cannabis Smoking on Respiratory Health." British Lung Foundation, November 2002. https://www.blf.org.uk/Files/5cbdf46e-8c70-4e75-b135-a06200de58a6/A_Smoking_Gun.pdf.vembe.

Abel, Earnest. *Marijuana: The First Twelve Thousand Years*. New York: Plenum Press, 1980.

Albanese, Catherine L. *America: Religions and Religion*. Belmont, CA: Wadsworth, 1992.

Alesia, Mark and Tim Evans. "Who is First Church of Cannabis Founder Bill Levin?" *Indianapolis Star*, June 27, 2015. http://www.indystar.com/story/news/2015/06/27/part-huckster-part-high-priest-pot-indys-counter-culture-icon-sparks-controversy/29287515/.

"Aloha and Welcome—e komo mai." The Hawai'i Cannabis Ministry, THC Ministry. http://www.thc-ministry.org/.

Americans United for Separation of Church and State. "Arizona Court 'Just Says No' to Religious Pot Defense," October 2009. https://www.au.org/church-state/october-2009-church-state/au-bulletin/arizona-court-%E2%80%98just-says-no%E2%80%99-to-religious-pot.

Andrews, Laurel. "Highly Informed: 13 Pressing questions about Alaska's marijuana legalization day." *Alaska Dispatch News*, February 24, 2015.

"Arizona Supreme Court to decide whether there is a Religious Right to Use Marijuana." Religious News Blog, January 7, 2009. http://www.religionnewsblog.com/2313/religious-marijuana-3.

Arizona v. Hardesty, 214 P.3d 1004 (2009).

Arweck, Elisabeth. *Researching New Religious Movements: Responses and Redefinitions*. London: Routledge, 2006.

The Assembly of the Church of the Universe, accessed September 17, 2015, http://www.iamm.com/templar.htm.

Associated Press, "Couple faces sentencing for medical marijuana 'ministry,'" *Honolulu Star Advertiser*, April 28, 2014. http://www.staradvertiser.com/news/breaking/20140428_Couple_faces_sentencing_for_marijuana_ministry.html?id=257050861.

"Baldasaro back in the race." CHCH, July 11, 2014, http://www.chch.com/baldasaro-back-race.

Barbin, Herculine. *Herculine Barbin: Being the Recently Discovered Memoirs of a Nineteenth-Century French Hermaphrodite*, Introduced by Michel Foucault. New York: Pantheon Books, 1980.

Baum, Dan. *Smoke and Mirrors: The War on Drugs and the Politics of Failure*. Boston: Little Brown, 1996.

Bayer, I. and H. Ghodse. "Evolution of International Drug Control, 1945–1995," *UN International Drug Control Programme, Bulletin on Narcotics* Vol. LI, Nos. 1 and 2 (New York: United Nations, 1999), 1–17.

Beeching, Jack. *The Chinese Opium Wars*. New York: Harcourt, Brace, Jovanovich, 1977.

Bell, Catherine. *Ritual: Perspectives and Dimensions*. New York: Oxford University Press, 1997.

Bell, Catherine. *Ritual Theory, Ritual Practice*. Oxford: Oxford University Press, 1993.

Bello, Joan. *The Benefits of Marijuana: Physical, Psychological and Spiritual*. Susquehanna, PA: Lifeservices Press, 2008.

Benard, Akeia. "The Material Roots of Rastafarian Marijuana Symbolism." *History and Anthropology* 18, no. 1 (2007): 89–99.

Bergaron, Elisabeth. "'New Age' or New Testament?: Toward a More Faithful Interpretation of 'Religion.'" *St. John's Law Review* 65, no. 1 (Winter 1991): 365–87.

Bergman, Robert. "Navaho Peyote Use: Its Apparent Safety," *The American Journal of Psychiatry* 128, no. 6 (1971): 695–99.

Bliss, Jessica. "Stephen Gaskin, Founder of The Farm, Dies at 79." *The Tennessean*, July 2, 2014.

Blumenauer, Earl and Jared Polis. "The Path Forward: Rethinking Federal Marijuana Policy." http://www.blumenauer.house.gov.

Bock, Alan. *Waiting to Inhale: The Politics of Medical Marijuana*. Santa Ana, CA: Seven Locks Press, 2000.

Book of Rites, chapter 54, verse 23, translated by James Legge. Beijing and Washington, DC: Intercultural Press, 2013.

Bourdieu, Pierre. *Outline of a Theory of Practice*. Translated by Richard Nice. Cambridge: Cambridge University Press, 1977.

Breathes, William. "'Holy Hippies' Tells Story of 1971 Pot-Fueled Spiritual Bus Caravan," *Toke of the Town*, July 25, 2011, http://www.tokeofthetown.com/2011/07/holy_hippies_book_tells_story_of_1971_pot-fueled_b.php/.

Bromley, David G. "Teaching New Religious Movements: Learning from New Religious Movements," *Teaching New Religious Movements*, ed. David G. Bromley. Oxford: Oxford University Press, 2007.

Budney, A. J., J. R. Hughes, B. A. Moore, and P. L. Novy, "Marijuana Abstinence Effects in Marijuana Smokers Maintained in Their Home Environment," *Achieves of General Psychiatry* 58 (2001): 917–24.

Burnett, John. "Roger Christie: Deal in Works for Pot Minister?," *Hawaii Tribune Herald*, June 12, 2011.

California Evidence Code Section 352. http://codes.findlaw.com/ca/evidence-code/evid-sect-352.html.

Cano, Regina Garcia. "South Dakota Tribe to open nation's 1st marijuana resort." Associated Press, September 29, 2015. http://bigstory.ap.org/article/b759278274a94be89e6e4f3793b8c009/south-dakota-tribe-open-nations-1st-marijuana-resort.

"Certified Couriers of the CoC." Church of Cognizance. http://danmary.org/tiki/tiki-index.php?page=Certified+Couriers+of+the+COC.

Chandyoga Upanishad (VI 14:3). In Limaye and Vadekar, eds. *Eighteen Principal Upaniṣads*. Poona: Vaidika Samsodhana Mandela, 1958.

Charone, Barbara. "Peter Tosh in *Creem Magazine*: 'Peter Tosh: He's the Toughest,'" in *Creem Magazine*, March 1979.

Chasmar, Jessica. "Marijuana church given tax-exempt status in Indiana: 'Somebody at the IRS loves us.'" *The Washington Times*, June 1, 2015. http://www.washingtontimes.com/news/2015/jun/1/marijuana-church-wins-tax-exempt-status-in-indiana/.

Chokshi, Niraj. "How Much Weed Is in a Joint? Pot Experts Have a New Estimate." *New York Times*, July 14, 2016.

Christie, Share. "9 Pillars of the Christie Mayor Campaign 2012," The-Last-Marijuana-Trial.com. http://the-last-marijuana-trial.com/9-pillars-of-the-christie-mayor-campaign-2012/.

"Church Credo." The Assembly of the Church of the Universe, http://www.iamm.clm/man-cu.htm.

"Church Mandate." The Assembly of the Church of the Universe. http://www.iamm.com/man-cu.htm.
"Church of Cognizance IOMM Membership Pledge," *Church of Cognizance Introduced*. http://www.coc.enlightener.net.
"Church of Cognizance: Pot Church Takes a Hit." Religion News Blog. http://www.religionnewsblog.com/15212/church-of-cognizance-pot-church-takes-a-hit.
"Church of the Universe Argues that Marijuana is a Sacrament Protected by Freedom of Religion." Centre for Constitutional Studies, July 9, 2010. http://ualawcc-sprod.srv.ualberta.ca/ccs/index.php/constitutional-issues/25-other/78-church-of-the-universe-argues-that-marijuana-is-a-sacrament-protected-by-freedom-of-religion.
"Church of the Universe." *Winnipeg Free Press*, February 8, 2011.
Clarke, Peter B., ed., *Encyclopedia of New Religious Movements*. London: Routledge, 2006.
Cohen, Jennie. "History in the Headlines, Drink Some Whiskey, Call in the Morning: Doctors & Prohibition." A & E Network, January 17, 2012. http://www.history.com/news/drink-some-whiskey-call-in-the-morning-doctors-prohibition.
Cohen, Peter J. "Medical Marijuana: The Conflict between Scientific Evidence and Political Ideology," *Utah Law Review* 2009, no. 1 (2009): 35–104.
Comitas, Landrow. "Occupational Multiplicity in Rural Jamaica," in *West Indian Perspectives: Work and Family Life*, eds. L. Comitas and D. Lowenthal. New York: Double Day, 1973, in A. Hamid, *The Ganja Complex*. Lanham: Lexington Books, 2002.
"Complaint." The First Church of Cannabis, Inc., Bill Levin, Herbert Neal Smith, and Bobbi Jo Young, *Plaintiffs v. State of Indiana*; Governor Mike Pence; Attorney General Gregory F. Zoeller; Indiana State Police Superintendent Douglas G. Carter; Chief Rick Hite, Indianapolis Metropolitan Police Department; Indianapolis Mayor Greg Ballard; and Marion County Sheriff John Layton Defendants, July 8, 2015, http://www.big.assets.huffingtonpost.com.
Coogan, Michael David, Marc Zvi Brettler, Carol A. Newsom, and Pheme Perkins. *The New Oxford Annotated Bible: New Revised Standard Version: With the Apocrypha: An Ecumenical Study Bible*. Oxford: Oxford University Press, 2010.
Cook, Michael. *Trinitarian Christology: That Power That Sets Us Free*. Mahwah, NJ: Paulist Press, 2010.
"Corita Kent: Biography," Corita Art Center. http://corita.org/about-corita.
Cozad, Laurie. "The United States Imposition of Religious Freedom: The International Religious Freedom Act and India," *India Review* 4 (2006): 59–83.
Daly, Mary. *Beyond God the Father: Toward a Philosophy of Women's Liberation*. Boston: Beacon Press, 1973.
de Bary, William Theodore and Irene Bloom, ed., *Sources of Chinese Tradition* 2nd ed., vol. 1. New York: Columbia University, Press, 1999.
"Declaration of Religious Belief." coc.enlightener.net, accessed on April 9, 2016, http://haoma.org/coc/documents/dclrtn1.htm.
"Declaration of Religious Sentiment." Church of Cognizance. coc.enlightener.net.
Deitch, Robert. *Hemp: American History Revisited*. New York: Algora Publishing, 2003.
"Did you know?" ProCon.org, April 19, 2013. http://medicalmarijuana.procon.org/view.resource.php?resourceID=000091.
"DMT." Treatment 4 Addiction: Online Recovery Resource Directory. http://www.treament4addiction.com.
Doniger, Wendy. *Dreams, Illusion, and Other Realities*. Chicago: University of Chicago Press, 1984.
Doniger, Wendy. *Siva: The Erotic Ascetic*. New York: Oxford University Press, 1981.
Doniger-O'Flaherty, Wendy. *Textual Sources for the Study of Hinduism*. Chicago: University of Chicago Press, 1990.
Douglas, Mary. *Leviticus as Literature*. Oxford: Oxford University Press, 1999.
Douglas, Mary. *Natural Symbols: Explorations in Cosmology*. New York: Pantheon Books, 1982.

Drug Policy Forum of Hawai'i. www.dpfhi.org.
"Drug Scheduling." U.S. Drug Enforcement Administration. https://www.dea.gov/druginfo/ds.shtml.
"Drug War Clock." Drugsense.org. http://www.drugsense.org/cms/wodclock.
"Drugs of Abuse." *A DEA Resource Guide*, 2015 Edition. https://www.dea.gov/pr/multimedia-library/publications/drug_of_abuse.pdf#page=72.
Dunhill, Alfred. *The Pipe Book*. London: A & C Black, 1924.
Durkheim, Emile. *The Elementary Forms of Religious Life*. New York: Free Press, 1912.
Dutton, Sarah, Jennifer De Pinto, Anthony Salvanto, and Fred Buckus. "Poll: Support for legal marijuana use reaches all-time high," *CBS News*, April 20, 2015. http://www.cbsnews.com/news/poll-support-for-legal-marijuana-use-reaches-all-time-high/.
Earleywine, Mitch. *Understanding Marijuana: A New Look at the Scientific Evidence*. New York: Oxford University Press, 2002.
Einstein, Albert. *Ideas and Opinions*. New York: Three Rivers Press, 1954.
Eliade, Mircea. *Mystic Stories: The Sacred and the Profane*. New York: Columbia University Press, 1992.
Eliade, Mircea. *Shamanism: Archaic Techniques of Ecstasy*. Princeton: Princeton University Press, 1964.
"Employment Division Department of Human Resources of Oregon versus Smith." OYEZ, Chicago-Kent College of Law at Illinois, April 17, 1990.
Ethiopian Zion Coptic Church." *CBS News—60 Minutes*, Volume xii, Number 7, October 28, 1979.
Evidence Code 352. leginfo.ca.gov.
"Evidence of Hate Crime." *A Chronology of COC History*. http://www.danmary.org.
"Family Oriented Monastic Orders Promoting Family," Church of Cognizance Introduced, accessed August 4, 2015, http://www.coc.enlightener.net.
Fichtner, Christopher Glenn. *Cannabinomics: The Marijuana Policy Tipping Point*. Northbrook, IL: Well Mind Books, 2010.
Fike, Rupert, ed. *Voices from the Farm: Adventures in Community Living*, 2nd ed. Summertown, TN: Book Publishing Co., 2012.
"First Amendment and Religion." http://www.uscourts.gov/educational-resources/educational-activities/first-amendment-and-religion.
"First Ever Congress of the United Cannabis Ministries." United Cannabis Ministries, October 28, 2005. http://ucm.enlightener.net/wiki/tiki-index.php?page=First+ever+Congress+of+the+United+Cannabis+Ministries.
Fisher, Gary L. *Rethinking Our War on Drugs: Candid Talk about Controversial Issues*. Westport, CT: Praeger, 2006.
Fletcher, Z. C. "The Hako: A Pawnee Ceremony," *22nd Annual Report, Bureau of American Ethnology* (1900–1901). Washington, DC: Government Printing Office, 1904.
Foucault, Michel. *The Archaeology of Knowledge*. Translated by A. M. Sheridan Smith. London: Routledge, 2002.
Foucault, Michel. *Discipline and Punish: The Birth of the Prison*. New York: Vintage Books, 1977.
Foucault, Michel. *The History of Sexuality, Vol. 1: An Introduction*. New York: Random House, 1978.
Foucault, Michel. *The Order of Things: An Archaeology of the Human Sciences*. London: Tavistock Publications, 1970.
Fowler v. Rhode Island. Justia US Law. http://www.law.justia.com.
"Freedom of Religion and the Establishment Clause." National Paralegal College. http://nationalparalegal.edu/conLawCrimProc_Public/FreedomOfExpression/FreedomOfReligion&EstCl.asp.
Frood, Arran. "Dope at the Wheel," *New Scientist* 173 (2002): 4.
Gallagher, Eugene V. *The New Religious Movements Experience in America*. Westport, CT: Greenwood Press, 2004.

Gaskin, Stephen. *Amazing Dope Tales*. Berkeley: Ronin Publishing, Inc., 1999.
Gaskin, Stephen. *Cannabis Spirituality*. New York: High Times Books, 1996.
Gaskin, Stephen. *Monday Night Class*. Summertown, TN: Book Publishing Co., 2005.
Gaskin, Stephen. *The Caravan*, Rev. ed. Summertown, TN: Book Publishing Co., 2007.
Gaskin, Stephen. *The Grass Case*. Summertown, TN: Book Publishing Co., 1974.
Geertz, Clifford. *The Interpretation of Culture: Selected Essays*. New York: Basic Books, 1973.
Ginzburg, Carlo. *The Cheese and the Worms*. Baltimore: Johns Hopkins Press, 1992.
"God Is God." *Assembly of the Church of the Universe*. http://www.iamm.com/69.htm.
Gore, Albert. "Church Group Swaps Views with Gaskin's," *The Tennesseean*, March 13, 1972.
Grant, William. "Rastafarian Culture," https://debate.uvm.edu/dreadlibrary/grant02.htm.
Greenberg, Brad A. "Temple Weeds out Tree of Life," *Los Angeles Daily News*, February 27, 2007.
"Greetings and Welcome to Dan & Mary's Monastery-HEMPorium," Church of Cognizance. http://danmary.org/tiki/tiki-index.php.
Grim, Ryan. "What 420 Means: The True Story Behind Stoners' Favorite Number," *Huffington Post*, April 20, 2013. http://www.huffingtonpost.com/2009/04/20/what-420-means-the-true-s_n_188320.html.
Grinspoon, Lester, James B. Bakalar, and Ethan Russo. "Marihuana: Clinical Aspects," in *Substance Abuse: A Comprehensive Textbook*, ed. Joyce H. Lowinson, Pedro Ruiz, Robert B. Millman, and John G. Langrod, 4th ed. Philadelphia: Lippincott Williams & Wilkins, 2005: 263–76.
Gross, Rita. *Feminism and Religion: An Introduction*. Boston: Beacon Press, 1996.
Grossman, Andrew. "Banks to be allowed to do business with marijuana dispensaries," *Wall Street Journal*, February 14, 2014. http://www.wsj.com/articles/SB10001424052702304434104579383150782034282.
Guo, Jeff. "How religious freedom laws were praised, then hated, then forgotten, then, finally, resurrected," *Washington Post*, April 3, 2015. https://www.washingtonpost.com/blogs/govbeat/wp/2015/04/03/how-religious-freedom-laws-were-praised-then-hated-then-forgotten-then-finally-resurrected/.
Gupta, Guarav. "Unconstitutional Restoration: The Religious Freedom Restoration Act and Religious Liberty in America," *Princeton University Law Journal* 12, no. 1 (1997), http://web.archive.org/web/20010411000039/http://www.princeton.edu/~lawjourn/Fall97/II1gupta.html.
Gyatso, Tenzin. *The Universe in a Single Atom: The Convergence of Science and Spirituality*. New York: Broadway Books, 2005.
Haglage, Abby. "The Rhode Island 'Church' Taking on the Law to Smoke Pot." *The Daily Beast*, August 7, 2016. http://www.thedailybeast.com/articles/2016/08/07/jesus-wants-me-to-smoke-this-joint.html.
Hall, David and Roger Ames. *Thinking Through Confucius*. Albany, State University of New York Press, 1987, 274.
Hall, Wayne and Thomas F. Babor. "Cannabis Use and Public Health: Assessing the Burden," *Addiction* 95, no. 4 (2000): 485–90.
Halper, Evan. "Mississippi, Home to Federal Government's Official Stash of Marijuana." *Los Angeles Times*, May 28, 2014. http://www.latimes.com/nation/la-na-pot-monopoly-20140529-story.html.
Hamid, Ansley. *The Ganja Complex: Rastafari and Marijuana*. Lanham: Lexington Books, 2002.
"Harris Poll: 81% Support for Legalizing Medical Marijuana in America." The Weed Blog, May 18, 2015. https://www.theweedblog.com/harris-poll-81-support-for-legalizing-medical-marijuana-in-america/.
"Hawaii Medical Marijuana Law." NORML. Norml.org/legal/item/hawaii-medical-marijuana.

Herer, Jack. *Hemp and the Marijuana Conspiracy: The Emperor Wears No Clothes*. Van Nuys: Hemp Pub., 1990.

Hiaasen, Carl. "Louv Story: Are Brother Louv and His Zion Coptic Church Facing the Last Judgment," *Miami Herald*, August 2, 1981.

"History of Marijuana Use: Medical and Intoxicant." Schaffer Library of Drug History. http://www.druglibrary.net.

"History, Beliefs, and Practices of the THC Ministry," The Hawai'i Cannabis Ministry, http://www.thc-ministry.org/?page_id=362.

Holden, Cindy. "Hollywood Judeo-Christian Cannabis Church Forced to Close—Arrested Reverend Claims Civil and Religious Rights Violated." http://www.californianewswire.com, December 11, 2006.

The Holy Bible, King James Version. New York: American Bible Society, 1999.

"Holy Herb Sacrament." The Religion of Jesus Christ. http://www.salvationanointed.com/about-the-church/the-holy-herb-cannabis-sacrament-of-the-religion-of-jesus-church/.

Hudak, John and Grace Wallack. "Ending the U.S. government's war on medical marijuana research." Center for Effective Public Management at Brookings, October 2015. https://www.brookings.edu/wp-content/uploads/2016/06/Ending-the-US-governments-war-on-medical-marijuana-research.pdf.

Idaho v. Cordingly. No. 39518 , Idaho Court of Appeals (March 21, 2013). http://caselaw.findlaw.com/id-court-of-appeals/1637233.html.

Ijvone, T., G. Esposito, D. De Fillippis, C. Scuderi, and L. Steardo, "Cannabidiol: A Promising Drug for Neurodgenerative Disorders," *CNS Neuroscience & Therapeutics* 15 (2009): 65–75.

"Individual Orthodox Member Monastery." *Church of Cognizance Introduced*. http://www.coc.enlightener.net.

Innes, Stephanie. "Church of Cognizance: Pot Church Takes a Hit," *Arizona Daily Star*, July 9, 2006.

Iversen, Leslie L. *The Science of Marijuana*. New York: Oxford University Press, 2008

Jelly-Schapiro, Joshua. *Island People: the Carribean and the World*. New York: Knopf, 2016.

Johnson, Cameron. "Drug Kingpin or Political Prisoner?" *Honolulu Weekly*, April 27, 2011. http://honoluluweekly.com/cover/2011/04/drug-kingpin-or-political-prisoner/

Kaplan, Aryeh. *The Living Torah*. New York: Maznaim Pub. Corp., 1981.

"Kaya: Bob Marley and Marijuana." Joewein.de. http://www.joewein.de/kaya.htm.

Kendall, Gavin and Gary Wickham. *Using Foucault's Methods*. New York: Sage Publications, 1999.

Kende, Mark. "Free Exercise of Religion: A Pragmatic and Comparative Assessment," *Drake University Legal Studies Research Paper Series*, Research Paper No. 11–30 (March 4, 2010).

Kerr, Keoki. "Marijuana Ministry in Hilo 'Busted' by Feds," *Big Island Video News*, July 11, 2010. http://www.bigislandvideonews.com/2010/07/10/marijuana-ministry-in-hilo-busted-by-feds/.

Kerr, Keoki. "Officials Unveil Big Island Marijuana Case," *KITV4 News*, July 9, 2010. http://www.kitv.com/Officials-Unveil-Big-Island-Marijuana-Case/5366164.

"Kim Davis: I Am Being 'Forced to Disobey God.'" *CBSDC*, September 14, 2015. http://washington.cbslocal.com/2015/09/14/kim-davis-i-am-being-forced-to-disobey-god/.

King, Bonnie. "DEA Holds THC Minister in Custody after Appeal," Salem-News.com, July 21, 2010. http://www.salem-news.com/articles/july212010/roger-christie.php.

LaFleur, William. *Liquid Life: Abortion and Buddhism in Japan* (Princeton: Princeton University Press, 1992.

Lavender, Paige. "On Bob Marley's Birthday, A Look at What He Had to Say about Government Opposition to Weed." *Huffington Post* online, February 6, 2015. http://www.huffingtonpost.com/2015/02/06/bob-marley-weed-government_n_6631410.html.

Leary, Timothy. *Politics of PsychoPharmacology*. Berkeley: Ronin Publishing, Inc., 1988.

Lemons, Stephen. "Arizona's Marijuana-Worshipping Church of Cognizance Seeks a Legal, Spiritual High." Phoenixnewtimes.com, March 6, 2009.

Levi-Strauss, Claude. *The Savage Mind*. Chicago: University of Chicago Press, 1966.

Lewis, Charles. "Church of the Universe: Marijuana as a Sacrament," *National Post*, June 16, 2010. http://www.news.nationalpost.com/holy-post/church-of-the-universe-marijuana-as-a-sacrament.

Lewis, Charles. "Updated: 'Pot Church' Member Sentenced to Three Months in Jail," *National Post*, May 30, 2011. http://news.nationalpost.com/holy-post/pot-church-members-to-be-sentenced.

Li, H. "An Archaeological and Historical Account of Cannabis in China," *Economic Botany* 28 (1924): 437–38.

"Lifestyle: The Lifestyle of a Legend." http://www.bobmarley.com/history/.

Lincoln, Bruce. *Death, War, and Sacrifice: Studies in Ideology and Practice*. Chicago: University of Chicago Press, 1991.

Lincoln, Bruce. *Discourses and the Construction of Society*. Oxford: Oxford University Press, 2014.

Liska, Ken. *Drugs and the Human Body: With Implications for Society*. Upper Saddle River, NJ: Pearson Prentice Hall, 2009.

London, Jeffery Matthew. *How the Use of Marijuana Was Criminalized and Medicalized, 1906–2004: A Foucaultian History of Legislation in America*. Lewiston, NY: Edwin Mellen Press, 2009.

Long, Charles H. *Significations: Signs, Symbols, and Images in the Interpretation of Religion*. Aurora, CO: The Davies Group, 1995.

MaCoun, Robert J. *Drug War Heresies: Learning from other Vices, Times, and Places*. New York: Cambridge University Press, 2001.

Maher, Bill. *Real Time with Bill Maher*, episode 377. HBO, February 12, 2016.

Mandal, Ananya. "Cannabinoid Receptors," *News Medical*, June 2, 2014. http://www.news-medical.net/health/Cannabinoid-Receptors.aspx.

Maraniss, David. *Barack Obama: The Story*. New York: Simon & Schuster, 2012.

Marez, Curtis. *Drug Wars: The Political Economy of Narcotics*. Minneapolis: University of Minnesota Press, 2004.

Marley, Bob. "Easy Skanking," *Kaya*, Island Studios, 1978.

Marley, Bob. "Pass It On," *Burnin'*, Harry J. Studios, 1973.

"Marijuana and the Bible," The Ethiopian Zion Coptic Church. http://www.druglibrary.org/Schaffer/hemp/potbible.htm.

"Marijuana Arrests By the Numbers." aclu.org. https://www.aclu.org/gallery/marijuana-arrests-numbers.

Marron, Kevin. "Counsel to the Damned," *Canadian Lawyer Magazine*, September 1996. http://www.iamm.com/damned.htm.

Martin, Douglas. "Stephen Gaskin, Hippie Who Founded an Enduring Commune, Dies at 79," *New York Times*, July 2, 2014.

Mason, Claire. *New Religious Movements: The Impact on Our Lives*. Chicago: Raintree, 2004

Mazur, Cynthia. "Marijuana as a 'Holy Sacrament': Is the Use of Peyote Constitutionally Distinguishable from That of Marijuana in Bona Fide Religious Ceremonies?," *Notre Dame Journal of Law, Ethics, & Public Policy* 5 (1991).

McGraw-Hill, *Dictionary of American Idioms and Phrasal Verbs*. New York: McGraw-Hill, 2005.

McKinley, Jesse. "Pat Robertson Says Marijuana Use Should be Legal," *New York Times*, March 7, 2012, http://www.nytimes.com/2012/03/08/us/pat-robertson-backs-legalizing-marijuana.html?_r=0.

"Medical Marijuana Policy in the US." Huntington's Outreach Project for Education at Stanford. http://web.stanford.edu/group/hopes/cgi-bin/hopes_test.

Mehl-Madrona, Lewis. *Coyote Medicine: Lessons from Native American Healing*. New York: Scribner, 1997.

Meland, Bruce. *There Was Marijuana in the Garden of Eden!: An Exposé on Marijuana and Hemp*. Bloomington, IN: XLibris Corporation, 2015.

Mernagh, Matt. "Church of the Universe Cannabis Court Ruling Fails," *Cannabis Culture Magazine*, February 7, 2011.

Metcalf, Bill. "Voices on The Farm: Adventures in Community Living (Book Review)," Rupert Fike, editor, in *Utopia Studies*, Vol. 10, No. 1, 2012.

Miles, Kathleen. "Just how much the war on drugs impacts our overcrowded prisons," *Huffington Post* online. http://www.huffingtonpost.com/2014/03/10/war-on-drugs-prisons-infographic_n_4914884.html.

Mills, James H. *Cannabis Britannica: Empire, Trade and Prohibition 1800–1928*. Oxford: Oxford University Press, 2003.

Milovanovich, Zoran. "Freedom of Religion," *Human Rights Issues in Criminal Justice*. http://www.lincoln.edu.

Morral, Andrew R., Daniel F. McCaffrey, and Susan M. Paddock, "Reassessing the Marijuana Gateway Effect," *Addiction* 97, no. 12 (2002): 1493–1504.

Murataeva, N., A. Straiker, and K. Mackie. "Parsing the Players: 2-Arachidonoylglycerol Synthesis and Degradation in the CNS," *British Journal of Pharmacology* 171 (2014): 1379–91.

Nicholson, Matthew. "Is O Centro a Sign of Hope for RFRA Claimants?" *Virginia Law Review* no. 95: 1281 (2009): 1281–1324.

Niman, Michael. "Out to Save the World: Life on the Farm," *High Times*, February 1, 1995. http://thefarmcommunity.com/high-times-1995/.

"Nine Pointed Star." The Assembly of the Church of the Universe. http://www.iamm.com/star.html.

"Nipatic Assembly of the Almighty and The Temple 420 of the Heartland Mission." Temple 420 Literature, received February 25, 2015.

Nura, John and Richard Perez-Pena. "Marriage Licenses Issued in Kentucky County, but Debates Continue," *New York Times*, September 4, 2015.

"Non-Medical Marijuana II: Rite of Passage or Russian Roulette?" National Center on Addiction and Substance Abuse at Columbia University. http://www.casacolumbia.org/addiction-research/reports/non-medical-marijuana-rite-of-passage-or-russian-roulette-2004.

O'Brien, Derek and Vaughan Carter. "Chant down Babylon: Freedom of Religion and the Rastafarian Challenge to Majoritarianism," *Journal of Law and Religion* 18, no. 1 (2002–2003): 220.

O'Connor, Thomas P., ed., *Religion, the Community, and the Rehabilitation of Criminal Offenders*. New York: Haworth Press, 2002.

"Origin of Mystery." Oxford Dictionaries Online. http://www.oxforddictionaries.com.

Otto, Rudolf. *The Idea of the Holy*. Translated by John W. Harvey. New York: Oxford University Press, 1958.

Pavia, Will. "Home of Reggae and Rastafarians Legalises its Favorite Herb." *The Times* (London, UK), June 14, 2014, Eire edition, 36.

"Peyote." Hallucinogens. http://www.hallucinogens.com.

Pollan, Michael. *The Botany of Desire: A Plant's-Eye View of the World*. New York: Random House, 2001.

Posadzki, Alexandra. "Court Rejects Church's Bid for Marijuana-Law Exemption." *Winnipeg Free Press*, February 8, 2011.

"Q&A: Legal Marijuana in Colorado and Washington." Brookings Institute. May 21, 2013.

"Quakers fight for religious freedom in Puritan Massachusetts, 1656–1661." Global Nonviolent Action Database. http://www.nvdatabase,swarthmore.edu.

Rabey, Rabey. "Cannabis Based Christian Compassion," *on Faith*, February 5, 2014.

Read, Kay Almere. *Time and Sacrifice in the Aztec Cosmos*. Indiana: Indiana University Press, 1998.

Reefer Madness, directed by Louis J. Gasnier (1936; United States: Grand National Studios).

"Report of the National Commission of Ganja." Office of the Prime Minister. Jamaica: Jamaica Information Service, 2000.

Repp K. K. and A. L. Raich. "Marijuana and Health: A Comprehensive Review of 20 Years of Research," Washington County, Oregon, Department of Health and Human Services, October 20, 2014.

Rhodes, Ron. *The Challenge of the Cults and New Religions: The Essential Guide to Their History, Their Doctrine, and Our Response*. Grand Rapids, MI: Zondervan, 2001.

Rmuse, "Hobby Lobby Ruling Opened Floodgates for Indiana Discrimination Law," Politics USA: Real Liberal Politics, April 1, 2015. http://www.politicususa.com/2015/04/01/hobby-lobby-ruling-opened-floodgates-indiana-discrimination-law.html.

Roderick, Bradley. "A Brief Look at the Roots and Development of the Nation of Islam," *Renaissance: A Monthly Islamic Journal* (1999). http://www.renaissance.com.pk.

Saad, Lydia. "Majority Continues to Support Pot Legalization in U.S.," Gallup, November 6, 2014. http://www.gallup.com/poll/179195/majority-continues-support-pot-legalization.aspx?utm_source=genericbutton&utm_medium=organic&utm_campaign=sharing.

Saliba, John A. *Understanding New Religious Movements*. Walnut Creek, CA: AltaMira Press, 2003.

Samahon, Tuan. "The Religion Clauses and Political Asylum: Religious Persecution Claims and the Religious Membership-Conversion Imposter Problem [notes]." *Georgetown Law Journal* 88 (May 2000): 2211–38.

Savage, Charlie and Jack Healy. "Trump Administration Takes Step That Could Threaten Marijuana Legalization Movement," *New York Times*, January 4, 2018.

"Scripture of the Church of Cognizance." *Church of Cognizance Introduced*. http://www.coc.enlightener.net.

Seligman, Adam B., Robert P. Weller, Michael J. Puett, and Bennett Simon. *Ritual and Its Consequences: An Essay on the Limits of Sincerity*. New York: Oxford University Press, 2008.

Seppa, Nathan. "Not Just a High," *Science News* 177, no. 13 (2010): 16–20.

"*Sherbert v. Verner*, Opinion of Justice Brennan, Legal Information Institute." Cornell University Law School. http://www.law.cornell.edu.

Shoemaker, Alan. *Ayahuasca Medicine: The Shamanic World of Amazonian Sacred Plant Healing*. Rochester, Vermont: Park Street Press, 2014.

Slemons, William. *Memorial Address on the Life and Character of Alpheus S. Williams* Washington, DC: Government Printing Office, 1880.

Small, Peter. "Smoking Cannabis Is a Religious Right, Court Told," *Toronto Star*, April 8, 2010.

Smith, J. Z. *Imagining Religion from Babylon to Jonestown*. Chicago: University of Chicago Press, 1982.

Smith, Jonathan Z. *Map Is Not Territory: Studies in the History of Religions*. Chicago: University of Chicago Press, 1993

Smith, Jonathan Z. *Relating Religion: Essays in the Study of Religion*. Chicago: University of Chicago Press, 2004.

Smith Phillip. "Marijuana: Arizona Court of Appeals Rejects Religious Defense." *Drug War Chronicle*, 546, August 8, 2008. http://stopthedrugwar.org/chronicle/2008/aug/08/marijuana_arizona_court_appeals.

Smith, Wilfred Cantwell. *The Meaning and End of Religion*. Philadelphia: Fortress Press, 1962.

Square Groupers: The Godfathers of Ganja, directed by Billy Corben (2011; Magnolia Pictures).

Stevenson, Douglas. *Out to Change the World: The Evolution of The Farm Community*. Summertown, TN: Book Publishing Co., 2014.

Streng, Frederick. *Understanding Religious Life*. Belmont, CA: Wadsworth Publishing Company, 1985.

Sullivan, Winnifred Fallers. "The Religious Expert in American Courts," *Archives de sciences sociales des religions* 155, July–September 2011.

Supreme Court of Arizona, en Banc. *State of Arizona, Apellee v. Danny Ray Hardesty, Appellant*, No. CR-08–0244-PR. Decided: September 8, 2009.

"Synthetic Cannabinoid Halts Progression of Multiple Sclerosis." NORML. http://norml.org/news/2012/03/01/synthetic-cannabinoid-halts-progression-of-multiple-sclerosis-study-says.

Tafari, I. J. "The Rastafari Successors of Marcus Garvey," *Caribbean Quarterly*, Vol. 26, No. 4, (1980): 9.

"Terms of Endearment." *Assembly of the Church of the Universe*. http://www.iamm.com/faq.htm#Endearments.

"The Global Religious Landscape." The Pew Research Center. http://www.washiontontimes.

"The Hawai'i Cannabis Ministry." TCH Ministry. http://www.thc-ministry.org/images/thcministry.brochure.pdf.

"The History and Development of the Leading International Drug Control Conventions." Canada: Library of Parliament. http://www.parl.gc.ca/content/sen/committee/371/ille//library/history-e.htm.

"The Temple 420 (Mission)—Cannabis and Christianity." Temple 420 Literature, received January 15, 2012.

Tillich, Paul. *Christianity and the Encounter of the World Religions*. New York: Columbia University Press, 1963.

Tillich, Paul. *The Shaking of the Foundations*. New York: Palgrave Macmillan, 2015.

"Timeline: The Use of Cannabis." *BBC News, Health*, June 16, 2005.

"Title 21 Code of Federal Regulations." U.S. Department of Justice, Drug Enforcement Administration. http://www.deadiversion.usdoj.gov.

Tokarev, Sergey. "Sincerity of Religious Belief." U.S. Civil Liberties, last modified May 9, 2012. http://uscivilliberties.org/dle101_utf8/themes/4488-sincerity-of-religious-belief.html.

Toots and the Maytals. *Pass the Pipe*, Island Records-Tuff Gong, 1979.

Town v. Florida, No. 55987, Supreme Court of FL 377 So. 2d 648 (Fla. 1979), November 1, 1979.

"Tree of Life," The Assembly of the Church of the Universe, accessed September 17, 2015, http://www.iamm.com/69.htm.

Twain, Mark. "Quotes," goodreads.com.

Tylor, Edward. *Primitive Culture*. London: John Murphy, 1903.

U.S. Department of Justice, "Controlled Substance Schedules." http://www.deadiversion.usdoj.gov/schedules/index.html.

"U.S. Federal Law." DMTSite. www.dmtsite.com/dmt/information/law.html

United States v. Ballard: 322 U.S. 78. (1944): Justia U.S. Supreme Court Center—Justia U.S. Law.

United States v. Macintosh. Legal Information Institute. http://www.law.cornell.edu.

United States v. David Meyers. No. 95–8079, U.S. Court of Appeals (10th Cir., September 6, 1996). http://caselaw.findlaw.com/us-10th-circuit/1074566.html#.

United States v. Quaintance, No. CR NO. 06–538 JCH. LEAGLE. http://www.leagle.com/decision/20061624471FSupp2d1153_11524.

United States v. Roger Cusick Christie, Sherryanne L. Christie, In the U.S. District Court for the District of Hawaii, CR. NO. 10-00384 LEK, Supplemental Declaration of Laurie Cozad, PhD.

United States v. Seeger, 380 U.S. 163 (1965).

Urantia Foundation, *The Urantia Book*. Chicago: Urantia Foundation, 1955.

"Use of the Word 'Marijuana' Increases in the US." ProCon.org. http://www.medicalmarijuana.procon.org.

Vandermeer, Jeremiah. "Canadian Government Will Appeal Court Ruling Striking Down Marijuana Laws," *Cannabis Culture Magazine*, April 18, 2011.

Vendidad or Laws against the Demons, Avesta—The Sacred Books of Zoroastrianism, Book 3, translated by James Darmesteter, edited by Joseph H. Peterson. Avesta.org, 1995.

Von Hartmann, Paul. "Aloha Denied: Prosecution or Predation? An Essay in Defense of Roger Christie, Imprisoned Big Island Cannabis Minister." *Honolulu Civil Beat*, May 12, 2012. http://www.civilbeat.com/2012/05/15817-aloha-denied-prosecution-or-predation/.

The Wailers. "Get Up, Stand Up," by Bob Marley and Peter Tosh, recorded April 1973, track 1 on *Burnin'*, Island Records-Tuff Gong, 1973.

Walsh, John. "Q&A: Legal Marijuana in Colorado and Washington." Brookings Institute, May 21, 2013.

Walters, John P. "No Surrender: The Drug War Saves Lives," *National Review* 56, September 14, 2004, 41.

Wang, Stephanie. "With court ruling, 'same-sex marriage just becomes marriage,'" *Indy Star*, June 26, 2015. http://www.stephaniewang@indystar.com.

Ward, Mitch. "White People Colored People, Los Angeles Craig X Rubin Marijuana Activist." 21stCenturyArtists Hollywood, updated April 20, 2016. https://www.youtube.com/watch?v=CUbUEILtpIk.

"Washington Drug Defense, 12 Little Known Consequences of a Marijuana Conviction or Arrest." Washington Drug Defense. Washington-drug-defense.com.

Weber, Max. *The Sociology of Religion*. Boston: Beacon Press, 1993.

Wenger, Tibor, Gabriella Moldrich, and Susanna Furst, "Neuromorphological Background of Cannabis Addiction," *Brain Research Bulletin* 61 (2003): 125–28.

"What Does 'Free Exercise' of Religion Mean under the First Amendment?" First Amendment Center. http://www.firstamendmentcenter.org/faq/frequently-asked-questions-religious-liberty.

"Why Rastas Don't Smoke Marijuana," January 6, 2011. The Dread Library.

Willoughby, Westel. *Opium as an International Problem*. Baltimore: Johns Hopkins Press, 1925.

Wilson, Bryan. "Introduction," *New Religious Movements: Challenge and Response, ed. Bryan Wilson and Jamie Cresswel*, 1–11. London: Routledge, 1999.

Winkelman, Michael J., and Roberts, Thomas B., eds. *Psychedelic Medicine: New Evidence for Hallucinogenic Substances as Treatments*. Westport, CT: Praeger Publishers, 2007.

Women of Reform Judaism, "Medical Marijuana as Mitzvah: A Study Guide." New York: Women of Reform Judaism, 2000. http://www.thc-ministry.org/benyehuda-dictionaryreference.html.

Wright, Annelise M. "Dude, Which Religion Do I Have to Join to Get Some Drugs? How the Supreme Court Got It Wrong in *Gonzales v. O Centro Espirita Beneficiente Uniao Do Vegetal*, 546 U.S. 418," *Nebraska Law Review* 86, no. 4 (2006): 987–1006.

Young, Jim. "Church of the Universe Argues That Marijuana Is a Sacrament Protected by Freedom of Religion," Centre for Constitutional Studies, July 9, 2010.

Young, Katherine K. and Paul Nathanson. "The Church of the Universe: Is It a Religion?" Affidavit filed with the Canadian Federal Court in the case of Christopher Bennet and the Attorney General for Canada, July 20, 2009. http://www.cannabisculture.com/files/Young_and_Nathanson_Opinion.pdf.

Zimmerman, Malia. "'Marijuana minister's' prosecution invigorates legalization fight in Hawaii," *Hawaii Reporter*, April 30, 2014. http://watchdog.org/141663/hawaii-marijuana-minister/.

Index

About the Author

Laurie Cozad received her MA and PhD in the history of religions from the University of Chicago Divinity School, where she specialized in Hinduism and Buddhism. She also received an MS at the School of Foreign Service at Georgetown University. She has been teaching, presenting, and writing for the past 20 years, primarily at the University of Mississippi. She presently teaches at Merrimack College. Her scholarly interests include cannabis religions, indigenous religions, religion and politics, gender studies, and discourse analysis.

www.ingramcontent.com/pod-product-compliance
Ingram Content Group UK Ltd.
Pitfield, Milton Keynes, MK11 3LW, UK
UKHW041628031026
15587UKWH00001B/130

9 781498 504041